Dear [...] you
may [...]
be [...]

Swaroopananda
29 June 2010

Vedanta and Vivekananda

Vedanta and Vivekananda

Swami Swahananda

Holy Mother
Mission

****

ISBN 13: 987-1-4507-2250-6

****

Published & printed by: Ramakrishna Monastery VSSC
                            19961 Live Oak Canyon Road
                            P.O. box 408, California
                            holymothermission@gmail.com

****

If you want to know more about the contents of this book email
swahananda@vedanta.org

Or visit our Internet sites:
To know more about Vedanta: www.vedanta.org
www.holymothermission.org

****

Publisher's Note

This book, Vedanta and Vivekananda, has been compiled mostly from published articles in journals and books. These are a collection of self contained articles and not a planned book. Those who are interested in a particular topic and not its entire philosophy or background may find these separate treatments more useful. These topics had been dealt with separately as lectures, essays, television talks and University lectures. There will be repetitions of ideas and language. They have often been retained for the sake of clarity and completeness of the topic.

The earlier writings have been rearranged and new ones added by Swami Swahananda. Thanks to Anuradha, and volunteers of Holy Mother Mission Trabuco, who have looked after the task of bringing out the book in their press. This book follows his previous book, Vedanta and Ramakrishna, published by Ramakrishna Mission Institute of Culture, Gol Park, Kolkata. For convenience it is printed in our Trabuco Monastery, but an Indian edition may come out later.

Ramakrishna Monastery VSSC
Publisher

TABLE OF CONTENTS

PARTS:

I Vivekananda

II Vedanta

III Religion

PART I

Vivekananda

PART I

Chapter 1

SWAMI VIVEKANANDA'S CONCEPT OF SERVICE

An address delivered at the University of Madras, Coimbatore campus.

Introduction

Swami Vivekananda lived only for about forty years. He was born on January 12, 1863 and passed away on July 4, 1902. A very short life indeed! Of those years again he worked for a decade only. Still he left such an indelible impression on the later generations that many writers thought it necessary to include his ideas in their specialized studies. Hence many Universities in India teach and do research on his philosophy, social thought, political thinking and even his literary and anthropological ideas. Several scholars from the West as well as from Russia are specially studying him. Max Mueller popularized the teachings of Sri Ramakrishna. Romain Rolland wrote on *Swami Vivekananda and his Universal Gospel.* Later in his book on the life of Mahatma Gandhi entitled *Lead, Kindly Light,* Vincent Shean wrote a chapter on Swami Vivekananda and Sri Ramakrishna. He signifies them there as 'Forerunners of Gandhi'. Another scholar Dr. Brown, in his book on the political thought of India called *The White Umbrella,* devotes a chapter to Vivekananda. In an interesting book *The Inevitable Choice,* the author Dr. Soper finds in the Swami's harmonizing ideas a great

challenge to all 'special' revelations. Many of the leaders of
India including Mahatma Gandhi, Aurobindo and Subhas
Chandra Bose felt his impact. Many political, social and
even revolutionary workers derived inspiration from his
writings. So tremendous has been the influence on posterity,
of this great son of Mother India! Hence it is worth studying
his major contributions regarding the doctrine of service,
which is of perennial interest and need.

'My life is my message,' Gandhiji used to say. This is true
of all great souls. It is much more true of spiritual personalities. As Swami Vivekananda said, Sri Ramakrishna was
content to live the life, the interpretation has to be given by
others, for such souls, 'one with the Infinite Spirit,' do not
take a single false step. It is not necessary to go into the details of the life of Swami Vivekananda, which is well-known.
There are many incidents in his life and in that of his Master
which show the sympathy, the consideration, the zeal for
serving fellow beings, which must have contributed a great
deal to the formulation and development of his famous
Gospel of Service which is our field of special study here.

'The child is father of the man,' says the old adage. True
to it, we find even in his boyhood days indications of his
social awareness, sympathy for fellow men and leadership
and understanding for suitable action. His father was a
magnanimous man, and his mother a soft-hearted, loving
woman. A large retinue of relations and dependents were
maintained in their house as their own children with all
affection and consideration. As a boy, Narendranath was

very kind-hearted. Whenever beggars would come to their house, he was sure to give off whatever came his way. Even shutting him up would not mend matters, for on hearing the voices of beggars he would throw things through the windows for them. Caste did not appeal to him. As a child, he experimented by smoking pipes reserved for lower castes as was the custom in those days, to see if he also lost his own caste! Once a sailor came to the help of Naren and his friends to raise a trapeze in their gymnasium. While lifting the trapeze, it fell down knocking the sailor unconscious. All the boys ran away thinking him dead but Naren nursed him, took him to a doctor and when he recovered, sent him with a little purse as a present. In his student days, he joined the Brahmo Samaj, which was advocating various social reforms. He was a voracious reader and became acquainted with the social thoughts of the masterminds of the West. And in his speeches and writings, we find references to many of these thinkers. His search for truth ultimately brought him to Sri Ramakrishna bringing fulfillment in his life. His boldness, as reflected in his total unconcern for his own safety was evident in an incident. Once when a boy was on the point of being run over by a horse carriage, the boy Naren rushed before the carriage and was successful in saving the boy and thereby earned the applause of the onlookers and gratitude of the parents. After the death of his father, Naren experienced much financial uncertainty and even poverty for sometime. As a mendicant, he underwent much hardship and saw the dire poverty of the people. This made him aware of the great sufferings through which our people pass.

Vivekananda's was a mother's heart. At the sight of
suffering he would be overwhelmed. When a famine was
raging in Bengal and his assistants were in doubt if they
would get enough money for conducting the Relief work,
he seriously thought of selling away the Belur Math property which he had just purchased to carry on the work of
bringing the spiritual heritage of eternal India to the people,
the work of which he dreamt for years, so intense was his
feeling. Deep sympathy is the key to all genuine service. So
he told his brother disciples at the Abu Road Station, just
prior to his leaving for the West, the following passionate
words:

'I have now traveled all over India, and lately in the
Maharashtra country and the Western Coasts. But alas! It
was an agony to me, my brothers, to see with my own eyes
the terrible poverty and misery of the masses, and I could
not restrain my tears! It is now my firm conviction that it is
futile to preach religion amongst them without first trying
to remove their poverty and their sufferings. It is for this
reason — to find some means for the salvation of the poor of
India — that I am now going to America!' (*The Life of Swami
Vivekananda:* By His Eastern and Western Disciples, 1915,
Vol. Ill, p. 141)

His sympathy for the poor and the lowly was immense.
Once a group of Santhal laborers were employed for work
in the Math. Often with tears in his eyes, he would hear
their tale of woe. Before they took their leave after finishing
the work, he arranged a feast for them.

Such was the heart of Vivekananda and so intense was

his feeling for the people that he once told Girish Chandra Ghosh: 'Look here, G. C., the thought comes to me that even if I have to undergo a thousand births to relieve the misery of the world, aye, even to remove the least pain from anyone, I shall cheerfully do it! I think, oh, of what use is my personal *Mukti* alone! I shall take everyone along that path with myself!' (ibid., pp. 166-167). Indeed it will be immensely fruitful to study the views of this great heart on the concept of service.

Origin of The Concept Of Service

Philosophical Basis

Search for unity has been the one passion of all mankind. This is more true of the Indian people. The Vedantic philosophy pointed out that unity of existence is a logical necessity and the saints and the Upanishads asserted that it is a reality. The visible universe, the individual and the ultimate reality are one and the same. 'All this is Brahman,' said the *Mundaka Upanishad(ll.* ii. 11). 'All this is Atman,' said the *Chandogya Upanishad* (VII xxv. 2). Again, This Self is Brahman,' said the *Brihadaranyaka.* (II. v. 19). This interest in the Self, or Soul, or Atman, is the pivot of Vedanta philosophy. The realization of the eternal Self is the goal of all activities of man. Whatever takes man towards that realization is spiritually beneficial. Vedanta is man- centered but man is nothing but the embodied Soul.

The whole point hinges upon our conception of man. In trying to define the real man, rationalism and science find it to be beyond their grasp. Vedanta, too, faced the problems and gave the unique conception of the Atman, the ultimate reality in man. Vedanta analyzed a visible man. What is he? Is he the body, or the mind, or something still finer? Real nature, according to philosophy, means that which does not change. A truly real thing must have been in the past, is now in the present and will continue to be in the future too. Is there anything in man that is constant? The body, we know, changes all the time and will not be there after a certain period of time. It is transitory. So it is not the reality. What about the mind? It, too, goes on changing. And even according to the Hindu philosophy, which accords some permanence to it, continuing from birth to birth, it dies out in final realization or in absorption. Is there anything real at all then in man? The materialists said, 'no'. They were assailed by the argument that a man is a 'self-evident fact and even if you cannot locate his fundamental reality he still exists and it is an axiom that nothing comes out of nothing'. Thus cornered, they said, 'We do not know its nature.' Now this is agnosticism. And, of course, 'We don't know' is a very safe position. Then the retort came, 'Do you know?' Vedanta said, 'Yes; we know it not through reason or physical analysis as such but through intuition, through spiritual absorption.' Sages down the ages have experienced it, and this experience is part of human heritage. And what is it? It is the Atman, the Self, the Spirit, the innermost spiritual core in man, which is his unchanging, real nature. The apparent man is the manifested real man, who is one with the Absolute, the Unity of existence. So service of man is really service to God. Hence it follows that, for Self-realization, disinterested service of man is necessary and perfect men must serve either to set an example or out of sympathy, or for both.

Buddhism spoke in favor of negating the soul whereas Vedanta saw the soul everywhere. The difficulty arose because of difference of concepts. In the Buddhist concept of Anattavada, the term soul stands for something which to a Vedantin is known as *antahkarana* or *ahamkara* (the mind stuff or the ego-sense). Hence the Soul, in the Buddhist sense, might be the seat of selfishness and egotism, but Vedantic Self stands for the essence, the Supreme Self behind the empirical. So, Swami Vivekananda speaks about manifesting the glory of the Atman and that precisely, according to him, is the purpose of life. Service of man helps in that manifestation.

'Ethics is unity', said the Swami, and he often pointed out 'that knowledge was the finding of unity in diversity, and that the highest point in every science was reached when it found the one unity underlying all variety, and this was as true in physical science as in the spiritual' (ibid., p. 206). Thus, according to him, the whole field of moral science was based on the unity of existence and all types of service had this idea of unity as their philosophical basis.

The same idea has been expressed by all religions, though sometimes more pointedly by some. The dictum, 'Love thy neighbor as thyself' or 'Do as thou would be done by' is the common advice of every faith.

By service, Vivekananda meant not only ameliorative service, but also all types of social action for all-round social welfare. Social reform and social work are all included in his doctrine of service. The major point in this doctrine is that we are to worship God in man by rendering service to the latter. In an inspiring poem he wrote:

From highest Brahman to the yonder worm, And to the very minutest atom,
Everywhere is the same God, the All-Love; Friend, offer mind, soul, body, at their feet.
These are His manifold forms before thee, Rejecting them, where seekest thou for God?
Who loves all beings, without distinction, He indeed is worshipping best his God.

He coined the word *Daridranarayana*, God in the form of the poor — and asked us to serve him, 'Where should you go to seek God, — are not all the poor, the miserable, the weak, Gods? Why not worship them first?' He believed that this type of service is doubly beneficial. If we forget God in the temple the whole service is practically a loss whereas in this kind of worship at least the sufferings will be physically mitigated. Thus it is a more useful type of worship, suitable to the modern temper too.

Religious attitudes to work

In order to appreciate Swami Vivekananda's contribution in this respect, it is worth recalling the various religious attitudes towards work that prevailed in different disciplines. Hinduism stressed the idea of *dana*, gift and *Istapurti*, social service. The traditional idea looked upon the duties of Varna and Ashrama as obligatory and a preparation for deeper spiritual life.

From the standpoint of deeper religion, there were and are four major approaches to work, depending upon the temperaments of men. The various spiritual disciplines of all faiths have been brought under *Jnana, Bhakti, Raja* and *Karma Yogas*. The intellectuals find analysis, discrimination and knowledge suitable to their taste. The emotional people like the expression of their emotions. The people who are temperamentally active want to do something tangible. Now these three, intellect, emotion and activity are the three possible functions of the mind. When the mind is at rest, i.e. it is free from all these three functions, *Raja-Yoga* experiences come in. Based on these four *Yogas*, or paths, to realization, different attitudes towards work have been prescribed.

From the standpoint of *Jnana-Yoga*, analysis leading to the knowledge that Atman alone is the reality is the major discipline. So work in this system is done with detachment, with the thought that the Self is untouched, *asanga*, and it is the body and the mind which are engaged in activities. Work is done for the purification of the mind in the preparatory stage. Many of these votaries try to apply the idea of one Spirit pervading everything and service to other creatures as service to the Spirit.

In the *Bhakti* system, every work is done with the idea of Divine service. This is done either through service to a deity or service to other creatures as God's creation. As Saint Tukaram puts it, 'God is our friend and through Him everybody is our friend.' The definition of Sage Narada that 'Whatever is done for God is devotion' has raised every activity to spiritual service, if done for God.

In *Raja-Yoga*, the stress is on deep concentration to realize the 'aloneness' of the Self, free from all defects of sufferings etc. To bring in concentration, a votary does every work with attention which keeps the mind in a field of thought. Gradually attention becomes more pointed and frees the mind from duality leading it to the realization of oneness.

In *Karma- Yoga*, work is done for work's sake. The objective is to practice non-attachment. The adherent to this discipline tries to free himself from agitation and anxiety and holds fast to the ideal of 'intense rest amidst intense activity and intense activity amidst intense rest.' The test for his non-attachment is that he has as much power of attachment as he has the power of detachment.'

Vivekananda harmonized the conflict among the different attitudes. Says he:

'Every man must develop according to his own nature. As every science has its methods, so has every religion. The methods of attaining the end of religion are called *Yoga* by us, and the different forms of *Yoga* we teach, are adapted to the different natures and temperaments of men. We classify them in the following way, under four heads:

(1) *Karma-Yoga* — The manner in which a man realizes his own divinity through works and duty.

(1) *Bhakti- Yoga* — The realization of the divinity through devotion to, and love of, a Personal God.

(2) *Raja- Yoga* — The realization of the divinity –through the control of mind.

(3) *Jnana- Yoga* — The realization of a man's own divinity through knowledge.

These are all different roads leading to the same centre — God. Indeed, the varieties of religious belief are an advantage, since all faiths are good, so far as they encourage man to lead a spiritual life. The more sects there are, the more opportunities there are for making successful appeals to divine instinct in all men.' (*The Complete Works*, Vol. V, p. 292)

Vivekananda visualized an ideal character by the blending of these different disciplines. He felt that development of man is at its best, in other words Self-realization is at its perfection, when human nature finds a many-sided expression in which *Jnana, Bhakti, Karma* all discover their respective limits and possibilities. He felt that by their combination, it was possible to produce a balanced character, free from the possible defects of each of these exclusive paths — the heartlessness of the intellectuals, bigotry of the emotionals, aloofness of the meditative and arrogance of the active. In a letter he writes:

'I agree with you so far that faith is a wonderful insight and that it alone can save, but there is the danger of its breeding fanaticism and barring further progress.

'*Jnanam* is all right, but there is the danger of its becoming dry intellectualism. Love is great and noble, but it may die away in meaningless sentimentalism. A harmony of all these is the thing required. Ramakrishna was such a harmony. Such beings are few and far between; but keeping him and his teachings as the ideal we can move on. And if amongst us, each one may not individually attain to that perfection, still we may get it collectively by counteracting, adjusting and fulfilling one another. This would be harmony by a number of persons, and a decided advance on all other forms and creeds.' *(Letters of Swami Vivekananda,* 1948, p. 88)

He held up his Master Sri Ramakrishna who was 'a synthesis of the utmost of philosophy, mysticism, and work' before society as the ideal to be emulated and said in another letter:

'About doctrines and so forth I have to say only this, that if anyone accepts Paramahamsa Deva as *Avatara* etc. it is all right; if he doesn't do so, it is just the same. The truth about it is that in point of character, Paramahamsa Deva beats all previous records, and as regards teaching, he was more liberal, more original and more progressive than all his predecessors. In other words, the older Teachers were rather one-sided, while the teaching of this new Incarnation or Teacher is that the best points of *yoga,* devotion, knowledge and work must be combined now so as to form a new society. . . . The older ones were no doubt good, but this is the new religion of this age — the synthesis of *yoga,* knowledge, devotion and work, the propagation of knowledge and devotion to all, down to the very lowest, without distinction of age or sex. The previous Incarnations were all right, but they have been synthesized in the person of Ramakrishna. For the ordinary man and the beginner, steady devotion *(nishtha)* to an ideal is of paramount importance. That is to say, teach them that all great Personalities should be duly honored, but homage should be paid now to Ramakrishna. There can be no vigor without steady devotion. Without it one can not preach with the intensity of a *Mahavira* (Hanuman).

Besides, the previous ones have become rather old.

Now we have a new India, with its new God, new religion and new Vedas.' *(The Complete Works,* Vol. VII, p. 493)

Swami Vivekananda's inspiration

Various opinions have been expressed regarding the inspiration behind Swami Vivekananda's gospel of service. True, there are various influences preparing a great man for delivering his special message. But even at an early age, the Swami had the intuitive knowledge of his high destiny, and he spoke to some of his college-mates that he would chalk out a new path for himself. But it is after meeting Sri Ramakrishna and his training under the latter and the experience of Oneness as a result, that he was convinced that he had a message to deliver and a mission to fulfill. The call did not come from any external agency but from his innermost self which was one with Reality, an experience about which he said that even if a fool entered into it he came out a sage. It is because of this that he spoke 'like one having authority and not as the scribes.' It is this which made Vivekananda a Prophet like the Prophets of old. *The Life of Swami Vivekananda* (Vol. IV, p. 169) tries to narrate the different influences on him:

'The chief formulative influences that went to the determining of his vision may be classified generally under the following heads: His Master's great prophecies regarding him; his training and his Realization; his knowledge of Western philosophies, history and Sanskrit scriptures; the constant study of the Divine life of his *Guru* before him in which he found the key to life and the verification of the Sastras; his travels all over his Motherland during which he availed himself of the constant opportunities of comparing her with what she had been and was, and of studying the life and thoughts of the people, their needs and possibilities, and the diversities of their customs and faiths; and mixing with princes and peasants, saints and scholars, he "grasped in its comprehensiveness", as Sister Nivedita says, "that vast whole of which his Master's life and personality had been a brief and intense epitome. These, then — the Sastra, the *Guru,* and the Motherland, — are the three notes that mingle themselves to form the music of the works of Vivekananda. These are the treasure which it is his to offer."

His meditation in Kanyakumari sitting on the last rock brought certain convictions in him regarding his future plan of work. In that hour of inspiration, he found his mission clear. He was to cross the seas and spread the light for the good of the world. Nay, there was something more. He was also to sacrifice his life for the sake of his poor countrymen. So intense was his anguish for the lot of the suffering millions! He was to evolve plans for the amelioration of their suffering. In that moment of supreme compassion, comparable to that of Buddha, even the bliss of absorption in the Absolute was rejected. To him, came the vision of the poor who were to be served as veritable gods with his life's blood in a spirit of worship. Vivekananda's gospel of service took a definite shape at that very moment. About this feeling he writes thus in a letter:

'My brother, in view of all this, specially of the poverty and ignorance, I had no sleep. At Cape Comorin sitting in

Mother Kumari's temple, sitting on the last bit of Indian rock—I hit upon a plan: We are so many *sannyasins* wandering about, and teaching the people metaphysics— it is all madness. Did not our *Gurudeva* use to say, "An empty stomach is no good for religion?" That those poor people are leading the life of brutes is simply due to ignorance. We have for all ages been sucking their blood and trampling them underfoot.' *(The Complete Works*, Vol. VI, p. 254)

It is clear that Swami Vivekananda's feelings played an important part in the formation of his gospel of service. Service originates from the fullness of heart. But the doctrine of service requires a saint to render validity and a philosopher to give language to it. Ramakrishna and Vivekananda jointly fulfill this task. And Vivekananda's message has been looked upon as the commentary of the Gospel of Sri Ramakrishna. But some felt his Master Sri Ramakrishna was only a mystic. It is Vivekananda who, familiar with the modern thinking, brought in these extraneous ideas from foreign sources. But facts would not bear the contention. While Vivekananda was, to be sure, impressed by the social work of modern type and admired the power of organization and the techniques, the original inspiration is rooted in the Gospel of his Master and in the tradition. It is characteristic of Hindu thought that in every age there was a dichotomy between knowledge and action, between *Jnana* and *Karma* and their ultimate reconciliation had to be made. From the Vedic age down to the present day, this dichotomy and reconciliation can be noticed. It is because Hinduism deals with the totality of life and experience that its scheme does not exclude any of the aspects. *Jnana* and *Karma*, knowledge and action, represent the two halves constituting life. Action stands for the manifoldness of experience and efforts for desired objects whereas knowledge stands for the denial of life and its desires and seeing the truth face to face. Both are necessary in a total scheme for life's fulfillment. The problem in every age of Indian history has been the reconciliation of the two, making action leading to knowledge. This made the view of life more comprehensive and synthetic.

In the Vedic age, the conflict arose between sacrificial rites and *Atma-vidya*, the spiritual wisdom. In the Upanishads, the Vedic gods were idealized into Brahman and the Vedic ceremonies into various meditations leading to final realization. Sri Krishna reconciled both ritualistic and secular activities. The *Mahabharata* gave the story of the butcher and the pious wife who by sheer performance of their duty got knowledge. With the rise of Acharya Sankara, superiority of knowledge was firmly established over ritualism which had powerful advocates in Kumarila, Mandana and others. Subservience of *Karma* to *Bhakti* was forcefully presented by Acharya Ramanuja and others. The modern age required a wider synthesis, for the question of the value of secular work has been brought to the forefront because of the tremendous social and organizational activity requiring the attention of individuals. To reconcile this with the supreme aim of life was the problem. Vivekananda took up the problem and his answer was the well-known doctrine of service, the worship of the Divine in man, which gave him a distinction

among the thinkers of modern times. He was not content
with merely giving the idea, he exhorted the people to work
for it and himself started several institutions in his lifetime.

Some writers see a sort of disparity between the thoughts
of Sri Ramakrishna and Swami Vivekananda, for Sri
Ramakrishna, the man of realization in fullness of *Bhakti*
and *Jnana*, once spoke disparagingly of *Karma*. Once when
Krishnadas Paul, a noted social reformer, said that doing
good to society was their principal duty, Sri Ramakrishna
retorted: 'God alone can look after the world. Let man first
realize God. Let him get Divine authority, and be endowed
with His power. Then and then alone he can think of doing
good to others.' Also to Shambhunath Mallick, he said,
'When God appears before you, would you seek schools
and hospitals of Him. Or beg for *Bhakti, Jnana,* etc.? Then
give up all these thoughts of hospital-building and think
of God alone.' Again he said, 'A man went to the Kali
temple at Kalighat and went on distributing money to
the beggars and in the process could not get time to see
the Mother!' Therefore it is argued that according to Sri
Ramakrishna, all work is an obstacle and if at all work is
to be done, it should be done after realization. But it has
been pointed out that the doctrine of service, an essential
teaching of Swami Vivekananda, is only another version
of the doctrine of the harmony of religions, an equally
essential teaching of Sri Ramakrishna, and that the one
cannot be without the other. The harmony of religions is the
most unique of Sri Ramakrishna's teachings and it stands
for the equal validity of all religions, if sincerely followed.

Religion stands for spiritual unfoldment and not for mere creeds and rituals. So whatever pushes a man forward towards final realization is religion. And in that sense, does not life itself become religion? In this sense only Swami Vivekananda said, 'Let every man have his own religion.' 'Religion is the manifestation of the Divinity already in man,' said he. So life with its joys and sorrows, good and evil, becomes the process of that manifestation. Hence the harmony is not merely of religions but of all lives. And Sri Ramakrishna realized this harmony, this oneness. The divinity of man is a fact with the saints. Others also can realize it, if they change their idea about man and serve him. Without the spirit of worshipful service, we cannot see the vision of the Divine in men, says a writer, and without that vision we cannot perceive every life as the unfolding of the Divine, which is religion.

When we look at the life of Sri Ramakrishna, we find that he gave direct support also even to the physical type of service. He himself exhorted Mathur Babu, his caretaker, to feed the poor in Deoghar during a famine. He felt his identity with a belabored boatman and with Nature in the form of green grass. These are instances of his complete identification with non-living as well as all living beings. The unity of existence of Vedanta became a reality with him and the service to humanity is only an application of this idea. A significant anecdote has thus been described in *The Life of Swami Vivekananda* (1955, p. 107): 'The general teachings which the Master imparted to his disciples Narendranath assimilated in a unique way. He was the readiest among them all in arriving at their true spirit. His soul was most attuned to the spiritual vibrations of the Master's words. Thus he read volumes where others read but pages of that Revelation unto men which was the life and gospel of Sri Ramakrishna. Really Naren possessed a rare insight to interpret Sri Ramakrishna's words. One instance will suffice. One day, some time during the year 1884, Sri Ramakrishna was seated in his room at Dakshineswar, surrounded by his disciples among whom was Naren. The conversation drifted to the Vaishnava religion. The Master gave the gist of the cult of Lord Gauranga and finished by saying: "This religion enjoins upon its followers the practice of three things, viz. relish for the name of God, compassion for all living creatures and service to the Vaishnavas, the devotees of the Lord. The real meaning of these precepts is this: That God is not different from His name. Therefore one should always repeat His name. God and His devotee, Krishna and the Vaishnava, are not separate from one another. Therefore everyone should show respect to all saints and devotees. Realizing this world as belonging to Sri Krishna utmost compassion should be shown to all creatures." Hardly had he uttered the words, "Compassion to all creatures," when he fell into *samadhi*. After a while he came back to a semiconscious state of mind and said to himself, "Compassion for creatures! Compassion for creatures! Thou fool! An insignificant worm crawling on earth, thou to show compassion to others! Who art thou to show compassion? No, it cannot be. It is not compassion for others, but rather service to man, recognizing him to be the veritable manifestation of God!" Everyone present there, no doubt, heard those words of Sri Ramakrishna uttered from the innermost consciousness of his soul; but none but Naren could gauge their meaning. When Naren left the room he said to the others, "What a strange light have I discovered in those wonderful words of the Master! How beautifully has he reconciled the ideal of *Bhakti* with the knowledge of the Vedanta, generally interpreted as hard, austere and inimical to human sentiments and emotions. What a grand, natural and sweet synthesis! The ordinary impression is that the culture of the knowledge of Vedanta demands an utter ostracism of society and humanity and a rooting out of all tender sentiments such as love, devotion, compassion, etc. The aspirant thus goes astray in cherishing an uncompromising hatred towards the world and his fellow creatures, thinking them as impediments in the way of spiritual attainments. But from those words of wisdom which Sri Ramakrishna uttered in an ecstatic mood, I have understood that the ideal of Vedanta lived by the recluse outside the pale of society can be practiced even from hearth and home and applied to all our daily schemes of life. Whatever may be the avocation of a man, let him understand and realize that it is God alone who has manifested Himself as the world and created beings. He is both immanent and transcendent. It is He who has become all diverse creatures, objects of our love, respect or compassion and yet He is beyond all these. Such realization of Divinity in humanity leaves no room for arrogance. By realizing it, a man cannot have any jealousy or pity for any other being. Service of man, knowing him to be the manifestation of God, purifies the heart, and in no time, such an aspirant realizes himself as part and parcel of God, Existence-Knowledge-Bliss Absolute. Those words of Sri Ramakrishna throw an altogether new light upon the path of devotion. Real devotion is far off until the aspirant realizes the immanence of God. By realizing Him in and through all beings and by serving Him through humanity, the devotee acquires real devotion. Those following the paths of work and *yoga* are similarly benefited by those words of the Master. The embodied being cannot remain even for a minute without doing any work. All his activities should be directed to the service of man, the manifestation of God upon earth, and this will accelerate his progress towards the goal. However, if it be the will of God, the day will soon come when I shall proclaim this grand truth before the world at large. I shall make it the common property of all, the wise and the fool, the rich and the poor, the Brahmin and the Pariah."

This shows how this remark of Sri Ramakrishna opened a new dimension to Vivekananda's thoughts. Even as a student, he said that he would preach this grand idea when the time came. The idea of harmony of religions, the divinity of the soul, the oneness of existence – all take their basis in the vision of the divine in man. The democratic principle of giving value to the individual has its firm roots here. To get that vision, it is not merely our concept of man that must change but our behavior too. Sri Ramakrishna said: 'I now really find that it is the Lord who is moving about in the forms of men, sometimes a saint, sometimes a fraud, at other times a knave. But all of them are God and none but God. So I say, God in the form of saint, God in the form of knave, God in the form of libertine.'

Sri Ramakrishna gave the spirit of service through these hints, the detailed work was left to his worthy disciple who gave it a language. Thus Swami Vivekananda raised *Karma-Yoga* to the status of an independent path. Down the ages it was considered to be secondary to *Jnana* and *Bhakti,* in spite of Sri Krishna's clear opinion *(Gita* III. 19) that through detached work alone the highest goal could be reached. Not only did Swami Vivekananda consider *Karma-Yoga* as the religious path suitable for this age but he exhorted people to adopt it without a shadow of doubt. The life work of Swami Vivekananda was to make spirituality intensely practical.

How this spirit of worship Swami Vivekananda transmitted to the service of the Motherland has been finely pointed out by Sister Nivedita in her 'Introduction' to *The Complete Works of Swami Vivekananda:* 'Here is the crowning realization, into which all others are resolvable. When, in his lecture on "The Work Before Us", the Swami adjures all to aid him in the building of a temple wherein every worshipper in the land can worship, a temple whose shrine shall contain only the word *OM,* there are some of us who catch in the utterance the glimpse of a still greater temple — India herself, the Motherland, as she already exists — and see the paths not of the Indian churches alone, but of all Humanity, converging there, at the foot of that sacred place wherein is set the symbol that is no symbol, the name that is beyond all sound. It is to this, and not away from it, that all the paths of all the worships and all the religious systems lead. India is at one with the most puritan faiths of the world in her declaration that progress is from seen to unseen, from the many to the One, from the low to the high, from the form to the formless, and never in the reverse direction. She differs only in having a word of sympathy and promise for every sincere conviction, wherever and whatever it may be, as constituting a step in the great ascent.'

Work And Workers

Spiritual motivation

What type of service did Swami Vivekananda want his people to render to society? And what type of training for workers did he visualize to work out that scheme? Religion is his fulcrum for all social action. His 'Practical Vedanta' or service of society with a religious motivation is, in a sense, an original contribution. It is not that the idea was not there. But it was Swami Vivekananda who forcefully presented the idea of looking upon man as God and serving him. Philosophically, there are two ways of looking upon the world. The negative way is to reject it, it being an illusion in the form in which it presents itself before us. The positive way is to look to its fundamental basis, the ultimate Reality which alone exists. This is the deification of the world as preached by Swami Vivekananda, as against the traditional negation of it. Both are true from different standpoints, but the deification has a tremendous social value. In all spheres, understanding among different groups is reached by overlooking the differences and stressing upon the common points. Men are equal, we say. We know they are not so in the purely physical sense but they are so in a special sense. From the standpoint of worship, too, this attitude is valid. To consider God as man will be idolatry, but to look upon man as God will be symbology and symbology is an accepted mode of worship in the religious system. So hard work with unselfishness plus the particular attitude is all that is necessary in this worship.

This worshipful attitude to men as God has been described as the socialization of the Absolute. The realization of the ultimate Reality is true religion, which in its expression is both individual and social. This realization is individual but men of realization see God everywhere as the Spirit, as the sum total of all souls. Seeing God in society thus becomes a spiritual discipline. When God is thus realized, service of society becomes service of God. It is then a distinct method of *sadhana*, which is nothing but the imitation of saints' experience and hence is not insincere. This is why Vedanta teaches the deification of the world, which has been very forcefully presented by Swami Vivekananda in his lecture on 'God in Everything.'

As a result of this attitude, there arises a tremendous social gain. The individual benefits from it by being freed from the dichotomy of sacred and secular, of contemplation and action. Men of social awareness find it more suitable. The difficulty of forgetting God or losing poise in the crowded program may be overcome by constant awareness and intensification of the attitude or by combining work and worship. The three stages of 'work and worship', 'work as worship' and 'work is worship' come to a spiritual aspirant step by step. Even the great devotees, who did not consciously follow work as a discipline, came to the realization that whatever we do is nothing but worship. This spiritual method of seeing the Divine in society and serving it is suited to the modern temper and is also available to those who lack faith. Socialization is a modern fad. Awareness of it is imperative for modern minds, and as Victor Hugo puts it, 'Nothing is so powerful in the world as an idea whose time has come.' That is the reason for the tremendous popularity and impact of Swami Vivekananda's *Karma-Yoga* and 'Practical Vedanta'.

This stress on spirituality is not merely for social workers; it is to play an important part in the lives of those who are to be regenerated. He felt that mass education must not disturb the religion of the people, which is essential for a complete life and which fosters the higher virtues so necessary for society. In all their changes, the central point is spirituality. True religion must light up the mind of man and give him all the strength that is necessary. So Swami Vivekananda said:

'Your duty at present is to go from one part of the country to another, from village to village, and make the people understand that mere sitting about idly won't do any more. Make them understand their real condition and say, "O ye brothers, all arise! Awake! How much longer would you remain asleep!" Go and advise them how to improve their own condition, and make them comprehend the sublime truths of the shastras, by presenting them in a lucid and popular way . . . Impress upon their minds that they have the same right to religion as the Brahmanas. Initiate all, even down to the Candalas, in these fiery *mantras*. Also instruct them in simple words, about the necessities of life, and in trade, commerce, agriculture, etc.' *(Swami Vivekananda on India and Her Problems,* Compiled by Swami Nirvedananda, pp. 71-72)

Patriotism

Swami Vivekananda was a lover of his country. To him patriotism was an expression of true worship and loving service to fellowmen, a means to the realization of the highest. It was merging of one's whole personality into the soul of his people. Everyone has to be a patriot. And what is his definition of a patriot?

'They talk of patriotism . . . First, feel from the heart. . . Through the heart comes inspiration. Love opens the most impossible gates; love is the gate to all the secrets of the universe. Feel, therefore, my would-be reformers, my would-be patriots! Do you feel? Do you feel that millions and millions of the descendants of gods and of sages have become next-door neighbors to brutes? Do you feel that millions are starving today, and millions have been starving for ages? Do you feel that ignorance has come over the land as a dark cloud? Does it make you restless? Does it make you sleepless? Has it gone into your blood, coursing through your veins, becoming consonant with your heartbeats? Has it made you almost mad? Are you seized with that one idea of the misery of ruin, and have you forgotten all about your name, your fame, your dearest ones, your property, even your own bodies? Have you done that? That is the first step to become a patriot, the very first step.' *(The Complete Works,* Vol. Ill, pp. 225-26)

Because of his deep love for his country, Swami Vivekananda has rightly been described as the 'Patriot-Monk of India.'

Sister Nivedita graphically describes in her book *The Master as I saw Him* (pp. 46-49) the dual aspect of Swami Vivekananda's genius as a lover of his country and as a teacher of spirituality and the inevitable conflict born of them:

'From the moment of my landing in India, however, I found something quite unexpected underlying all this . . . It was the personality of my Master himself, in all the fruitless torture and struggle of a lion caught in a net. . . .

'But wherein lay the struggle? Whence came the frequent sense of being baffled and thwarted? Was it a growing consciousness of bodily weakness, conflicting with the growing clearness of a great purpose? . . . Banished to the Himalayas with shattered health, at the very moment when his power had reached its height, he had written a letter to his friend which was a cry of despair.

'To what was the struggle actually due? Was it the terrible effort of translating what he had called the "super-conscious" into the common life? Undoubtedly he had been born to a task which was in this respect of heroic difficulty. Nothing in this world is so terrible as to abandon the safe paths of accepted ideals, in order to work out some new realization, by methods apparently in conflict with the old. . . Certainly in years to come, in the last five and a half years, particularly, which were his crowning gift to his own people, he stood for work without attachment, or work for impersonal ends, as one of the highest expressions of the religious life. And for the first time in the history of India an order of monks found themselves banded together, with their faces set primarily towards the evolution of new forms of civic duty.'

How to reconstruct India

Much before the independence of India Swami Vivekananda appeared on the Indian firmament with his original ideas for reconstructing India. The paramount necessity was to arouse enthusiasm of the enduring type coupled with a clear vision of the future. An understanding of the Indian temperament and fundamental aspiration has to be there for proper propelling of the national zeal. Tremendous *rajasic* mentality had to be created and to hold the zeal together, a consciousness of India as a synthetic whole had to be presented before the society. Lack of unity is a bane to newly freed zealous countries, as we see before our eyes. Unity would be achieved, true nationhood would be a fact, if we could create an inner consciousness of a common ideal, common struggle and common feeling among the different constituents of the nation. Patriotism is a means but often it is bedeviled by parochialism because of its stress on group interest. Unity of purpose and striving could be brought in India minus the bad effects, if it could be inspired by a higher ideal. The spiritual quest itself could be made the motive power of Indian nationalism, spiritual realization being its goal. Improving of material standards of life, economic growth, industrial development, scientific progress, — all would find their proper place in the total scheme of all-round regeneration of India. That is what Swami Vivekananda wanted. So he exhorted Indians to live up to the ideal to bring about the model society where material and spiritual forces are well balanced. True spiritualization is a slow process. But a mere political nationality is apt to be belligerent to keep the internal different forces together for work, if it is based on pacts and compromises. In trying to accumulate strength for progress, tremendous *rajasic* zeal has to be released; material happiness has to be brought, it is true, but not at the cost of the spiritual ideal. Then India would have an imperfect civilization and would collapse sooner than expected like some of the predominantly materialistic civilizations of old. This danger of rejection of India's spiritual culture may come from three directions, he thought in the last years of the last century:

(a)   The land could be converted to an exotic religion.

(b)   The lower castes could create a different religion.

(c)   A totally non-religious group could arise. The first, the efforts to convert the country to Christianity have failed, as failed Islam in olden days. The danger of the second has also passed off. The third danger of materialistic secular democracy and extremely anti-spiritual dialectic materialism still continues. Secular democracy will bring in indifference and the aggressive second is bound to bring in conflict and civil war. The only solution lies in their being spiritualized, retaining most of their economic and social program. With this perspective, we can very easily understand why Swami Vivekananda was so anxious to retain the spiritual values. The method he suggested was to make the motive power of the national upheaval to be idealistic in nature and content and practice of *Karma-*

(a) *Yoga*, detached, unselfish action, for workers. Aiming high, they will at least practice enlightened self-interest as against gross selfishness. As it is commonly said, the most likely way of achieving a goal is not aiming at the goal itself but at some goal beyond it. Of course, for this a section of the people must be essentially dedicated to the spiritual ideal and will at the same time embody the best aspirations of the nation. They are not to be otherworldly but disinterestedly serviceful. They will be the fittest instruments to uphold the spiritual ideal before the nation. Not only that, the ideal has to be preached to other nations to bring the world round this ideal, thus paving the way for a peaceful, lasting, spiritual civilization. With that idea, he founded the Ramakrishna Math and Mission which would serve as the suitable model.

Heritage

In regenerating India, Swami Vivekananda often spoke of going back to the past cultural heritage. Why did he glorify the past so much? Swami Vivekananda's idea was that to create enthusiasm in a huge nation it was necessary to arouse the national pride. And what have Indians to be proud of except this cultural heritage? He said:

'Nowadays, everybody blames those who constantly look back to their past. It is said that so much looking back to the past, is the cause of all India's woes. To me, on the contrary, it seems that the opposite is true. So long as they forgot the past, the Hindu nation remained in a state of stupor; and as soon as they have begun to look into their past, there is on every side a fresh manifestation of life.'

(The Complete Works, Vol. IV, p. 324)

The hypnosis of centuries of subjection made Indians weak. So rang out his message of strength based on the idea of superiority of India's cultural heritage. 'Back to the Upanishads!' 'He who thinks that he is weak is weak: he who believes that he is strong is already invincible!' The *Gita* to him, was 'a mine of strength.' Indians would arise anew when they assimilate this strength, this faith of the Upanishads. The sense of superiority of their cultural heritage would remove the hypnosis and put energy in his countrymen. That was his idea.

India can remain united only on the common ground of her sacred traditions. He said, 'The common ground that we have is our sacred traditions, our religion.' Nationality, to him, was not merely political, of having powers and rights and privileges but a sacred ideal 'whose innermost striving was to express its own conception of ideal manhood'. The political significance of nationality was necessary but his stress was on unity based on heart and spirit rather than on mind. He was international in outlook because of his realization of the oneness of existence. Yet he was the very personification of the true Indian spirit.

Imitation

It was not required of modern India, according to him, to change her social or religious institutions, but all that was required was to put them in a position to work out the current problems in the light of the national ideals. He was against meaningless imitation. He knew that our Indian social system has many defects and they must be rectified. But he was against throwing off of our own age-old system and borrowing wholesale any new system including that of the West. He said:

'A child of but yesterday, destined to die the day after tomorrow comes to me and asks me to change all my plans and if I hear the advice of that baby and change all my surroundings according to his ideas I myself should be a fool, and no one else. Much of the advice that is coming to us from different countries is similar to this. Tell these wiseacres, "I will hear you when you have made a stable society yourselves. You cannot hold on to one idea for two days, you quarrel and fail; you are born like moths in the spring and die like them in five minutes. You come up like bubbles and burst like bubbles too. First form a stable society like ours. First make laws and institutions that remain undiminished in their power through scores of centuries. Then will be the time to talk on the subject with you, but till then, my friend, you are only a giddy child."' (*The Complete Works,* Vol. III, p. 133)

Swami Vivekananda's love for India was unlimited. To him, all India was sacred and wonderful and he defended even Indian manners and customs often while training up his Western disciples:

'The Swami was defiant in the defense of the culture of his people. He was ready to beat down mercilessly any other than a living interest in everything connected with the people of his land and thundered against anything that sounded like patronizing. He would turn upon the Western disciples if they were guilty of stupid criticism. He demanded that they should come to the task of the understanding of India without prepossessions and with sincerity, and that India must be understood in the light of the spiritual vision. He upset any notion they might have had as to his country being either old or effete, and he often said that only a youthful nation could so readily have assimilated the ideals of a foreign culture. He made them see India, in the light of its ideals and ideas, as young, vital and powerful, as one throughout in the religious vision. He made them see that India's culture was incomparable, being developed through thousands of years of trial and experimentation till it had attained the highest standard ever reached by humanity, and consequently possessed an unshakable stability and strength. He made them see the *why* of every Indian custom. And they saw that though India was poor, it was clean and that poverty was honored in the land where religion was understood to be renunciation, and that here poverty was not necessarily associated with vice, as it is so often in the West. To the Swami all India was sacred and wonderful. And later on as he wandered with his disciples from city to city and province to province, he would recount to them the glories and the beauties of the land. The Swami was anxious that his Western disciples should make an impartial study of Indian problems. They were not only to see the glories, but also to have especially a clear understanding of the problems of the land and bring the ideals and methods of Western scientific culture to bear upon the task of finding a solution.' (*The Life of Swami Vivekananda:* by His Eastern and Western Disciples, pp. 553-554)

Swami Vivekananda was fully conscious of the merits

of the Western ideal but he wanted India to retain her feet firm on the ground of her own ideal and then learn the useful things from other nations. Like his Master, he was a great harmonizer. He wanted the combination of the best of the West and the East, of materialism and spirituality, of action and contemplation. So he said:

'We talk foolishly against material civilization. The grapes are sour. Even taking all that foolishness for granted, in all India there 'are, say, a hundred thousand really spiritual men and women. Now, for the spiritualization of these, must three hundred millions be sunk in savagery and starvation? Why should any starve? How was it possible for the Hindus to have been conquered by the Mohammedans? It was due to the Hindus' ignorance of material civilization . . . Material civilization, nay, even luxury is necessary to create work for the poor. Bread! Bread! I do not believe in a God, who cannot give me bread here, giving me eternal bliss in heaven! Pooh! India is to be raised, the poor are to be fed, education is to be spread, and the evil of priest craft is to be removed. No priest craft, no social tyranny! More bread, more opportunity for everybody! Our young fools organize meetings to get more power from the English. They only laugh. None deserves liberty who is not ready to give liberty.' (The Complete Works, Vol. IV, p. 368).

Education

In bringing in the regeneration of India, Swami Vivekananda put the maximum emphasis on training and education. Education is the pivot of Swami Vivekananda's idea of reform. 'Education is the panacea for all social evils', he used to say. So in trying to improve the lot of the socially oppressed, he was not enamored of the prevalent social reforms, for they were only surface reforms. He wanted to go deeper and bring in a total change in their outlook and thus root out the cause of degeneration. And what was the method for bringing in that total change which removes all dullness, makes men aware of a higher and better life? It was education. He wrote:

'Traveling through many cities of Europe and observing in them the comforts and education of even the poor people, there was brought to my mind the state of our own poor people and I used to shed tears. What made the difference? Education was the answer I got. Through education comes faith in one's own Self, and through faith in one's own Self the inherent Brahman is waking up in them, while the Brahman in us is gradually becoming dormant.'

'In New York I used to observe the Irish colonists come — downtrodden, haggard-looking, destitute of all possessions at home, penniless and wooden-headed, — with their only belongings, a stick and a bundle of rags hanging at the end of it, fright in their steps, alarm in their eyes. A different spectacle in six months, — the man walks upright, his attire is changed. In his eyes and steps there is no more sign of fright. What is the cause? Our Vedanta says that that Irishman was kept surrounded by contempt in his own country — the whole of nature was telling him with one voice, — "Pat, you have no more hope, you are born a slave and will remain so." Having been thus told from his birth, Pat believed in it and hypnotized himself

that he was very low, and the Brahman in him shrank away.
While no sooner had he landed in America than he heard
the shout going up on all sides, — "Pat, you are a man as we
are, it is man who has done all, a man like you and me can
do everything: have courage!" Pat raised his head and saw
that it was so, the Brahman within woke up. Nature herself
spoke, as it were, "Arise, awake and stop not till the goal
is reached."' *(Swami Vivekananda on India and Her Problems:*
Compiled by Swami Nirvedananda, pp. 68-69)

Education in its turn makes the mind free from all
superstitions and hypnosis before tyranny and oppression
and so freedom was his spiritual goal as well as prescription
for social upliftment. Educate and give liberty was his
prescription for the masses. He said:
    'The chief cause of India's ruin has been the monopolizing
of the whole education and intelligence of the land among
a handful of men. If we are to rise again, we shall have to
do it by spreading education among the masses.' (Swami
Vivekananda: *Education,* p. 69)
    'Who will bring the light to them — who will travel
from door to door bringing education to them? Let these
people be your God — think of them, work for them, pray
for them incessantly — the Lord will show you the way.
Him I call a *mahatman* (great soul) whose heart bleeds for
the poor, otherwise he is a *duratman* (wicked soul). ...So
long as the millions live in hunger and ignorance, I hold
every man a traitor who, having been educated at their
expense, pays not the least heed to them! I call those men
who strut about in their finery, having got all their money

by grinding the poor, wretches, so long as they do not do anything for those two hundred millions who are now no better than hungry savages!' *(The Complete Works,* Vol. V, p. 58)

Qualities to imbibe

On various occasions, Swami Vivekananda recommended various qualities for the all-round development of social workers. But these same qualities are to be implanted in all the members of society. So he spoke about the development of strength, confidence, faith, zeal, fearlessness and other qualities. The first and foremost duty of a social worker is to rouse self-respect, zeal and enthusiasm in the people. Details of social activities will then very easily be looked after. To do that man must be made aware of the infinite source of energy lying within him. Divinity of the self is to be preached first. Every other thing that human beings need, such as economic rehabilitation and so on, should be offered only after the human mind has been flooded with the idea of man's true being.

For service, Swami Vivekananda visualized two types of workers, monastic and lay, both having purity of character, perfect unselfishness, tremendous missionary zeal and a higher spiritual outlook. Monks are specially to be trained to live and preach the universal religion of Vedanta in foreign countries as well as in India. The Indian work of monks will have a bias for service — physical, intellectual and spiritual. The lay workers will specially serve in the so-called secular fields. He did not consider sacred and secular service to be different. Sister Nivedita nicely puts in her *Religion and Dharma* that the grand ideal of *sannyasa* should be practiced in civic life too. Scientists, executives, social and political workers, all should have the social application *of sannyasa* by practicing detachment with zeal and determination coupled with complete unselfishness.

Since Swami Vivekananda wanted specially the youth to serve the nation, he asked them to build up a strong body and an equally strong character. He said, 'It is character that pays everywhere.' 'Men, believing young men, sincere to the backbone are wanted. A hundred such and the world becomes revolutionized.' To be a true reformer, he said, three things are necessary. 'The first to feel; do you really feel for your brothers? . . . Are you full of that idea of sympathy? If you are, that is only the first step. You must think next if you have found any remedy. The old ideas may be all superstition — but in and around these masses of superstition are nuggets of gold and truth. Have you discovered means by which to keep the gold alone, without any of the dross? One more thing is necessary. What is your motive? Are you sure that you are not actuated by greed of gold, by thirst for fame or power?' *(The Complete Works,* Vol. IV, pp. 158-159)

'Renunciation and service are the national ideals of India,' said Swami Vivekananda. He wanted national workers to develop this spirit. The essential thing is renunciation. Without renunciation none can pour out his whole heart in working for others. The man of renunciation sees all with an equal eye, and devotes himself to the service of all.

Nothing will be able to resist truth and love and sincerity.'
(Swami Vivekananda on India and Her Problems: Compiled by
Swami Nirvedananda, p. 33)

Strength

Strength was a special message of Swami Vivekananda.
It was a central principle round which he gathered his
ideas. It was he who gave the famous equation, 'Strength
is religion, religion is strength.' Strength is the watchword
of our scriptures. Quoting the *Katha Upanishad,* he exhorted
them to be 'optimistic, strong, firm and intelligent.' Strength
is necessary, for it gives ability to follow a program.

'Weakness is sin,' he said. Inhumanity and selfishness
are born of weakness. 'We lie, steal, kill and commit
other crimes because we are weak.' In his enthusiasm, he
dramatically said that playing football is better than reading
the *Gita.* He did not want India to be militarily weak, though
he was proud of India which never went out to conquer.
His exhortation of strength was not a glorification of mere
force or violence. It is not destructive. It is for making peace.
'I have always spoken of strength, not of revenge,' he said.
The other factor in the composition of the strength of
his idea is the intellectual power. Education is not the
collection of information but liberation of inexhaustible
inner potentialities of man. But, of course, the unfailing
abiding source of strength is the Atman and spiritual
strength. It is a tremendous ethical force generating
harmony and inspiring heroic self-sacrifice. His ideals for
the people of India were strength, courage, fearlessness

and service with the Lord at the centre of all work. These
characterize true manhood. Manliness, according to him,
is the whole of piety. To follow strength and fearlessness
in all circumstances is manliness. It is to uphold whatever
is true and uplifting. This is *dharma*. This is righteousness.
To act manly was the agitation of the moment too.

As a Vedantin, he knew that real strength lies in the
Self. The body has its limitations, the mind, too, is not
paramount. But it is the Atman which is the repository
of all strength, all hope, all energy. By attuning oneself to
the Self, one could gain strength, hope and energy. That is
why he exhorted his followers to spread this message of
the glory of the Atman from door to door.

Self-confidence is the one virtue he wanted his countrymen to imbibe. It was necessary for the progressive and
the backward, for the educated and the ignorant, for the
rich and the poor. In trying to assert self-confidence, even
if a man became proud, Vivekananda would not mind. He
went further in his passionate moments. Sister Nivedita
mentions him saying: 'Yes! The older I grow, the more
everything seems to me to lie in manliness. This is my new
gospel. Do even evil like a man! Be wicked, if you must, on
a grand scale !'

An important aspect of real strength, of manliness, is the
capacity to face the problems of life. He was all for fighting
Nature, for all progress in civilization came through it. He
said:

'It is rebellion against Nature, struggle for self-
preservation that differentiates Spirit from Matter. Where

there is life, there is struggle, there is the manifestation of the Spirit. Read the history of all nations and you will find that that is the Law. It is only this nation which drifts with Nature, and you are more dead than alive. You are in a hypnotized state. For the last thousand years or more, you are told that you are weak, you are nobodies, you are good for nothing and so on, and you have come to believe yourselves as such.' (*Life of Swami Vivekananda*, op. cit., pp. 490-491)

'At one time, before the trip to Amarnath, when someone had asked him, "Sir, what should we do when we see the strong oppress the weak?" he had made reply, "Why, thrash the strong, of course!" "Even forgiveness", he said on a similar occasion, "if weak and passive, is not good: to fight is better. *Forgive* when you can bring legions of angels to an easy victory. . . The world is a battle field, fight your way out." Another asked him, "Swamiji, ought one to die in defense of right, or ought one to learn never to react?" "I am for no reaction", replied the Swami slowly, and after a long pause added, " — for *sannyasins*. Self-defense for the householder!"' (ibid., pp. 593-594)

Gandhiji has popularized the idea of non-violence being applied in national life. Swami Vivekananda was all for sacrifice which is a higher virtue, but still he exhorted the youth of India to cultivate the qualities suitable for a competitive life. He said: 'Darwin's theory is applicable to the animal and vegetable kingdoms, but not to the human kingdom where reason and knowledge are highly developed. In our saints and ideal men we find no trace of struggle whatever, and no tendency to rise higher or grow stronger by the destruction of others. There we find sacrifice instead. The more one can sacrifice the greater is he. The struggle of a rational man is with his internal nature. The more he succeeds in controlling the mind the greater is he. On being questioned, "Why then do you emphasize so much the need of our physical improvement?" — the Swami thundered: "Are you men? You are no better than animals, satisfied with eating, sleeping and propagating, and haunted by fear! If you had not had in you a little rationality, you would have been turned into quadrupeds by this time! Devoid of self-respect, you are full of jealousy among yourselves, and have made yourselves objects of contempt to foreigners! Throw aside your vain bragging, your theories and so forth, and reflect calmly on the doings and dealings of your everyday life. Because you are governed by animal nature, therefore I teach you to seek for success first in the struggle for existence, and to attend to the building up of your physique, so that you may be able to wrestle all the better with your mind. The physically weak, I say again and again, are unfit for the realization of the Self! When once the mind is controlled and man is the master of his self, it does not matter whether the body remains strong or not, for then he is not dominated by it.'" (ibid., pp. 615-616)

It shows that he was aware of the higher ideal and wanted the best among us to practice it. From a philosophical height of detachment, he viewed the Indian method as fightlessness. 'You are quite wrong', he said again, 'when you think that fighting is a sign of growth. It is not so at all. Absorption is the sign. Hinduism is the very genius of absorption. We have never cared for fighting. Of course we struck a blow now and then, in defense of our homes! That was right. But we never cared for fighting for its own sake. Everyone had to learn that. So let these races of newcomers whirl on! They'll all be taken into Hinduism in the end!' (ibid., p. 651)

A very important aspect effacing Nature' is to cultivate the restraint of the senses. It is not strength and freedom that make one glide along easy and unprincipled path. So mastery over the mind and the senses must be acquired and the power of deep concentration must be developed. So he said:

'Herein is the difference between man and the animals — man has the greater power of concentration. The difference in their power of concentration also constitutes the difference between man and man. Compare the lowest with the highest man. The difference is in the degree of concentration. This is the only difference.' (*The Complete Works*, Vol. VI, p. 37)

'How has all the knowledge in the world been gained but by the concentration of the powers of the mind? The world is ready to give up its secrets if we only know how to knock, how to give it the necessary blow. The strength and force of the blow come through concentration. There is no limit to the power of the human mind. The more concentrated it is, the more power is brought to bear on one point; that is the secret.' (ibid. Vol. I, pp. 130-31)

Fearlessness is the one quality Swami Vivekananda liked to see in the youth of the country. It is the greatest glory of the Upanishads, that they visualized the highest Reality as *Abhayam,* fearlessness itself.

Faith is the other most important quality which Swami Vivekananda wanted our people to imbibe. The Upanishads and the *Gita* are full of praise for cultivating this faith. 'Whatever one's faith so one is', says the Upanishad. 'A man of faith gets knowledge', says the *Gita*. So he said:

'Faith, faith, faith in ourselves, faith, faith in God — this is the secret of greatness. If you have faith in all the three hundred and thirty millions of your mythological gods, and in all the gods which foreigners have now and again introduced into your midst, and still have no faith in yourselves, there is no salvation for you. Have faith in yourselves, and stand up on that faith and be strong; that is what we need.' (ibid., Vol. Ill, p. 190)

As Goethe puts it, 'Give me the benefit of your convictions, if you have any, but keep your doubts to yourself, for I have enough of my own.' The world wants to hear a man of conviction and if that conviction is based on his realization of man's fundamental nature, his appeal becomes irresistible. That is the secret of Swami Vivekananda's tremendous impact on scores of people in the country and outside. 'All the scholastic scaffolding falls,' said Napoleon, 'as a ruined edifice, before one single word — faith.'

Swami Vivekananda exhorted even the newly ordained monks to have faith and set themselves to the service of fellow men.

To them, he said, 'Be fearless, be ready, from today, to lay down your life for your own *Moksha* and for the good of others.' (*Life of Swami Vivekananda*, op. cit., p. 500)

Monks are to be ideal workers and other social workers, too, must practice the virtue of detachment. 'Again and again he would say that only a great monk can be a great worker. "Only the unimpassioned and unattached do most for the world," he would say. "Who can claim to be a greater worker than Buddha or Christ?" In the Swami's eyes there was no work which was secular. All work was sacred. All work was worship. "We must combine the practicality and the culture of the finest citizenship with the love of poverty, purity and thorough renunciation that characterize the true monk and man of God!"' (ibid., p. 625)

Society

Swami Vivekananda was as much a sociologist as a religious teacher. In one of his letters to a lady-disciple, we get glimpses of his ideas on the origin of custom, widow-remarriage, liberty and the psychology of religious consciousness. In it, he writes:

'Rishi, Muni or God—none has the power to force an institution on society. When the needs of the times press hard on it, society adopts certain customs for self-preservation. Rishis have only recorded those customs. As a man often resorts even to such means as are good for immediate self-protection, but which are very injurious in the future, so also, society not infrequently saves itself for the time being, but these immediate means which contributed to its preservation turn out to be terrible in the long run.'

'For example, take the prohibition of widow-marriage in our country. Don't think that Rishis or wicked men introduced the law pertaining to it. Notwithstanding the desire of men to keep women completely under their control, they never could succeed in introducing those laws without betaking themselves to the aid of a social necessity of the time.' Similar is the case, with the caste system, and other social customs. 'So, if it be necessary to change any social custom, the necessity underlying it should be found out first of all; and by altering it the custom will die of itself. Otherwise, no good will be done by condemnation or praise.'

'Liberty,' said Swami Vivekananda, 'does not certainly mean the absence of obstacles in the path of misappropriation of wealth etc. by you and me, but it is our natural right to be allowed to use our own body, intelligence or wealth according to our will, without doing harm to others; and all the members of a society ought to have the same opportunity for obtaining wealth, education, or knowledge. . . .'

'Who constitute society? The millions, or you, I and a few others of the upper classes?' "Raise self by self." Let each one work out one's own salvation. It is freedom in every way, i.e. advance towards *Mukti* is the worthiest gain of man. To advance towards freedom — physical, mental and spiritual — and help others to do so is the supreme prize of man. Those social rules which stand in the way of the unfoldment of this freedom are injurious, and steps should be taken to destroy them speedily. Those institutions should be encouraged by which men advance in the path of freedom.' (ibid., pp. 618-20)

His concept of service led him to a concept of society which was the fore-runner of socialist thoughts in India. He was a socialist, 'not because it is a perfect system, but because half a loaf is better than no bread. The other systems have been tried and found wanting. Let this one be tried — if for nothing else, for the novelty of the thing.' But he was not a socialist in the ordinary sense of the term, for he was anxious for all-round welfare to retain the spiritual values.

He wanted the combination of all that is best in every old social group. He wrote, 'If it is possible to form a state in which the knowledge of the priest, the culture of the militia, the distributive spirit of the commercial, and the ideal of equality of the rest can all be kept intact, minus their evils, it will be an ideal state.' He thought of harmonizing the two special characteristics of the two important communities of India, the social equality of the Muslims and the thinking faculty of the Hindus and would fondly express this idea with the expression, 'Islamic body and Vedantic brain.' He feared that in the age of the common man there may be lowering of cultural standards. So he wanted abolition of privileges and voluntary sharing of the enjoyable goods of life. It is not merely equal opportunities, it is giving an extra consideration to the poor and the down-trodden. 'Our Mission,' he said, 'is for the destitute, the poor and the illiterate peasantry, and laboring classes; and if after everything has been done for them first, there is spare time, then only for the gentry.' (Swami Vivekananda: *Caste, Culture and Socialism*, pp. 84-92)

In social reform, he did not believe in condemnation or in sudden change. Growth is always gradual. Take a man from where he stands and from there give him a lift.'

Masses

Swami Vivekananda was one of the earliest leaders who thought about improving the lot of the masses, for it is they who are the backbone of society. So he wrote in a letter:

'Preach the idea of elevating the masses by means of a central college, and bringing education as well as religion to the door of the poor by means of missionaries trained in this college. Suppose some disinterested *sannyasins*, bent on doing good to others, go from village to village, disseminating education, and seeking in various ways to better the condition of all down to the *Chandala*, through oral teaching, and by means of maps, cameras, globes and such other accessories, — can't that bring forth good in time?' *(Swami Vivekananda on India and Her Problems,* op. cit., p. 72)

'Keep the motto before you — "Elevation of the masses without injuring their religion." Remember that the nation lives in the cottage. But, alas ! Nobody ever did anything for them. . . Can you raise them? Can you give them back their lost individuality without making them lose their innate spiritual nature? Can you become an Occidental of Occidentals in your spirit of equality, work, energy, freedom and at the same time a Hindu to the very backbone in religious culture and instincts? This is to be done and we will do it.' *(The Complete Works,* Vol. V, pp. 29-30)

He exhorted our young men to render service to their fellowmen. In one of his letters written from America, he wrote to Alasinga Perumal, 'Trust not the so-called rich, they are more dead than alive. The hope lies in you – in the meek, the lowly, but the faithful. Have faith in the Lord; no policy, it is nothing. Feel for the miserable and look up for help – it shall come. I have traveled twelve years with this load in my heart and this idea in my head. I have gone from door to door of the so-called rich and great. With a bleeding heart I have crossed half the world to this strange land seeking for help. The Lord is great. I know He will help me. I may perish of cold or hunger in this land, but I bequeath to you, young men, this sympathy, this struggle for the poor, the ignorant, the oppressed.'

'It is not the work of a day,' he wrote further, 'and the path is full of the most deadly thorns. But Parthasarathi is ready to be our *Sarathi,* we know that; and in His name and with eternal faith in Him, set fire to the mountain of misery that has been heaped upon India for ages – and it shall be burned down. Come then, look it in the face, brethren, it is a grand task and we are so low. But we are the sons of Light and children of God. Glory unto the Lord, we will succeed.' *(Letters of Swami Vivekananda,* pp. 70-71)

What are his ideas about mass contact which is a popular slogan now? Swami Vivekananda's exhortation to his educated countrymen was full of suggestions for mass communication. For that, qualified workers are of utmost importance. They must be strong, vigorous, believing young men, fired with the ideal and armed with the spirit of sacrifice and selflessness. The content of this education will be secular as well as spiritual knowledge. For that, he wanted to set in motion machinery that would bring noble ideas to the door of everybody. The villagers have to be taught hygiene etc. and they also must be conversant with the cultural heritage and also the day-to-day happenings. Education will be best, if it is given through religion. The medium should be the vernaculars. Education should be given orally by telling stories, history etc. and occasionally through different village theatrical programs. Globes, charts, posters etc. have to be profusely used. Swami Vivekananda was one of the earliest thinkers to suggest the use of modern methods including the audio-visual. He wanted the talks to be simple, interesting and direct. The teachers must go to the villagers instead of expecting the villagers to come to them. As a technique, they must know how to come down to the level of the villagers. This is a tremendous task. But this is a duty. This is their debt to the community.

Caste

Pursuing his concept of service, Swami Vivekananda devoted himself to discussing the burning questions of the masses, of the caste system and of women. The underlying principles of social organizations have to be understood before a social program is evolved. To him, caste in its broad sense of division was a universal phenomenon. It is in the nature of things that societies will be divided into groups. When they are crystallized and become hereditary, they are called castes. Mr. Packard in his well-known book *The Status Seekers* cites examples of hereditary stratification of professions from the American business world. In many countries, it is money, instead of heredity, that brings in the division. In modern society, we take an individual as a unit whereas in India a community embodied in caste was accepted as a unit. A man, though not free to go up the ladder alone, could do so along with the group. He pointed out:

'The law of caste in every other country takes the individual man or woman as the sufficient unit. Wealth, power, intellect or beauty suffices for the individual to leave the status of birth and scramble up to anywhere he can. Here the unit is all the members of a caste community. Here too, one has every chance of rising from a low caste to a higher or to the highest; only, in this birth-land of altruism, one is compelled to take his whole caste along with him. In India, you cannot on account of your wealth, power or any other merit, leave your fellows behind and make common cause with your superiors. If you want to rise to a higher caste in India, you have to elevate all your caste first, and then there is nothing in your onward path to hold you back.'

The caste system served the Indian society well in times of need by providing it a great measure of stability. 'No doubt,' says Sydney Law in his *Vision of India* about *caturvarnya*, 'that it is the main cause of the fundamental stability and contentment by which Indian society has been braced up for centuries against the shock of politics and the cataclysms of nature.'

While Swami Vivekananda thus defended the original

purpose of the caste system, he denounced the abuses into which it had fallen. The crystallized, hereditary caste system of the present day, the 'don't-touchism, received its strongest condemnation at his hands. But he believed in leveling up rather than leveling down. 'The solution is not by bringing down the higher, but by raising the lower up to the level of the higher.' The only way to bring about the leveling of castes is to appropriate the culture, the education, which is the strength of the higher castes.'

In trying to remove the evils of social differences, Swami Vivekananda was against all strife, for that will weaken the nation. So he said:

'Therefore, it is no use fighting among the castes. What good will it do? It will divide us all the more, weaken us all the more, degrade us all the more. The solution is not by bringing down the higher, but by raising the lower up to the level of the higher. And that is the line of work that is found in all our books, in spite of what you may hear from some people whose knowledge of their own scriptures and whose capacity to understand the mighty plans of the ancients are only zero. What is the plan? The ideal at one end is the *Brahmana* and the ideal at the other end is the Chandala, and the whole work is to raise the Chandala up to the *Brahmana*. Slowly and slowly you find more and more privileges granted to them.' *(Swami Vivekananda on India and Her Problems,-op.* cit., p.84)

Swami Vivekananda was against class war. Instead, he wanted to bring out the best qualities of the higher and privileged castes and classes. He was not prepared to denounce the forward groups for their progress. While describing the role of Brahmana, he said: 'It is true he was the earliest preacher to the Indian races, he was the first to renounce everything in order to attain to the higher realization of life, before others could reach to the idea. It was not his fault that he marched ahead of the other castes. Why did not the other castes so understand and do as they did? Why did they sit down and be lazy, and let the Brahmanas win the race?'

'But it is one thing', he said, 'to gain an advantage, and another thing to preserve it for evil use. Whenever power is used for evil it becomes diabolical; it must be used for good only. So this accumulated culture of ages of which the Brahmana has been the trustee, he must now give to the people at large, and it was .because he did not give it to the people, that the Mohammedan invasion was possible. It was because he did not open this treasury to the people from the beginning, that for a thousand years we have been trodden under the heels of every one who chose to come to India; it was through that we have become degraded, and the first task must be to break open the cells that hide the wonderful treasures which our common ancestors accumulated; bring them out, and give them to everybody, and the Brahmana must be the first to do it: There is an old superstition in Bengal that if the cobra that bites, sucks out his own poison from the patient, the man must survive. Well then, the Brahmana must suck out his own poison.' (ibid., pp. 86-87)

What Swami Vivekananda wanted is the abolition of all

privileges based on caste. He went further in his lectures on 'Privilege' and 'Vedanta and Privilege' and said that all types of privileges based on birth, health, education and spirituality are based on tyranny and exploitation. So he said:

'It is in the nature of society to form itself into groups; and what will go will be these privileges! Caste is a natural order. I can perform one duty in social life, and you another; you can govern a country, and I can mend a pair of old shoes, but that is no reason why you are greater than I, for can you mend my shoes? Can I govern the country? I am clever in mending shoes, you are clever in reading Vedas, that is no reason why you should trample on my head; why if one commits murder should he be praised and if another steals an apple why should he be hanged? This will have to go.' (ibid., pp. 79-80)

If at all privileges are necessary, the balance must tilt towards the backward. So he said:

'If the Brahmin has more aptitude for learning on the grounds of heredity than the Pariah, spend no money on the Brahmin's education, but spend all on the Pariah. Give to the weak, for there all the gift is needed; if the Brahmin is born clever, he can educate himself without help. . . This is justice and reason as I understand it.'

The philosophy of Vedanta can give back people their lost self-respect if properly cultivated. 'Each Hindu, I say, is a brother to every other, and it is we, who have degraded them by our outcry, "Don't touch," "Don't touch!" And so the whole country has been plunged to the utmost depths of meanness, cowardice and ignorance. These men have to be lifted; words of hope and faith have to be proclaimed to them. We have to tell them, "You are also men like us and you have all the rights that we have.'" (ibid., pp. 82-83)

Women

In trying to define the national ideal and suggesting remedies for social evils, Swami Vivekananda's attention was naturally drawn to the plight of women. He wanted their progress, for the progress of a nation depends upon the progress of its women. He wrote about the imperative need of women's progress in the following way:

'All nations have attained greatness, by paying proper respect to the women. That country and that nation which do not respect the women have never become great, nor will ever be in future. The principal reason why your race has so much degenerated is that you had no respect for these living images of Shakti. Manu says, "Where women are respected there the gods delight; and where they are not, there all works and efforts come to naught." (*Manu-Samhita* II. .56) There is no hope of rise for that family or country where there is no estimation of women, where they live in sadness.' (ibid., p. 95)

Again he wrote: 'Can you better the condition of your women? Then there will be hope for your well-being. Otherwise you remain as backward as you are now. The uplift of the women, the awakening of the masses, must come first, and then only can any real good come about for the country, for India. If the women are raised, then their children will by their noble actions glorify the name of the country — then will culture, knowledge, power and devotion awaken in the country.' (ibid., p. 95) But he cautioned that we should not judge their condition through the eyes of others having different standards of morality and outlook of life.

'We should not allow the sudden influx of European criticism, and our consequent sense of contrast, to make us acquiesce too readily in the notion of the inequality of our women. Circumstances have forced upon us, for many centuries, the woman's need of protection. This and not her inferiority, is the true reading of our customs. Could anything be more complete than the equality of boys and girls in bur old forest universities? Read our Sanskrit dramas — read the story of Sakuntala, and see if Tennyson's "Princess" has anything to teach us!'

Again: 'In Malabar the women lead in everything. Exceptional cleanliness is apparent everywhere and there is the greatest impetus to learning. When I myself was in that country, I met many women who spoke good Sanskrit, while in the rest of India not one woman in a million can speak it. Mastery elevates and servitude debases. Malabar has never been conquered either by the Portuguese, or by the Mussalmans. The Dravidians were a non-Aryan race of Central Asia, who preceded the Aryans, and those of Southern India were the most civilized. Women with them stood higher than men.' (ibid., pp. 92-93)

But women's position deteriorated and betterment of their lot was necessary. Regarding this, his view was that women must be given education and then 'let them decide their future.' He would, however, like the ideal of Sita to be kept up. The women of India must grow and develop in the foot-prints of Sita, and that is the only way.' He was enamored of the Sita ideal and said:

'Sita is the very type of the true Indian woman, for, all the Indian ideals of a perfected woman have grown out of that one life of Sita; and here she stands these thousands of years, commanding the worship of every man, woman, and child, throughout the length and breadth of the land of Aryavarta ... All our mythology may vanish, even our Vedas may depart, and our Sanskrit language may vanish forever but so long as there will be five Hindus living here, even if only speaking the most vulgar *patois*, there will be the story of Sita present, mark my words. Sita has gone into the very vitals of our race. She is there in the blood of every Hindu man and woman; we are all children of Sita.' (ibid., p. 89)

'I know', he further continues, 'that the race that produced Sita — even if it only dreamt of her — has a reverence for woman that is unmatched on the earth. There is many a burden bound with legal tightness on the shoulders of Western women that is utterly unknown to ours. We have our wrongs and our exceptions certainly, but so have they.' (ibid. p.91)

What should be the type of education for girls? Swami Vivekananda casually mentions some: 'History and the Puranas, religion, arts, science, house-keeping, cooking, sewing, hygiene — the simple essential points in these subjects ought to be taught to our women. It is not good to let them touch novels and fiction. But only teaching rites of worship won't do; their education must be an eye-opener in all matters. Ideal characters must always be presented before the view of the girls to imbue them with a devotion to lofty principles of selflessness. The noble example of Sita, Savitri, Damayanti, Lilavati, Khana and Mira should be brought home to their minds and they should be inspired to mould their own lives, in the light of these. Along with other things they should acquire the spirit of valor and heroism. In the present day it has become necessary for them also to learn self-defense. See how grand was the Queen of Jhansi! With such an education women will solve their own problems.'

'We must see to their growing up as ideal matrons of home in time. The children of such mothers will make further progress in the virtues that distinguish the mother. It is only in the homes of educated and pious mothers that great men are born.'

'Studying the present needs of the age, it seems imperative to train some of them up in the ideal of renunciation, so that they will take up the vow of lifelong virginity, fired with the strength of that virtue of chastity which is innate in their life-blood, from hoary antiquity. Along with that they should be taught sciences and other things which would be of benefit, not only to them but to others as well, and knowing this they would easily learn these things and feel pleasure in doing so. Our motherland requires for her well-being some of her children to become such pure-souled *brahmacarinis.*' (ibid., pp. 97-99)

Exhortation

Thus, freeing men from the tyranny of hierarchical,

hereditary caste and leveling them up, amelioration of sufferings wherever they are, betterment of women, defense of the weak and uplifting the masses to build a radiant society, reconstructing India through 'the development of industry', 'improved methods of agriculture which is the noblest profession' and all possible help from the West in science and technology — all these were included in Swami Vivekananda's concept of social service. He gave the basic ideas, the detailed work was left to the workers. But service has to be undertaken not as levers to power or fame or for a name in history but as service to God Himself to satisfy the yearning of the soul. When one takes up service in this spirit, one can be free from the aberrations that would, otherwise, vitiate the endeavor. This is spirituality. This is practical Vedanta. After explaining the system of Vedanta in his famous Lahore Lecture, Swami Vivekananda exhorts young men to practice this practical spirituality. He said:

'Raise once more that mighty banner of Advaita, for on no other ground can you have that wonderful love, until you see that the same Lord is present everywhere. Unfurl the banner of love! "Arise, awake, and stop not till the goal is reached." Arise, arise once more, for nothing can be done without renunciation. If you want to help others, your little self must go. . . Your ancestors gave up the world for doing great things. At the present time there are men who give up the world to help their own salvation. Throw away everything, even your own salvation, and go and help others. Ay, you are always talking bold words, but here is practical Vedanta before you. Give up this little life of yours. What matters it if you die of starvation — you and I and thousands like us — so long as this nation lives?

The nation is sinking, the curse of unnumbered millions is on our heads, those to whom we have been giving ditch-water to drink when they have been dying of thirst and while the perennial river of water was flowing past, the unnumbered millions whom we have allowed to starve in sight of plenty, the unnumbered millions to whom we have talked of Advaita and whom we have hated with all our strength, the unnumbered millions for whom we have invented the doctrine of *Lokachara* (usage), to whom we have talked theoretically that we are all the same and all are one with the same Lord, without even an ounce of practice. "Yet, my friends, it must be only in the mind and never in practice!" Wipe off this blot. Arise and awake.' (*The Complete Works*, Vol. Ill, pp. 430-31)

Merits of the Concept

Two Urges

Atmanam viddhi — know thyself — is the command of our sages. *Gnothi Seauton* is the old Greek adage. In India as well as in many other countries of the world, the realization of the Ultimate Reality is put forward as the sum-mum bonum of human life. From the beginning of history the different religions have shown us the way to realization. The Hindu conception of the value of life puts spiritual redemption as the supreme objective. The pining restlessness of the mystics, their hunger for realization or their impatience with the 'dark night of the soul' indicates the intense yearning of humanity for transcending the limitations of finite existence.

But there is another side of the picture. Man is not all

spirit, he has a body and it has its demands. Ministering to these needs is the task of society. So the sociologists, the economists and above all the politicians, all enjoin that every member of society must render service to it. With the intensive propaganda of non-religious doctrines, social betterment for its own sake has become the cry of the reformers whereas spiritual perfection is the eternal cry of the soul. Whenever the ethical and spiritual sense has reached higher developments in men, there is a dichotomy of thought: individual and collective. These two trends of thought pervade the entire field of human life in modern times. In secular life they manifest as egoism and altruism and in social context they reveal themselves as individualism and socialism.

Problems of Exclusive Followers

There is an inner conflict even among the exclusive followers of the two paths. Spiritual redemption requires hard training. It depends upon the shifting of our centre of interest from the world of our limited self to the ultimate Reality. That means a complete re-orientation of our outlook on life. All our efforts must be suffused with the idea of the Divine and all work that distracts our mind from it must be shunned. Constant awareness of the Reality slowly takes possession of the aspirant and all other work drops off. He becomes unfit for ordinary work. Even in the preparatory stage, he has to live in the presence of God and must have a great longing for Him, which is the main condition for realization. If he is to ask for a boon, he is to ask for God and not for hospitals. But life on earth is a series of compromises. In these days of collective planning and global economics, the society exerts a tremendous influence. A corrupt or backward society drags the ordinary aspirant down from the higher pursuits. So even for the cultivation of spiritual values a good society is essential. That is why the aspirant feels that the kingdom of heaven must be brought down on earth. There might be geniuses who fought against their degrading circumstances and became saints. But for less determined people, the quality of society is a great influencing factor in spite of their idealism. On the other hand, social gospels such as humanism take note only of man and society; and unenlightened by the vision of higher realities, they seek, to imprison the spiritual aspirations of man in a narrow mundane sphere. As a result, the unsatiated hunger of the soul manifests itself now and then and the resulting conflict drives many social workers into indecision and inaction. In the absence of an abiding background for their ethical zeal, some turn cynics after a few unpleasant experiences in social service, although they might have started with great enthusiasm in the beginning of their life. The quality of service also often goes down, for the personal factors and self-interest intrude. So the workers feel that to keep the flow of enthusiasm constant and unimpaired, it is necessary to have an enduring faith. And a greater amount of constancy and devotion could be mobilized by directing the zeal to a non-material goal.

Necessity of Harmonizing The Two Views

So far we see both are exclusive. Though a section of people can completely ignore the call of their conscience and the other the demands of society, the vast majority of humanity requires both. It may be necessary to have the whole-timers for both the pursuits, people who will be absorbed in one kind of pursuit. They are expected to be the specialists. But for others, a harmony is urgently called for. To meet the conflicting demands and guide the people in their double vocation, a proper philosophy is essential. It is a view of life, a philosophy, a faith that gives real value to all our pursuits, the recognition of which rouses us to action. Such a philosophy can be properly evolved and evaluated, if we know the demands of social workers upon the individual and the complaints they make against religious pursuits.

Demands of Society And Charges Against Spirituality

Society demands creative and productive work in the material sense from all its members. For that, the focal point of all the members of society must be society itself. Otherwise the social awareness and the resulting urge will lessen. The social stability being the immediate concern of the social and political workers, they fear, rightly or wrongly, that the hunger for higher life and the belief in eternal existence after death shift man's interest from social life and thus foster the spirit of individualism. It might have been all right, they say, in the medieval Europe when lack of unity among common men rendered them helpless in changing the whole society and that must have been the reason, according to them, for the good people of those times to cut themselves off from the vicious society and seek perfection in self-culture. But now, to progress on all fronts, a social sense must be created. An urgent awareness of the social problems and a strong determination to solve them require the full attention and energy of every individual. So higher pursuits are considered as obstacles to the realization of these objectives.

Answer of Spirituality

The spiritual aspirants answer that the religious view of life can be brushed aside only after establishing that the higher reality does not exist and the life after death is not a fact. But that is the province of metaphysics, and not of science or politics. The hunger for the infinite, of a life beyond death, is eternal and universal. Even if it does not conform to the social conceptions of the day, it has every right to live as long as search for reality or truth is not considered a taboo by the temporal authority that finds it inconvenient to its idea of social progress.

Fear Meaningless

But the fear of the social gospellers is meaningless. Every religion speaks of love and service. This is not for a moment to deny that institutionalized religions have practiced social exclusiveness or narrow dogmatism; religions — apart from 'real' religion or as they are distinguished from Religion with a capital 'R' — have an immense capacity to raise false issues; instead of promoting spirituality they often talk of spiritualism and occultism, and they may also promote obscurantism and be illogical. But Religion that integrates the head with the heart can meet science and even spur science. Spirituality can be the driving force for new discoveries. A man who is truly spiritual and believes that he is the spirit has conquered the fear of death; he can dive to the bottom of the ocean, live in the frozen area to work for his fellow beings. This is the content of spirituality. It is this force that has propelled man over the centuries to his onward march. Forgetting this fact, we often tend to deny that the greatest service to humanity has been rendered by people imbued with faith in the Higher Reality. How faith works wonders has been powerfully and graphically presented by Dr. Radhakrishnan in his *Recovery of Faith:*

'Human societies like human beings live by faith and die when faith disappears. If our society is to recover its health, it must regain its faith. Our society is not beyond curing, for it suffers from divided loyalties, from conflicting urges, from alternating moods of exaltation and despair. This condition of anguish is our reason for hope. We need a faith which will assert the power of spirit over things and find significance in a world in which science and organization seem to have lost their relationship to traditional values.'

Saints Also Work

The religions of the world point to an important fact. Men of realization might in the beginning of their pilgrimage negate the world, but as they advance, *Karma* develops with the preponderance of *sattva*. With the fullness of the heart, not only their mouths speak, their hands also work, their love for humanity, especially the suffering section of it, knows no bounds. They help thousands of people both physically and spiritually and they in their turn take up the burden of the suffering humanity on their own shoulders. Romain Rolland speaking about Sri Ramakrishna's sympathy draws out the point very clearly:

'If he did not try to detach himself from life, as so many mystics do, to avoid sufferings, it was because of universal love, which was to him a second sight, revealed to him, in a flash, in the presence of human misery, that "Jiva is Siva" — that the living being is God — that whoever loves God must unite himself with him in sufferings, in misery, even in errors and excesses, in the terrible aspect of human nature.'

Basis of the Harmonizing Philosophy

This universal love and sympathy was evident in all great souls whose only absorption was God. This was true of Christ, of Ramanuja, of Chaitanya, and of a galaxy of saints and seers of the world. Realized souls see the world from the standpoint of realization and tell us that the world is nothing but Brahman, the substratum of all existence. For ordinary men, ethical principles are formulated on the basis of these truths, as Swami Vivekananda has done in formulating his 'Practical Vedanta':

'This is the gist of all worship — to be pure and to do good to others. He who sees Siva in the poor, in the weak, and in the diseased, really worships Siva; and if he sees Siva only in the image, his worship is but preliminary. He who has served and helped one poor man seeing Siva in him, without thinking of his caste, or creed, or race, or anything, with him Siva is more pleased than with the man who sees Him only in temples.'

This application is necessary. To have the best ideal of service to the world, our philosophy of service must be grounded in the transcendental Reality to give it a permanent value. Our pursuit in ordinary life should not be based upon the ephemeral values alone; it must lead us gradually to the highest truth.

Let us see what happens when we take up questions like 'social service,' or 'social justice' simply as a mundane affair, denying them a higher morality. Wilfred Cantwell Smith opines in his *Islam in Modern History* that in practice as well as in theory, they who start by denying transcendence end up by denying value. The Marxist doctrine had started as a humanist movement. But we find today that social justice, which the Marxists had first set out to achieve, has become in the hands of the Communist parties an ideological weapon to serve the purposes of a nihilistic mundane power. The Marxist movement had repudiated transcendental norms by which it could be judged, and has, therefore, eventuated rather quickly in an enterprise with no norms at all.

A Philosophy

Based on this higher realization, a philosophy has been formulated in the dictum *Atmano moksartham jagaddhitaya ca* — for one's own salvation and for the good of the world.' This twin ideal gives the best practical ideal for most of us who do not believe in the mere reforms bereft of a higher ideal or unrelated to our own supreme good and yet are not spiritually developed enough to be devoted exclusively to the religious pursuit. Swami Vivekananda showed very clearly in his *Karma-Yoga* that it is not mere work that purifies our mind but the spirit behind it. In he words of Shakespeare, 'There is nothing either good or bad, but thinking makes it so.' The mere act of making a garland is not spiritual but the motive that it is for the sake of the Lord that makes it so. Similarly, merely giving medicine or education to the suffering or ignorant is not spiritual but the accompanying thought that God is in man, makes the whole work a worship. This kind of attitude towards work purifies the mind. It is from this subjective standpoint of purifying one's own mind that all social services gets their spiritual value. Purification of the mind in the ultimate analysis is the objective of all spiritual disciplines. In the purified mind dawns knowledge or love of God.

Distinguished from Philanthropy

This view should not be identified with philanthropic ideals of humanism or charity. It is not humanism. For, in humanism, man is the centre and society the circumference, whereas this view has its centre in man-God and its field of work is the whole of humanity. In the latter, therefore, service cannot degenerate into charity. A man becomes charitable either to get rid of the beggar or to get name and fame or if it is a purer motive, out of sympathy. Even sympathy is not enough. The ideal of service of man as God brushes off the concealed feeling of condescension. It is inspired by reverence and humility. As Swami Vivekananda said: 'Let the giver kneel down and give thanks, let the receiver stand up and permit.' A worshipper can only serve and adore, not pity and help. He is not puffed up with success, he is not mortified with failure, for he considers himself an instrument of God.

No service is small to him, for all work is God's service
and he takes as much care of the means as of the end?
This spirit saves religious movements from being choked
by social programs and it elevates social movement into
spiritual Sadhana thus saving them from frustration. Sri
Ramakrishna, or for that matter all men of God, denounced
the philanthropy of the self-lauding type, which was not
service as spiritual discipline. In a way, it may be considered
a new outlook and a new way of salvation. But in reality,
its basis is the ancient scriptures, particularly the Vedanta.

Vedantic Scheme

The Vedantic view proclaimed the spiritual unity of the
world and men with God. When Sri Shankara gave the gist
of the whole Vedanta in a single line, 'Brahman alone is real,
the world is unreal and the jiva is nothing but Brahman,'
he stressed also the idea that embodied souls are one with
Brahman. For ages we have laid stress upon the unreality of
the world. But it remained for Swami Vivekananda to draw
our attention to the other part of the saying, the oneness of
man and God. In Vedanta, the world is conceived as the
body of *Virat*, the highest manifestation of God. And service
to living beings must be done with a worshipful attitude
towards them. The reverential outlook towards social duty
is further inculcated by the idea of *Svadharma*. Its purpose
is twofold: individual purification and duty to others. The
hard school of duty will teach man self-control and one-
pointedness which along with self-dedication will make
him free from all desires and then he will be free from all

duties. *Sannyasa* dissolves all obligations but it is not the beginning of spiritual life, it is the end. If it precedes, it must be coupled with unselfish work. In the presence of such an ideal man, the whole society is surcharged with the fragrance of love, holiness and unselfishness. Then welfare of society naturally follows. That is the history of all great movements. Their realization inspires men with faith, hope and charity and when these virtues come, is it difficult to have men dedicated to social service?

God-intoxicated life improves society

From this consideration, the spiritual ideal, even if bereft of direct physical service, should be the guiding force for all social work. As Toynbee remarks in his *Civilization on Trial* that 'seeking God is itself a social act' for it makes not only the aspirants but all members better men free from egoism which is a prime necessity for all altruistic activities. Sorokin in his *Reconstruction of Humanity* very pertinently observes: 'A society consisting of only thoroughly egoistic members could not survive and no peaceful or creative society could be made up of wholly egoistic members.' He further says that impure altruism, based on pleasure or utility only does not carry us far but genuine altruism is pure even in its motivation: altruistic actions are performed for their own sake, quite apart from any considerations of pleasure or utility. To produce altruistic type of humanity, society must be oriented that way. 'Altruistic individuals,' says he, 'cannot be reared in a *milieu* of egoistic culture and social institutions.'

Higher ideal of service

So even for doing more service, the ideal must be grounded on higher principles. Toynbee, in the aforesaid book, very pertinently observes: 'It is a paradoxical but profoundly true and important principle of life that the most likely way to reach a goal is to be aiming not at the goal itself but at some more ambitious goal beyond it.' So the social reformers, who consider the social betterment to be the urgent need, would do quite well even for the sake of the greatest measure of success in their immediate undertaking to get it connected with higher ideals. This will give an added motive force to their work and save the workers from frustration which is inevitable in all social undertakings. As we have said earlier, only the ideal of work for the sake of one's own spiritual good can save them from that frustration. Even from the psychological standpoint this combination is good. Dr. Jung divides men into two broad categories of introverts and extroverts, though normally a man's temperament is a mixture of the two. So this twofold ideal will meet the needs of these temperaments also.

Sources of Enthusiasm

Since the reconstruction of society demands, from all members of society their full attention to the production of material goods, the modern conception of good life is not to cultivate certain subjective virtues but the creation of a good society assuring plenty and prosperity. To produce in plenty it is necessary to create enthusiasm in people. It may be done by encouraging self-interest. But there is a great danger in stressing too much this aspect of human nature. Egotism and selfishness are quite strong in an unregenerate human being. It is by training and culture that a man becomes socialized and fit to be a good member of society. If the main incentive of unselfish behavior is withdrawn, no amount of self-interest, enlightened or otherwise, can hold the people together for a long time. Hinduism tried to solve this problem by attuning human aspiration to the Divine. The four objects of attainment, viz. virtue, wealth, desire and emancipation *(Dharma, Artha, Kama, Moksha)* are interrelated. Man is not denied the joys and material goods of life. He is to labor hard for wealth and fulfillment of desires. But it must be done with a due sense of propriety, discrimination and regard for the ultimate end. All these ideals must not be thrown into the winds. This is *Dharma*. It steers man through wealth and desire to emancipation.

Ideal of Individual Perfection

Dharma lays stress on individual perfection by shifting the emphasis to a non-material objective. And by doing so, it contributes a great deal in lessening unhealthy competition and thus paves the way for social cohesion and unity. This scheme of fourfold objectives of life harmonizes the urges for individual perfection and social salvation. To keep the incentive of social welfare intact, it is necessary to ground it on a firm basis. In the ultimate analysis, it will be found that a man is a true servant of society in proportion to the perfection of his character. As Tolstoy said: There is only one way of serving mankind, and that by becoming better yourself.' Moreover, a society is the summation of individuals. It is high time that our social gospellers gave up harping on the unhealthy separation between these two ideals. If so much of unselfishness and spirit of sacrifice is met with in modern society in spite of preaching the doctrines of selfishness, it is because of the moral standard attained by the efforts of our unselfish, idealistic and God-loving ancestors. The modern non-religious yet socially aware man is like a baby on a monument enjoying the panoramic view forgetting that his stature has increased because of the basis, the contemporary social *milieu*, which is a product of centuries of spiritual culture. Secularist gospels will be considered audacious, if they claim to be a substitute for spiritual values. Their message is one-sided; they cannot visualize! A meeting ground between religion and science; they cannot see that in pure minds, intuition and emotion need not conflict with reason; that scientific knowledge demands the supreme effort of the heart as well.

Let us look to the future and guide the nation towards a more abiding, more permanent welfare. What our social workers need is the vitalizing influence of a burning faith in spirituality. There is not another such potent force to turn an egocentric into a cosmocentric. Reform by consent may not be as quick as reform by compulsion. But force, coercion and violence cannot work for social cohesion.

Conclusion

With the progress of quick transport, the contact of different nations has brought this conflict of ideals to the forefront. The predominantly meditative and spiritual civilization of the East meets the aggressively active civilization of the West. It is not possible to stay in one's own corner any more. In the words of Jawaharlal Nehru, 'A living philosophy must answer the problem of the day.' And it must satisfy both these urges represented by the two civilizations; a synthetic culture is the demand of today. There has been scarcely any great culture without a great religion as the foundation,' says Sorokin. Here is a new ~ religion or rather a new interpretation of the old, which can satisfy the needs of the age and urge the members of society to engage themselves in social reform that is very urgent and which at the same time can lead them to that freedom which is the eternal hunger of the soul. Let us then adopt this method of service and strive for the higher goal. Swami Vivekananda will encourage us with his oft-quoted exhortation, 'Arise, awake, and stop not till the goal is reached.'

PART I

Chapter 2

WHY VIVEKANANDA?

Swami Vivekananda's clarion call left an indelible impression on the minds of the youth of the last generations. The present generation of youth naturally often hears about him from them. But it is not always that boys know about him, for often they are just growing into manhood and trying to know about the different values of life. A young college boy, fresh from school, once put the question: Why Vivekananda? The idea is, what is the necessity of knowing about another person of old, when there are so many other great living men? The question is pertinent. Two points are involved in it. First, why should we read the lives and teachings of great men? And then, what is the speciality of Vivekananda? The answer to the first question is, because it makes us real men. The words of great men give us a direction, inspire us, stir up our nobler emotions, generate hope and implant faith. In trials and tribulations we look at similar experiences of great men and regain strength of mind, so that we do not break down under their pressure. And knowing the life and teachings of great men is possible only through books on and by them.

Our boys read many books, no doubt. But books are of various types to suit the variety of tastes and temperaments. They may be good, bad or indifferent. For purposeful reading it is necessary to choose the right type of books. Especially in younger days it is necessary to be acquainted with ennobling thoughts. In the prevalent atmosphere of increasing materialism, rank hedonism and cynical disbelief in nobler life, it is not easy to know of the higher values. So instructions are necessary. Examples are still more so. But in the absence of proper instructors books are very valuable, especially because too much nearness to imperfect teachers takes away much of the appealing quality. So it is noble books primarily that can transmit the higher ideas to young boys at their impressionable age, for books are free from the defects of the conveying medium. Of course, good men there are in every walk of life. And they surely can transmit the essential goodness and humanity of man to the younger generation. But what we are stressing is that the refreshing, salutary influences of noble writings are immense. Worthy and ennobling reading is therefore essential. Books are said to either divert and entertain, inform and instruct, or inspire and elevate. It is necessary therefore to choose the right type of books. The baneful effect of unhealthy literature can be counteracted only by them.

How a book can change a life and powerfully influence a nation can be seen from the example of Gandhiji. He became acquainted with Ruskin's 'Unto the Last' and Tolstoy's writings and his ideas took a shape. Devendra Nath Tagore by chance came across a leaf of the Upanishad and his life took a turn. Many such cases can be cited.

So we see that young men and women must be acquainted with the writings of the leaders of society.

Such books will be a fine and potent vehicle to cleanse and transform their ideas and impulses, endeavors and attainments. These are books which educate, enlighten and edify. Boys should know several of them. And they of course will have their favorite authors. We feel, however, along with a general reading of others, a boy should thoroughly read one idealistic author of repute. Thoroughly knowing the ideas of one thought-leader gives clarity of thinking and systematic way of approach.

'Lives of great men all remind us, that we also can make our lives sublime.' Our life is like a lamp. The lamp of life is to be ignited from another lamp. Hero-worship is inborn in man. It is more pronounced in younger days. Children follow the elders. They often live in a make-believe world. The adolescents become gradually aware of social norms. This awareness is often painful. Definite guidance is a necessity. But gradually the budding youth is oppressed by the why of things. Even things which are accepted by elders as norms are also enough to create these questionings in them. These cannot be answered always by elders, for it is humanly impossible to answer all. Books satisfy their inquisitiveness and quell the doubts. If these books are of great men honored in society, they become more impressive. If they are written by holy men of realization their effect will be still more.

While it will do if a boy reads any of the well-known writers of serious thoughts, Swami Vivekananda, we feel, has a special claim. It is because he has spoken about the fundamental thoughts of mankind. And that too in such a language that they can stir up all young men. Swamiji has been described as the awakener of souls. The purpose of all reading, all education is just that. Once inner awakening comes, the rest will follow of themselves. Of his writings Romain Rolland says:

'I cannot touch these sayings of his, scattered as they are through the pages of books at thirty years' distance, without receiving a thrill through my body like an electric shock. And what shocks, what transports must have been produced when in burning words they issued from the lips of the hero!'

Enthusiasm is a great necessity in creating impressive characters. Swami Vivekananda's writings and speeches have the capacity of creating immense enthusiasm. Once enthusiasm is created, it may seek its expression through various channels in accordance with the aptitude of the man. Writers, social workers, students and many others of various walks of life have found that Swamiji's writings generated an unbounded enthusiasm in them, which expressed itself in their particular fields. Enthusiasm to be fruitful requires a steady attitude of optimism and hopefulness. The problems of life, especially in the economically underdeveloped countries, are apt to make the stout hearts disheartened. The message of hope is a special quality of Swamiji's writings. He spoke about the essential goodness of man. He had drawn our attention to the underlying aspect of human personality. That is why in his writings we find so much glorification of the Atman which is the true, unchangeable nature of man. Even a glimpse of that understanding is apt to make a man hopeful, bold and pure. Infinite energy and unlimited enthusiasm will naturally follow. Moreover, his direct energizing words also give these qualities in an abundant measure. As a sample, read the following lines:

'Up, up, the long night is passing, the day is approaching, the wave has risen, nothing will be able to resist its tidal fury. Believe, believe, the decree has gone forth, the fiat of the Lord has gone forth - India must rise, the masses and the poor are to be made happy. Rejoice! The flood of spirituality has risen. I see it is rolling over the land resistless, boundless, all-absorbing; Every man to the fore, every good will be added to its forces, every hand will smooth its way, and glory be unto the Lord!'

Is faith necessary? Abundant faith in oneself and in the destiny of India will be generated if we read:

'Have faith in yourselves, and stand upon that faith and be strong; that is what we need. "We are the Atman, deathless and free; pure, pure by nature. Can we ever commit any sin? Impossible!" – Such a faith is needed. Such a faith makes men of us, makes gods of us. Have faith that you are all born to do great things! Each one of us will have to believe that every one else in the world has done his work, and the only work remaining to be done to make the world perfect has to be done by himself. This is the responsibility we have to take upon ourselves. Give up the awful disease that is creeping into our national blood, that idea of ridiculing everything, that loss of seriousness. Give that up. Be strong and have this Shraddha, and everything else is bound to follow.'

Along with energy and hope, strength is a predominant quality his writings give. In fact, he has been described as a prophet of strength. As strength is urgently necessary for everybody this message has a great value. 'Strength is life, weakness is death,' was that message. His religion is a religion of strength. Even in the Upanishads he found this message of *Abhih*, fearlessness, coming out like a bombshell.

'Our young men must be strong. Religion will come afterwards. Be strong, my young friends; that is my advice to you. You will be nearer to Heaven through football, than through the study of the Gita. You will understand the Gita better with your biceps, your muscles, a little stronger. You will understand the mighty genius and the mighty strength of Krishna better with a little of strong blood in you. You will understand the Upanishads better and the glory of the Atman, when your body stands firm upon your feet, and you feel yourselves as men. What I want is muscles of iron and nerves of steel, inside which dwells a mind of the same material as that of which the thunderbolt is made. Strength, manhood, Kshatravirya plus Brahmateja.'

Is patriotism necessary? Swamiji's writings are full of patriotic fervor. Love of the country is a predominant note there. His exhortations are potent enough to fill the minds of our youth with the love of the nation and its people. In our country where so much poverty, illness and ignorance persist, it is necessary for the advanced people to feel for them. Do they need a plan of work? They will have it too.

'Feel from the heart. What is in the intellect or reason? It

*goes a few steps and there it stops. But through the heart comes
inspiration. Love opens the most impossible gates; love is the gate
to all the secrets of the universe. Feel, therefore, my would-be
reformers, my would-be patriots! Do you feel? Do you feel that
millions and millions of the descendants of gods and of sages have
become next-door neighbors to brutes? Do you feel that millions
are starving to-day, and millions have been starving for ages? Do
you feel that ignorance has come over the land as a dark cloud?
Does it make you restless? Does it make you sleepless? Has it
gone into your blood, coursing through your veins, becoming
constant with your heart-beats? Has it made you almost mad?
Are you seized with that one idea of the misery of ruin, and have
you forgotten all about your name, your fame, your wives, your
children, your property, even your own bodies? Have you done
that? This is the first step to become a patriot, the very first step.'*

Swamiji is essentially international as all religious people
ought to be. So his nationalism too is such that it does not
militate against consideration for other nations of the world.
And so he advocated removal of all exclusiveness.

*'We cannot do without the world outside India; it was our
foolishness that we thought we could, and we have paid the
penalty by about a thousand years of slavery. We have paid the
penalty; let us do it no more. All such foolish ideas that Indians
must not go out of India, are childish. They must be knocked on
the head; the more you go out and travel among the nations of
the world, the better for you and your country. If you had done
that for hundreds of years past you would not be here today,
at the feet of every nation that wants to rule India. The first
manifest effect of life is expansion. You must expand if you want*

to live. The moment you have ceased to expand, death is upon you, danger is ahead.'

Is love of the past necessary for getting clear vision and proper direction? Swamiji's love of ancient India and its great heritage is second to none.

'Nowadays, everybody blames those who constantly look back to their past. It is said that so much looking back to the past is the cause of all India's woes. To me, on the contrary, it seems that the opposite is true. So long as they forgot the past, the Hindu nation remained in a state of stupor; and as soon as they have begun to look into their past, there is on every side a fresh manifestation of life.'

Do we want our children to be rational, strong, virile and at the same time possessed of purity and abundant sympathy? Swamiji's writing is full of all these ideas. So we see that Swamiji's writings are capable of giving us the fundamental virtues of hope, enthusiasm and strength, etc. A man endowed with these basic qualities is fit to face life squarely and he will not be cowed down by its troubles and turmoil, dangers and difficulties, despairs and frustrations. It is because of these qualities of his writings we feel that in younger days our boys and girls should be acquainted with them. Thereby strong characters will be formed. And once many such characters are formed, the society may experiment with any type .of political and social organization or idea;" it is bound to progress. The bane of modern times, as is often said, is the general collapse of values, or the crisis of character. With the high achievements in acquiring the advanced tools of civilization, it is urgent that modern man has the noblest reaches of culture. Then will the earth be a veritable heaven which is the goal of all social workers. We strongly believe Swami Vivekananda's writings have the requisite qualities for bringing in such higher virtues in society and hence recommend them with all the force at our command to the young men and women of India.

PART I

Chapter 3

VIVEKANANDA TO MODERN YOUTH

The meeting of Vivekananda with Sri Ramakrishna in 1880 A.D. is considered as a meeting of the modern with the ancient, of the West with the East, of energy with contemplation, of humanitarianism with spirituality. Narendranath Datta, as Vivekananda was called, born in an aristocratic family of Calcutta in 1863, was robust and turbulent as a boy, with a sharp memory and a keen power of observation. He was brought up in a religious and cultural environment. As a budding youth, he became the representative of modern youths having the intellectual conflict born of the clash of the two opposing ideals of the East and the West but he became a seeker after Truth with a strong moral character, mainly because of the Brahmo influence. The meeting with Sri Ramakrishna changed the whole course of his life. He renounced the worldly life, traveled throughout India and with the encouragement of a few Madras youths went to America and had the phenomenal success in 1893 in the Parliament of Religions of the world and raised the status of his country by placing her in the role of the teacher. His success caused a great emotional upheaval and roused the dormant qualities of all his countrymen. He passed away too early at the age of 39 in 1902 and within five years of his passing, that energy burst forth in the form of volcanic eruptions of the Revolutionary Movement to free the country from foreign yoke, under Aurobindo and Tilak. The Indian

National Congress also was vitalized. From that time onwards hundreds of youths received inspiration from the clarion call of this 'patriot-saint', and there followed the Renaissance of life and letters in almost all the provinces of India.

Vivekananda's love for the youth was unbounded. To him youth was a stage full of promise and possibilities. He wanted a band of fiery young men sacrificing their lives for the regeneration of the country. The harmonious development of the hand, head and heart is necessary. He wanted young men with muscles of iron and nerves of steel. To encourage the boys to pay close attention in acquiring more physical fitness, he said that they could understand the Gita better by playing football. The idea is, with better health and consequently with improved faculty of thinking, the life-giving messages of the Gita could be assimilated better. Is there any use of all the training unless 'there is the nervous association of all the energizing ideas? Our education is successful only when the ideas we know from our books and from our elders enter into our very veins and impel us to contemplate on them and finally induce us to action. Our routine is too much overcrowded with theoretical information, undigested and unconnected with life. The age-old tradition of India is to combine study with contemplation, work with meditation. The modern education is off its balance because of the lack of this calming and soothing influence. The occidental educationists and their prototypes in India must learn this grand lesson from the educationists of ancient India called Rishis. Swami Vivekananda wanted for this purpose to regenerate the ancient gurukula system with the brahmacharya ideal of austerity, piety and continence for the students. In fact the conception of the four stages of life (ashramas) is a grand gift our forefathers gave to the moderners. As a student one is to prepare oneself for the future life. Then is a stage of enjoyment sanctioned by dharma which is equivalent more or less to the modern conception of ideal civic duties. The third stage is to retire from the family and to be more conscious of the outside world and the ultimate values of life, which Bankimchandra, the composer of the *vandemataram,* interprets as philanthropic and social activities to suit modern conditions. In the fourth stage one is to retire from all worldly activities and enjoy the well-earned rest devoted wholly to the contemplation of God. Life spent with a constant awareness of the higher values will save us from frustration which is inevitable if we are too-much self-centered. The secular West is not yet able to find a suitable substitute for this. Swamiji wanted us first to be thoroughly acquainted with our ancient culture and then to march towards the grand future which, he saw in his vision, is sure to come. In fact, the predominating note in his life is a love for India and its cultural heritage. Hundreds of youths visit nowadays the foreign countries who might be the cultural ambassadors of their country. But alas! Few boys know about themselves and their fathers. The world gives scant recognition to the weak defeatists with inferiority complex. Most often, we forget this little truth.

To Swami Vivekananda losing faith in one's self means losing faith in God. 'We are the children of the Almighty,' he said, 'we are sparks of the infinite, divine fire. How can we be nothings? We are everything, ready to do anything, we can do everything and must do everything.' Thus his was a positive gospel of -manliness- and self-reliance which put enthusiasm in those who came in touch with his personality or teaching.

Vivekananda preached the glory of the divine nature of human beings and wanted people to manifest their potential divinity. The awareness of one's real nature is a great motive force. Far from making people impractical and irresponsible, it gives man a bold and healthy attitude towards life. It supplies him with a calm, resolute determination to strive for individual and collective perfection. Attachment clouds man's vision; a detached outlook clears it and endows man with a capacity to look at things and issues objectively. Objectivity is the primary virtue for correct estimation. So understanding of one's divine heritage leads one to maximum efficiency and minimum waste of mental energy in fretting and fuming, worrying and beating the breast.

He was a monk through and through. He loved India for 'if India is to die, religion will be wiped off from the face of the earth.' India was great because of her spiritual heritage. She must regain her pristine glory by gripping the ideal of the all-renouncing Siva. 'Give and take' is the law of nature. India must give in order to get. What has she got but her cultural heritage, her love for renunciation, devotion and God-intoxication? If she is not to play the role of a novice all the time, she must keep her spirituality living, nay, she must make it dynamic. That can be done by shifting the stress on the mere other-worldliness to seeing God in humanity preached by Vedanta and sacrificing oneself for its service. That is the implication of Vedanta necessary for modern times. And it is suitable to modern temper also. If the scientific spirit does not allow a modern man to accept the finality of things, let him take this principle as a hypothesis or a working formula and see for himself through his detached pursuit of the mystery of the ever-unfolding universe, whether the never-changing mystery of its substratum is revealed to him or not.

Swami Vivekananda was an apostle of freedom. Freedom is our aspiration. 'To be freer is the goal of all our efforts.' What is liberation? It is a state where absolute freedom reigns. Who is God? He is the 'embodiment of freedom. So seeking God is striving for freedom. Only, this freedom has a wider connotation. It is all-embracing. Political, social, cultural and other freedoms are only the fragmentary aspects of real freedom. They also have a place in Vivekananda's scheme of all-round regeneration. But we must have a wider vision so that we do not become, because of our limited perspective, narrow, selfish, jingoistic or exclusive. The attachment for our family must bloom forth into the attachment for the society, devotion to our culture into the devotion to the world culture and love for the country into the love for the universe. The greater receptacle does not exclude the lesser one. On the other hand, the lesser is the portal of the greater. Through the finite to the infinite, that is the way. So Vivekananda found no conflict in loving both his country and the world.

He did not want to mould all people into the same pattern. Unity in variety is the law of nature. It is the sauce of life. It is the condition of growth too. So let men and societies grow in a variegated manner. But let them not circumscribe their ideal, let them grow to their fullest stature. And if they do so, they will see that all of them find their meeting ground in infinity. Innumerable are the gateways to the infinite. Once a man or society gets a -glimpse-of-that infinitude, it will be found that world-understanding, fellow-feeling or brotherhood of man has already been achieved.

Vivekananda was against all privilege, not merely of hereditary caste. Man may work in different spheres in accordance with the social necessity and that is inevitable for the proper functioning of the social organism. But on that account there must not be any vested interests in regard to the enjoyable goods of the world. The Vedantic conception of the atma-samya, the equality of all men because the same Soul resides in all, is the basis of his firm view in favor of the bhoga-adhikara-samya, the equality in the rights of enjoyment. All privilege is based on tyranny. Where privilege is more, tyranny also is intense. So he wanted the abolition of all privileges, physical, intellectual and spiritual.

He was convinced that 'no individual or nation can live by holding itself apart from the community of others.' He affirmed that the degeneration of India started when the Indians secluded themselves from the world-current. India must rebuild herself by advancing in political, economic and social spheres. When she has effectively done that, the world will listen to her eternal, spiritual message. Democracy in India cannot be secular in the sense of anti-God or non-godly. So in the Indian context the word secular is slowly acquiring a new meaning of freedom of conscience and religious pursuit as against its original meaning. This is due to the impact of spiritual forces and the resulting climate created by saints and seers of India. As long as the religions are living, as long as they can produce saints, there is no fear for them, for they will be in a better position than the faith-less secularism to inculcate all the noble qualities on which a social structure stands. It may not be impossible to build a society without an avowed religious faith, but when we have it 'in our blood', why go against it? It is better to deepen the existing channel than dig a new one.

Swamiji viewed Hinduism as all-inclusive. The note of optimism and affirmation is predominant in it. Those who want the material goods of the world, let them follow the path of abhyudaya, success. And those who are not drawn by the joys of the world and hanker after something higher, let them follow the path of nihsreyasa, Freedom. Once when asked to give the gist of Indian culture in the briefest possible manner, he only repeated the two words pravritti and nivritti. These two paths include all the aspirations and efforts of men. Science, philosophy, technology, all have a place in the Hindu scheme of life. Here the spirit of inquiry is not throttled and the endeavor, for improving the standard of living is not questioned. Only, they should not stifle the higher aspirations of man, that's all. The Indian culture is not merely a particular way of life, a special outlook, a distinctly formulated philosophy, it is a total vision of reality, an appraisal of life in its totality, an appreciation of its values and their recognition in a specific scheme and order.

Vivekananda fervently believed that the life-force of India is in her spiritual culture and the regeneration of India will be possible only through the vitalizing of her spiritual life. Aurobindo, Gandhi, Rabindranath, in fact all great Indians, also believed strongly in this. We must take into account the versions of these master minds before we hurry into conclusions being enamored of the external glaze of the materialistic, Western way of life and its immediate, apparent success. By spiritual culture, Vivekananda, of course, never meant the quarrelsome outer crust of modern denominational religions. We must remember, as has been told already, that he was against all caste-privileges, religious, intellectual and economic, and denounced them in virulent language.

Now India is a free country. There are a lot of things to do in all the fields of activity. But there are some disrupting forces sown in this soil by vested interests, which threaten the unity of India. Swamiji with his rare insight into history found out that even when there was no unified political government in India there was an underlying unity because of the spiritual culture and the Sanskrit language, the vehicle of that culture. So giving up all petty, local self-interests we must join together for the progress of the nation. To do that we must be thoroughly imbued with the national ideals of renunciation and service. The ideal of working for one's own supreme good and for the good of the world gives us the noblest practical ideal. The ideal of working for others without a thought of oneself is too high an ideal for most men. We are too self-centered to do this consistently and continually except in moments of our spasmodic enthusiasm. Swamiji knew of this human weakness. So he connected the good of the one with the good of the many by pointing out to us the unity of existence in the universe. The unity of existence is a statement of fact. It neither can be proved nor disproved conclusively by our intellect. It is verifiable in our heart of hearts and in the realization of the mystics. Even if it is a theory herein only lays the basic reason, why man should love his neighbor as himself and not cut his throat. The utilitarians, the humanists and even the dialectical materialists must accept this today or tomorrow to keep the incentive of men intact to work not only for the individual but also for the sake of the society. To achieve the brotherhood of man without the fatherhood of God is futile. The sooner we understand this the better for the country. When we understand this inherent unity, the suffering people will no longer be our objects of pity to be given a pice with neglect but veritable 'Gods in the form of the poor, the ignorant, the downtrodden. This is the doctrine of Daridra-narayana which can save the world from the threatening class-war of the Marxists.

A new world order is coming to the old weary world. The eternal spirituality of India is reinterpreted by its modern mouthpiece, Swami Vivekananda, to suit modern conditions. To accept this we must be bold. Fearlessness (abhih) is the word coming like bomb-shell from all the Upanishads. To conceive of a revolutionary ideal like this we must be extremely fearless and to make this practical we must have deep love for the country and its culture. In fact, his 'plan of campaign' (a lecture delivered in Madras) is to deluge the land with spirituality. Therein only lies the key to open the closed hearts of the people.

A spiritual personality like Vivekananda cannot be claimed as the exclusive asset of any particular race or clime. Vivekananda stands for universal religion and world culture, and his sublime message goes for humanity at large. His nationalism is the outcome of India's attempt to express herself in modern times. Yet it has a universal significance for all lands, inasmuch as it sets forth a lofty ideal, gives a new angle of vision and reveals a spiritual outlook — in brief a rare cultural heritage which can satisfy both the East and the West. We must try to translate this ideal in the life of the individual and society. This is the message of Vivekananda to modern youths.

PART I
Chapter 4

GOD OR HUMANITY?

With the development of secularism, belief in God has been undermined. The agnostic attitude is now spreading throughout the world. But secularism and agnosticism began quite early in the West. The Western knowledge had to advance ignoring the overall influence of Christian theology. As a reaction, there was a tendency among philosophers to overthrow God and religion. But social philosophers noted that man required a faith to be animated to selfless action. So they wanted Humanity to replace God. Thus Positivism and Humanism were born.

The different branches of knowledge are compartmental. They intensively study a particular aspect of nature or society. Hence the conclusions they arrive at have often no reference to God or religion. These studies have nothing to say for or against religion, for it is outside their province. The scientists of the twentieth century realize the limitations of science.

As W. N. Sullivan says: *'Science deals with but a partial aspect of reality. There is no faintest reason for supposing that everything science ignores is less real than what it accepts. ... We are no longer taught that the scientific method of approaching is the only valid method of acquiring knowledge about reality. Eminent men of science are insisting, with what seems a strange enthusiasm, on the fact that science gives us but a partial knowledge of reality, and we are no longer required to regard as illusory, everything that science finds itself able to ignore.'*

Prof. W. J. Sollas, the noted geologist, says: *'In matters of philosophy and Religion, Science is not the arbiter: the final judgment on ultimate questions must always rest with philosophy and Religion themselves.'*

Prof. Lecomte, the noted botanist, goes farther saying: *'Incompatibility between Science and Faith exists only in the minds of those who want such an incompatibility.'*

But still the confusion in thought that has been brought about by scientific philosophy based on partial truth continues to hold the field in some quarters. The modern political thought also claims to be scientific and either ignores God as in secularist democracy or fanatically opposes Him as in totalitarian Communism. But being concerned about human beings, it knows the uses of belief in God and so tries to place Humanity itself on the pedestal.

The question naturally arises: Is it a better choice? Should Humanity replace God? It is true as Goethe contends, that 'the deepest, nay, the one theme of the world's history is the conflict of faith and unbelief.' The remarkable epochs of human history are the epochs of faith. Faith might have marched under different names and varying forms but it has always marched in the van of the noblest movements of humanity. The main spring of human activity in all the important epochs of history in which man has shown the

highest powers of his spirit is the belief in the spiritual
and moral order, as well as in the indestructibility of the
human spirit and the imperishability of human virtue, both
being grounded *in* the Supreme Power, unseen, eternal and
omnipotent.

How do the positivists and humanists look at this great
historical phenomenon? They doubt its essential reality
and consider it as the outcome of the desire to gratify
certain wants of the human mind. They have installed
Humanity in place of God and consider it to be real and
efficacious. They consider it sufficient to draw the affection
and adoration of the people by providing inspiration for
all practical endeavors. These positivist thinkers tell us
that God must be dethroned and thereby the world loses
nothing, for Humanity supplants Him and does all His
functions. The beauty and nobility of life engendered by
belief in God will be retained and enhanced by being related
to Humanity which is positively real and scientifically
verifiable. Our sense of awe and sublimity can be awakened
by this Supreme Being of Humanity in whom 'we live
and move and have our being' and in whose bosom we
rise and disappear like bubbles. The inheritance of ages is
with us. It is more lovable because it is more accessible. So,
they contend, Humanity reconciles the demands of reason
with the longings of the heart and takes its stand on the
unassailable basis of fact and experience. Thus they make
Humanity the goal of religion.

But can Humanity really be the object of worship and
can its worship help man to conquer his impulses to

realize the ideal of duty? If we study different religions we find that an invisible Being has always been the object of worship. It has been transcendental all the time. Even Fetishism does not worship mere objects of nature but all these are conceived as inhabited by some invisible, indwelling spirit. The idea in the higher religions is still more developed. The old Indian thinkers describe the eternal spirit, the only object of adoration, in such words as 'There eyes cannot penetrate, nor speech nor mind.' *(Kena Up.* 1.3.)

The mistake of the positivists lies in this that they confuse the two planes of devotional activity, for while God works in the invisible sphere, Humanity works in the scientific or phenomenal sphere. If the religion of the past is to be the basis, and it must be so if their theory of evolution is universally applicable, the positivists' religion of Humanity is without a foundation. This is its logical irregularity. Practically too Humanity cannot be the object of worship. Worship means entering a mood of purity and holiness. But Humanity in its positivistic aspects is not ennobling at all but disgusting': As Prof. Huxley puts it, 'I know no study which is so utterly saddening as that of the evolution of humanity.' It is impossible to worship a Being whose record is as bad as ours and who cannot be proud of its sense of justice and righteousness.

Again, the Power that we can worship must not only be righteous, it must be eternal and self-existent too. But Humanity is not so, it is a mere ephemeral product of evolution. Humanity is only a bubble in the eternal stream of creative power unlimited in space or in time. It will be the height of folly to ignore the unlimited source and worship the transient thing.

It is possible to worship Humanity no doubt, but only as an expression of the Divine. It has been sanctioned by the greatest philosopher-saint of India. Acharya Shankara gave the gist of the Vedanta philosophy in the famous saying: 'Brahman alone is real, the universe is ultimately unreal and the individual soul is no other than the Universal Soul'

For all these years-we gave more stress on the first part. Swami Vivekananda, the patriot-saint of India, has exhorted us to give due recognition to the second part of the saying that jiva is really Siva and service to humanity with that idea is really service to God. To get rid of the soul behind the universe as the positivists do and then exhort us to worship the latter is to ask us to worship the corpse from which the soul has departed. The concrete mass of men and women cannot evoke that love and respect but Humanity with a Divine ideal and Providence manifesting itself in mankind and its history can evoke reverence and adoration. But to men to whom the visible is all and grave the end of existence, there can be nothing sacred. And without sacredness the world will be full of death and corruption.

Thus Humanity is incapable of being an object of worship and veneration. Neither has it the power of inspiring by itself any lofty enthusiasm or heroic devotion giving rise to acts of self-immolation. Inculcation of a sense of duty and moral purpose has been recognized as the great contribution of religion. But will humanistic religion, banishing belief in Providence and a future life, be able to nourish the moral life of the community? Will it furnish the community with an adequate stimulus for moral aspiration? The religion of Humanity, divorced from all belief in the supernatural, has never yet been practiced. It is contended that there are individuals leading an unselfish life without any religious faith. 'Morality without religion' is their slogan. But they forget that it is possible now only due to the prevailing religious atmosphere which influences them unconsciously. The general level of the time and the heritage has a strong influence on individuals.

Moreover, the arguments of the positivists are all directed to Personal God. They generally accept the Impersonal. And Swami Vivekananda points out:

'*A man who understands and believes in the Impersonal — John Stuart Mill, for example — may say that a Personal God is impossible, and cannot be proved. I admit with him that a Personal God cannot be demonstrated. But He is the highest reading of the Impersonal that can be reached by the human intellect, and what else is the universe but various readings of the- Absolute? It is like a book before us, and each one has brought his intellect to read it, and each one has to read it for himself.*'

The Personal God rooted in the Impersonal can be satisfying to many rational minds. Hence it is better we hold on to our ancient, eternal God instead of taking a new, weaker one.

People respect things of permanent nature more than those of transient type. Their souls aspire to serve the universal and the abiding and feel more enthusiastic when they are sharing the works of God. But the enthusiasm of man believing with the positivists that Humanity is an infinitesimal bubble on an infinitesimal globe destined to pass away soon compared to the positivist's (i.e., scientist's, geologist's or astronomer's) time, suffers a total collapse. Without immortality and effects of the actions of man abiding, it will be the height of folly to practice self-sacrifice. And when this idea comes in, the devotion to duty will be undermined.

What makes us love our fellowmen and desist from the path of vice? It is the conviction that the same Divinity dwells in us. The principle of right living and right doing implies a supreme Intelligence pervading all and unifying all, to which we are 'strung together like pearls'. But for it the universe would be a chaos and moral life a delusion. The Religion of Humanity, not recognizing God and life after death and the divine spark in the individual, take away the basis of morality. It withholds from man all his motive power for selfless action and makes him a solitary and loveless being with no consolation for the present and no hope for the future.

PART I
Chapter 5

THE NEW WORSHIP

*'Do you know how I see? Trees, plants, men, animals, grass —
these and all other things I see as different coverings like pillow
cases, some made of fine cotton and others of coarser stuff, some
round in shape and others square. But within .all these pillow
cases there is one and the same substance, cotton. In the same
way all the objects of the world are stuffed with the unconditioned
Satchidananda. I feel as if the Mother has wrapped Herself in
different clothes, and is peeping out from them.'*

Thus said Sri Ramakrishna about his realization of the
Absolute in all created things. This is the cardinal message
of Vedanta too. The unity of existence, the same Brahman
permeating and manifesting as the entire universe is the
foundation on which the basic doctrine of the divinity
of man stands. It is from this standpoint that Swami
Vivekananda said that it is a sin to call men sinners.

*'Ye are the Children of God, the sharers of immortal bliss, holy
and perfect beings. Ye divinities on earth – sinners! It is a sin to
call a man so; it is a standing libel on human nature. Come up, O
lions, and shake off the delusion that you are sheep; you are souls
immortal, spirits free, blest and eternal; ye are not matter, ye are
not bodies; matter is your servant, not you the servant of matter.'*

When Rabindranath Tagore read this, he remarked

that this may really be called a 'message'. Now when we look upon humanity from this angle, it becomes an object of worship for us. It is not apotheosizing humanity but recognizing its real nature. In a different way the humanity has been raised to the pedestal of God by the humanists and positivists also. It has a natural appeal to modern man when the air is surcharged with the idea of the importance of the dignity of common man. But the positivistic conception of humanity, though quite evident, does not draw spontaneous adoration of a spiritual quality. But real devotion comes when we look upon man as the manifestation of God and while serving the former, look at his divine core. Hence Swami Vivekananda preached the gospel of service to man and said:

'May I be born again and again, and suffer thousands of miseries so that I may worship the only God that exists, the only God I believe in, the sum total of all souls, – and above all, my God the wicked, my God the miserable, my God the poor of all races, of all species, is the special object of my worship.'

Such service is as much a part of spiritual discipline as the old methods are. It appeals to our common sense too. Flowers are plucked, garlands are made. This is done by the devotee as well as the garland-seller. The devotee's act is considered a devotional exercise while the garland-seller's is not. It is because of the difference of motives. As the devotee aims at serving God the garland-making does become a worship. It becomes a continuous worship if he is aware of God during the process and thereby the best results can he reap. All the religious teachers draw our attention to this. Swami Brahmananda says:

'Before you begin to work, remember the Lord and offer your salutations to Him. Do the same from time to time while you are working, and also after you have finished. Spend all your time thinking of the life, teachings and commandments of Sri Ramakrishna. Know in your heart of hearts that all the work you do is for His sake.'

(*Spiritual Teachings*, p. 156.)

Sri Ramakrishna too has the story of a farmer and Sage Narada. Once finding Narada a little conceited Lord Vishnu asked him to visit a great devotee. Narada went there and found an agriculturist who rose early in the morning, pronounced the name of Hari (God) only once, and taking his plough, went out and tilled the ground all day long. At night, he went to bed after pronouncing the name of Hari once more. Narada said to himself, 'How can this rustic be a lover of God? I see him busily engaged in worldly duties and he has no signs of a pious man about him.' Then Narada was tested with a cup of oil. When he finished going round the city with the cup, the Lord asked him: 'Well, Narada, how many times did you remember me in the course of your walk round the city?' 'Not once, my Lord,' said Narada, 'and how could I, when I had to watch this cup brimming over with oil?' The Lord then said, 'This one cup of oil did so divert your attention that even a great devotee like you did forget me altogether. But look at that farmer, who, though carrying the heavy burden of a family, still remembers me twice every day.'

This is a very important point to remember and cultivate, to think of God during the work and offer salutations after the work is over. Even in ceremonial worship, which the orthodox conception regards as real worship, it is practiced. Hence we see that after performing the worship of a deity according to the scriptural directions, the sadhaka is enjoined to offer the fruits of his puja or japa to the deity. 'Krishnarpanam astu', let even its result be offered to the Lord. However, once he offers the result to God, it comes back hundredfold to him. It is true of both good and bad action. Hence Bhima of Mahabharata warns Yudhisthira not to offer bad actions to Sri Krishna.

This warning solves an important problem of ours, whether results of all the actions can be offered to God or not. It is true that for an evolved soul every act is worship, but so long as we are conscious of the dual throng of this world, we must observe this rule of offering good things only. This attribute helps us not to forget in our unevolved stage the immense importance of ethical values. Of course, as a sadhana, we may follow the behavior of men of realization and consider all actions as prompted by God, and lessen our idea of agent-ship.

Spiritual discipline may be practiced with different attitudes prescribed by different methods of sadhana. The attitudes may be broadly classified into three groups. They are the attitudes of the followers of Bhakti, Jnana and Karma yoga. Concentration, the main instrument of Raja-yoga, is the life of all the three sadhanas. When a devotee does work to please God and remembers Him in the beginning, middle and end of the work and offers the fruit of it to Him, he has the attitude of Bhakti-yoga. His work is really a part of Bhakti-sadhana. When a man visualizes God in all created things and serves them seeing God in them, it may be described as a happy mixture of Bhakti and Jnana. A strict Jnana yogi, however, regards all actions as performed by his body and mind from which he knows himself to be separate. He may work at the behest of his Guru but really he is not identified with anything at all. A man following strict Karmayoga practices detachment and unconcern about success or failure. And it has been pointed out by Swami Vivekananda that in this way also the highest realization is attained.

Swamiji further showed that really these four yogas are interconnected. A spiritual aspirant following the path of Knowledge must have great love for the Ideal, deep concentration and suitable action for attaining the goal. A devotee too must have a clear understanding of the nature of God, whole-souled meditation on Him and must work for His satisfaction. A Raja yogi must know of his goal and the wayside pitfalls, have intense liking for the Ideal and practice sadhana also. A Karma yogi must observe the pros and cons about his project, have deep devotion to it and full concentration to attain his objective. For all these years spiritual aspirants following a particular method of sadhana laid exclusive stress on it forgetting all the while that unknowingly they were practicing the other disciplines too. Swamiji therefore pointed out that in each were ingrained the others but a quicker development will take place if all the four are consciously practiced. The growth too will be more balanced and perfect.

Swamiji saw this ideal combination in Sri Ramakrishna and bowed down to him as a perfect incarnation of God.

'Such a unique personality, such a synthesis of the utmost of philosophy, mysticism, emotion, and work, has never before appeared among mankind. The life of Sri Ramakrishna proves that the greatest breadth, the highest catholicity and the utmost intensity can exist side by side in the same individual, and that society also can be constructed like that, for society is nothing but an aggregate of individuals. The formation of such a perfect character is the ideal of this age.'

This is an ideal which can be practiced in other walks of life too. A businessman must have a clear understanding about his particular business, a genuine interest in the profession, and the capacities of deep concentration and sustained action. Then only he may be confident of success. This is an ideal type for modern times. Our worship too will be all-rounded like this. Then only a perfect character will be formed, and vistas of spiritual visions will be opened up.

This all-round sadhana has a great social implication. The primary function of religious discipline is saint-making. But in the process it creates characters that are the prop of society. When such individual characters are formed, different functions of social reconstruction may safely be handed over to them. As Mahatma Gandhi says:

'I would feel that if we succeed in building the character of the individual, society will take care of itself. I would be quite willing to trust the organization of society to individuals so developed.'

(Gandhi Marg, January '59. p. 10.)

Society consists of individuals. And when individuals become better, society also automatically becomes better.

In modern times, however, there is more stress on social rather than individual betterment. The lot of the common man is the concern of all. So a conscious striving is made on all fronts. But unless good individuals are available, all undertakings will meet with failure. Moreover, political workers are too conscious of their party considerations. Their concern for man even is toned down by their party interests and any means is considered acceptable, which augments the latter. As an effect, the best results are not achieved. Hence for such results a combination of purity of individual character and passion for the service of society must be achieved. This happy combination has been provided for us by the new method of worship of God in man. In this worship, self-interest is brought to the minimum; so results will be better. As it stresses on direct service to humanity, there will be clear material gain too. As worship, it will bring out more devotion and greater attention and steadfastness. So from the social standpoint it will always be welcome. From the religious standpoint too it will be equally fruitful.

Of course, because of our age-old habit and tradition we instinctively feel a sanctity and holiness when we visit a shrine or perform worship. It may take some time for individuals, and even some generations for the common man of society to develop such a feeling of sacredness. So it will be necessary to practice the orthodox, age-old method of worship too. In fact, new worship will require new rituals, new meditations, new offerings. They will not be really new ones, but only the application of the old ones in the new setting. Till such rituals acquire sanctity the old practices must be continued. When all this is said and done, it must be admitted that there are different types of people. And so the new worship will not completely replace the old, but provide scope for different temperaments. Variety is the spice of life. A drab, dreary uniformity is against human nature. It will have no life and will not create the spontaneous enthusiasm of all, which is the main spring of all religious action or worship. The history of mysticism makes it clear to us that diverse manifestation of devotion are seen in the 'lives of mystics. A uniform code is apt to stifle the growth of that life and an efflorescence of devotion.

Hence worship will have two significant developments in modern times. While the ancient and well-tried methods will remain in all their variety and richness, a new application of the same principles in the new set-up will be made, satisfying values held in high esteem by contemporary thinking and fulfilling the aspirations of modern man. The new worship will be the worship of God in man. It will embrace all the four different yogas in making that worship perfect and satisfying to diverse natures. Those who have lost their faith in the existing religions will thereby find a new religion satisfying their beliefs yet which is not a mere mental construction but supported by the philosophy of Vedanta and rooted in the realization of the ancient sages as well as the modern saint Sri Ramakrishna.

PART I

Chapter 6

ON READING VIVEKANANDA

The birthday of Swami Vivekananda is approaching and it will be observed with suitable celebrations. Though there are various ways of paying our respects to a great man, the best method is to popularize his life and teachings, and attempts to do so will surely be made by the organizers.

Books play a dominant role in creating a clear understanding of Swamiji's ideas. But reading is ultimately an individual affair. It is the individual who is to read and be benefited by the books. Often we are only generally informed about a great man, not thoroughly knowing his views. So it is necessary that a great effort be made to read Swami Vivekananda's *Complete Works*.

Many people think that they do not have enough time for this undertaking. The volume of Swamiji's writings may scare them. But if we calculate, we find that if a person reads for 15 minutes a day, he will be able to finish reading the *Complete Works* in two years. There are 5400 pages in nine volumes. The last six volumes are a little easier than the earlier ones. On the average, a person can read about six pages in fifteen minutes, so the reading can be completed over a two year period. The works are available in Indian languages also, and the speed will be greater if they are read in the mother tongue.

So we hope that those who have some liking for Swamiji may read his works daily for fifteen minutes and finish the whole collection by the celebration. This reading can, of course, be done any time, but we are speaking of a special occasion, and an occasion gives special interest and a time limit. Both of these are great incentives. We have found that daily reading suits most people best, though there are some who find it convenient to read the works in a shorter time, devoting several hours a day to the task. Absorption in the Swamiji's thoughts and enthusiasm for the reading are their great help. I remember a brilliant student of engineering who finished the old seven volumes in five weeks during a vacation. Of course, he had an earlier background of religious reading. But for most students and working people, it will be convenient to read the works slowly. The assimilation also will be better, especially if there are occasional recapitulations. It will require determined patience and sustained enthusiasm.

The writings of Swamiji are capable of helping men and women in all walks of life. We hope there will be a determined attempt on the part of the general admirers of Swamiji to be thoroughly acquainted with his writings by reading them for a few minutes a day. And people who have already drunk deep of this perennial source should make others aware of this fountain of energy, strength, and bliss.

PART I

Chapter 7

VIVEKANANDA AND SPIRITUALITY

Swami Vivekananda's life is familiar to all. Born in 1863, in a well-to-do family in Calcutta, he was brought up in a very liberal atmosphere, his father being a liberal man, an advocate, a lawyer, and knowing several languages. He was a healthy boy, developed his body very well and in fact was a good wrestler. Then when he grew up as a young man he came in touch with the thoughts of the well-known philosophers of India and especially the West. And naturally a little doubt came into his mind. That was the period of the agnostics. Of course agnosticism is prevalent everywhere, at every age, but in Bengal of those days -Calcutta was the capital of India - this was especially noticeable. But then Swami Vivekananda as a boy had that deeper search for truth and had a moral fiber. Tremendous changes in society were being brought by the preachings of the Brahmo leaders headed by Keshab Chandra Sen and others. Vivekananda, then called Naren, was a member of the Brahmo Samaj for quite some time, got his inspiration from them. He was a good singer, a good debater and one of the most brilliant students of those days. It is said that once when he was a student in the school, one of the most noted speakers of India, who was president of the National Congress, Surendranath Banerjee, came to his school, and just to test the boys, he wanted one of the boys to come up and speak on a topic he was giving on the spot. And it is said Naren got up and spoke on that topic. He had a tremendous memory, photographic memory. It is said that because of his various extracurricular interests he did not study much. A day before the examination he found that he had not studied the Euclid Geometry - four parts in those days. The story goes that he sat through the whole night and whole day, and next day appeared in the examination creditably. So these are some of the stories told about him. A natural urge for knowing the truth, a good moral fiber, very fine body, some of the finer artistic qualities - this was the boy Naren. This search for the ultimate reality of things, search for truth brought him to Sri Ramakrishna in 1880. He had gone from teacher to teacher, well-known men of the day, to find out whether God existed or not. And the story is told that when he went to Sri Ramakrishna, for the first time he found a teacher who definitely said, "Yes, I have seen God. Not merely I have seen Him, I see Him much more clearly than I see you. And moreover I can help you to see Him." So that gave a sort of jolt in the beginning to Naren, and it took about a year for the young man to accept him fully as his Master. In fact he did not believe Sri Ramakrishna's words in the beginning, but still this man was something of a novelty. Then Naren began to undergo spiritual practices under the guidance of Sri Ramakrishna.

When Sri Ramakrishna fell ill he was taken to Kashipur Garden House, and a batch of young men gathered round him and began to serve him. After Sri Ramakrishna passed away, this batch of young men in their teens and early twenties left their homes and started what was later called the Ramakrishna Order of Monks. And Swami

Vivekananda was their leader. But then the intensification of experiencing truth and the desire to know the motherland, prompted most of the brothers, including Naren, to go out on pilgrimage, an accepted part of the monastic discipline in the Indian context. Naren, now Swami Vivekananda, for the next six years roamed about mostly on foot, the length and breadth of India, from Kashmir to Kanyakumari, from the North to the Southernmost tip of India. There he arrived at Kanyakumari where there is a temple to Mother Kumari, the Divine Mother as a small girl. It is an especially holy place. There near that temple just near the shores of the sea where the three seas meet, there were two rocks a little away from the shore. The story is told that the Swamiji swam across to one of the rocks and sat in meditation for a day. There came to him the idea of crossing the seas, to preach the gospel of Vedanta and do something for the poor masses of India. Some time ago a fine temple has been brought on that rock, after six years of massive effort by some of the enthusiastic followers of Swami Vivekananda, not members of our order, but also admirers of the great Swamiji.

So he went to America to attend the Chicago Parliament of Religions, which was a part of the world Expo, in commemoration of Columbus's discovery of America, Tercentenary. There right in the first lecture he made such an impression that overnight he became a very well-known public figure. For two years he roamed about the whole country delivering the message of Vedanta, went back to India, started the Ramakrishna Mission, which has its American branches known as Vedanta Societies.

Once more he came to America, this time with the hope he could recoup his health. At that time he came to the West coast also and spoke in some of the cities of California. In India and the West, gradually centers began to grow up, and after his passing a large number of institutions came up. Thousands of young men were inspired by his message, and especially by his writings, a movement continuing to grow even after his passing. As regards his writings, many are familiar with Romain Rolland's often quoted statement, "I cannot touch these sayings of Vivekananda, scattered as they are through the pages of books at thirty years' distance, without receiving a thrill to my body like an electric shock. And what shocks, what transports must have been produced when in burning words they issued from the lips of the hero!" That's what Romain Rolland writes in *Swami Vivekananda, Universal Gospel.*

He passed away in 1902, barely a life of thirty-nine years. But then his lectures and some of his writings have been collected and preserved, which have become a sort of an inspiration through all these years. Most of the top leaders of India, especially between 1893 and 1920 were inspired by Swami Vivekananda's writing. Practically all of them.

Anyway, Swami Vivekananda's writings have a message, spoken in such a language that even now it is meaningful. Ninety-five percent of his writings and lectures are often reproduced because they are not limited by local color. Every problem he faced from such a universal standpoint and in such a way that time has no hold on his sayings. Most of our writings are very topical, but he always dealt with the eternal nature of things, and even when he dealt with topical things he spoke in such a language they are potent and inspiring for all times. Take for example, the following lines:

"Hold on yet a while, brave heart
If the Sun by the cloud is hidden a bit,
If the welkin shows but gloom
Still hold on yet a while, brave heart,
The Victory is sure to come. "

Vivekananda, like the leaders of every movement naturally has a special liking for youth, because youth has that vitality and the capacity of following an ideal with a total abandon, not caring for themselves or their future. They can take up an ideal and devote their entire life for the realization of that ideal. Naturally every movement appeals to youth. Vivekananda, because he himself was a young man had a special appeal to the youth of India. And in Indian context he gave a sort of a social program.

He was a patriot, but a patriot of such a type that his patriotism never went against the interests of the other parts of the world. But his idea was through the finite to go to the infinite, as the Vedanta propounds. So through the finite idea of a country you go to the realization of your world citizenship. It is not that you jump to the universal idea, disregarding the part that you have to play in your limited circumstances. A man is born in a society in a particular environment, in a particular family. So through all this, gradually transcending the limitations of these limiting institutions, Vivekananda propounded an ideal which will take man step by step to the realization of that one world which is the vision of all the concerned thinkers of the world.

Here are some of his ideas. The important point to remember is this: Vivekananda was primarily a spiritual personality, but he had a deep social concern also. Half of his sayings were exhortations to young men to lay down their lives for the service of poor people, for the downtrodden, for the ignorant. Now there are many political and social thinkers who have done that, but Vivekananda's special contribution was to supply a philosophy behind service. It is not merely the interest created in the mind of a man living in a particular time that brought him to this understanding. He was grounded in spiritual realization and he had the experience of his teacher's deeper spiritual realization. With the help of this he gave a philosophy to us, a philosophy of service and social action, not losing the basic philosophical core of Vedanta. And that is the special message of harmonizing work and worship.

There is a dichotomy in religious thinking. People who turn religious find that external activity brings a sort of jarring effect on their minds. And normally that is accepted in religious circles that to be deeply religious you will have to avoid too much activity. Action versus contemplation is an age-old struggle in every religion. Again, social workers and social gospelers want the full attention of the people so that every individual member of a society could render his best to the society. And that is how in secular democracies a sort of indifference is practiced towards religious or spiritual pursuits. And in aggressive communistic countries where the social gospel is supreme a sort of anti-religious or anti-spiritual movement is always in the forefront.

But Vivekananda as a spiritual personality based his social gospel on spirituality. Why spirituality? He said, "Without it the whole world would be destroyed". And then he added, "The whole of the Western World is standing on a volcano, which may burst even tomorrow unless it shifts its basis of life from materialism to spirituality." That was a warning given by Vivekananda in 1897, and we must remember at that particular stage the Western World was quite smug in its victory and security. A sense of security was prominent, and an idea that society was continually progressing, having a boom in the acquisition of the wherewithal of life, and the luxuries of life. At that time in that age people never thought their society could go to pieces. Within twenty years the First World War broke out that shows Vivekananda's insight into the workings of the society. And he exhorted India also not to be lured by the enticing things of life developed through science and technology of the West, and never to give up its hold on spirituality. And to India he said if you give up spirituality, then your life's strength, the seed of your life will be destroyed. In one place he said if India dies, spirituality will die from the face of the earth. Spirituality in the West as well. He was speaking not out of patriotism here. He was pointing out that India down the ages has kept this torch or flame of spirituality alive. India, you know, through all these thousands of years has hugged the spiritual message to its heart. And he said we should not lose hold of that. Spirituality was Vivekananda's message, and he exhorted people by pointing out the spiritual core of one's Self.

Naturally his teaching was through the philosophy of Vedanta. It was practically Vivekananda who gave new life and energy to the philosophy of Vedanta. The Orientalists of course came in and translated the books of Vedanta, but Vivekananda came and popularized the Vedanta teachings in a language understandable and appealing to ordinary people. He pointed out, as the Vedanta does, that man's nature is Divine. He said - a frequently quoted line - "Each soul is potentially Divine".

The Vedanta argues like this: Man has a body, body is transient; man has a mind, mind is changing. Then what is the core of man which is permanent, which is not transient, which ever exists? It is the discovery of Vedanta, it is the realization of his master, Sri Ramakrishna, and it is his own realization also, that man is ultimately Divine in nature. He is the Spirit in essential nature. The other aspects of man are always changing, but the real core is the Spirit that is in every person. So this real nature of man, as it is put in Sanskrit, is the Atman. He said that any training that you give to man, any idea or any social program that you give him must be based on these three aspects of man. If it is only localized to cater to the needs of the body it will be a partial gospel, if it is only for the mind, again partial. Body-mind combined, which is normally done, is also based upon the partial aspect of man's nature. Man will be satisfied only when all these three aspects of man's nature will be looked after. So spiritual training is essential in any educational scheme according to Vivekananda. Body, of course, must be looked after, mind must be looked after; but much more important than these two, is to look after the Spirit, which is not always palpable to the average person. That was the special idea which formed the superstructure of his thought.

Swami Vivekananda has been known as the prophet of strength. Often in Indian context we present him more as a man preaching strength. Strength, he felt, is necessary everywhere in the world. Strength in three levels. He was in favor of introducing different physical exercises for body building. There was a very interesting controversy in later days. Mahatma Gandhi raised a question. Swami Vivekananda in one place exhorted young people to build up their body by saying, "You will understand the *Gita* better by playing football" - very dramatic way of putting it. The idea was that a man who gives attention to his body and builds up his body, with that strength of body and added vigor, he will understand the message of the *Gita* better. And not merely understanding, he will be in a position to apply the message of the *Gita* in actual life. There is no dearth of ideas. Many of us know many ideas, but the dearth of the ability of putting those ideas in action is what he wanted to remedy the social problems. So he spoke about building up the body. And, in fact, in the early days in many of our centers we generally provided physical exercise for young people. When such exercise was taken up by Indian society our stress on it was lessened.

Now the strength of Vivekananda was not based merely upon physical strength. He wanted intellectual development and moral development. But more important than all these, again, was a spiritual development. Strength really comes not from the weaker part of the human personality. Man's body can be made very strong, but sometime or other it will deteriorate. Mind can be made very strong, but still some of the defects may persist. But what is the source of strength? The source which never fails, Vivekananda tried to present before society. That the real strength is not in the body, the real strength is not in the mind but in the Spirit.

Some of you might be familiar with Sando's book. Sando was a very famous physical culturist, one of the earliest physical culturists in the West. His book, I think, was *Strength and How to Create It*. And there he propounded a very interesting theory. After a lifetime of developing a system of physical exercise he says, "It is the brain that develops the muscle." If you want to develop a muscle, say biceps, you need not do anything, he says, except think that the muscle is developing, and it will develop. This is a physical culturist speaking. Of course to help your mind develop this muscle you can put a little pressure, a little pain experience. So you give a little pressure to the muscle, and this pain brings more mind to the muscle. Then he improved it even further. Put a little weight in the hand and exercise As a result more pain will come and more mind will go to the muscle. Thus there will be quicker development. That is how the dumbbell was invented. And Sando was the man who did it. Later he introduced spring dumbbell, which requires more attention, plus weight, plus pressure. What I was driving at is this, though his real objective was to develop the physical body, he found that it is the brain which really directs the development of the body.

Vivekananda through his Vedantic training, realized this point much earlier, and said, "We want muscles of iron and nerves of steel." Mental strength can be developed directly and with the spiritual idea also. So to exhort people to develop the mental strength he said that through daily exercise you can make the mind so strong that whatever you want to achieve you can achieve. It is not necessary to have a God for this, your mind has that potentiality. This mind, by daily suggestion, by daily contemplation, by daily identification with your real nature, which is the spirit, can bring out that strength.

So that is the Vedantic method of prayer, not asking for anything. In normal prayer what we do is speak about our difficulties, "I have got this pain, that pain," and after saying it half a dozen times, "We say O God, save me from this pain." But the Vedantic method is different, and it is much more psychological. It is assertion: suddhoham, buddhoham, niramayoham. "I am pure, I am with knowledge, I am free from disease and defects." These are Vedantic prayers. They assert your real nature with statements such as these. Telling yourself all the time I am diseased, I am diseased will not cure the disease, medicine is necessary. Telling all the time I am weak, I am weak will not cure the weakness. Strength is necessary. And strength doesn't come by thinking of weakness all the time. That is the rationale of Vedantic prayer, assert your real nature, do not harp on your weakness, your sins and your defects. So that is what he emphasized for developing strength.

However, he went so far as to say that if a man is not aware of his spiritual nature, let him develop at least the body. And gradually a time will come when he will go to the higher realization of his real nature. So strength is one of his great messages. He said when you search for spiritual truths shun like poison, whatever is secret. Because there are many theories, many systems, sometimes they speak too much of secrecy and all that. He said it is debasing, and that which is debasing shun as poison.

Again, there are some people, some religious sects which stress surrendering to an individual, and through him to get results suddenly. He was very much against this also. He said you don't give up your independence in any of these matters. Learn from all the teachers you can, but retain your independence, because if somebody else does a thing for you, in the process you become weakened. So hypnotism and such things, he wanted young people to shun like poison. The main test of anything, any religious truth or social truth was for him whether it makes you strong. If it makes you strong day by day, then it is good. If not, even if its objective is good, it is not good for you. That is how he presented it.

A corollary of this idea for Indian context, and for the young people in general throughout the world, he said, is that the major problem in the human mind is fear. Fear of insecurity, fear of the future, fear of the uncertainties. He said that fear can be removed and neutralized by improving the social institutions. If you analyze the history of mankind from nomadic days, man, stage by stage was in search of some sort of security. Thus he built up various institutions, as that gives at least some sort of physical security. But that security is no enough. Something more is necessary. Real security comes from the spiritual security of realizing one's own undying nature. Fear is a common instinct with every living being, but when a man is identified with his real nature, what he discovers is that he is by nature the Spirit, the Atman, which never dies. A tremendous strength comes to him. Fear is cut at the root. Of course even in other situations, everyday situations, he said we should cultivate fearlessness. Cultivate fearlessness even in the physical level. In this way stage by stage you go to the highest realization. This idea will give you real strength. It is the greatest glory of the Upanishads, the ancient books of the Vedanta, that God is identified with Fearlessness, with Immortality itself; Abhayam, Amritam, these are the terms given. In many of the Upanishadic sayings, they don't mention the word God at all, but rather they give Amritam, Immortality; Abhayam, Fearlessness Itself. That is the real condition, that is the real nature of God or the real nature of the Atman, which is man's essential nature. So this idea of fearlessness, cultivation of fearlessness was one of his special ideas.

Again, based upon this, he exhorted men, especially young men, budding young men to confidence and that confidence ultimately is rooted in his real nature. He was very fond of repeating the word Shraddha! We have known in the Katha Upanishad, Nachiketa went to learn the truth and was even willing to learn the truth from the God of Death. That is the story. And he said we want this Shraddha, this faith like that of Nachiketa. Now this word Shraddha is not merely faith as we understand the word. It is an affirmative attitude towards things, a positive attitude towards things. Often we are dispirited, we feel dull, we feel uncertain about things. Vivekananda was all for cultivating what is the positive attitude. The affirmative attitude is the meaning of the word Shraddha. It is faith in oneself, and faith in God. There is a famous saying of his, *The old religion said he is an atheist who did not believe in God, but the new religion says, he is an atheist who does not believe in himself.* Of course all the time he was expecting that when a man tries to know his real nature even if it is in the physical level, gradually he will try to understand what really he is himself. That was Vivekananda's great emphasis; be affirmative towards everything.

In one of his letters he says that there is no strength in the negative attitude. We know from our experience that a man with a negative attitude cannot inspire others and really we cannot inspire ourselves." So he said, *No negative, all positive. I am. God is. Everything is in me. Be conscious of this truth, and manifest this truth in your life.* That is how Vivekananda exhorted people to cultivate this affirmative attitude towards things.

Of course nowadays we often speak about scientific attitude of neutrality, but in real life it is very difficult to cultivate that scientific attitude. Normally if a thing is presented before you, you add your emotions behind it, round it. If you are a man with an optimistic idea you are optimistic, if you have pessimistic ideas you become pessimistic. Often the example is given of half a glass of water. In this classical example the optimist will say, "Ah, half a glass of water." A pessimist will say, "Ah, half a glass of water is finished." A real scientific truth is simply half a glass of water, no emotions. But human nature is to mix up emotion in it. So Vivekananda said if it is in your nature to mix emotion in a situation, and you cannot get away from it, cultivate a positive attitude. Vedanta speaks of the real nature of things, and in the statement of the real nature of a given situation, a neutral attitude is the best. But if you cannot cultivate neutrality, then cultivate the affirmative or positive attitude. That is the idea of Shraddha, which was presented in the Katha Upanishad, and which Vivekananda was very fond of quoting.

He used to quote from the Taittiriya Upanishad, that young men by the thousands are wanted with certain qualifications. These are Asthishtha, Dradhistha, Balishtha and Medhavi. (Tai.2.8.1.) Balishtha is one having strength. Dradhishtha is firmness, one who can engage himself for a longer time, an athlete, for example, who can sustain his strength. Medhavi, intelligent, a person who has cultivated his mind. But the first qualification is Asthishtha, which means he must be optimistic by nature. A man may have strength, he may have enduring strength, he may be skilled and intelligent, but if he is pessimistic by nature he is not going to achieve anything in life, nor will he be of service to society. So that is why he wanted optimistic young men to go for service to society.

His spiritual message is seen in three levels. It helps individuals, it helps society, and it is for finding truth. Spirituality which is exhausted only in social gospel is not real spirituality. If my function is merely the functioning of scavengers, that would not be enough. He said those are the social scavengers who just work for society. Real spirituality is deeper than this. It is the application of a spiritual principle in social context, but that should not be the be-all and end-all of a person. Physical culture should go to social help, but that should lead to the spiritual realization. That is how Vivekananda programmed the development of a struggling soul.

Religion is useful for the individual to help him in his weaker moments, to give him strength to conduct his life, and to inculcate certain virtues for the good of society, and then religion must also take him stage by stage from this to the trans-social level of finding out the truth. If there were no real truth, ultimate truth, if there were no God, then the entire spiritual message would be of no use. It is merely an exhortation of a social gospeler but would not be the real truth. But Vivekananda asserts that the ultimate truth of life is there and the purpose of life is to realize that ultimate goal of truth. So all the work that is there in the physical and mental realms are all meant for developing the individual. Through all these developments he will go stage by stage to the truth. Truth is nothing but God, and that means in popular language to realize God or realize one's own real nature. So that is the purpose he had. But then stage by stage he wanted that this spirituality will take man to that realization.

Vivekananda emphasized mental development. In the preliminary stage body plays a very important part, but once the mind is developed, body becomes less significant. Of course we cannot neglect the body, but mind and soul become so strong that physical aspect becomes important. He stressed self-mastery. In the matter of self-mastery he recommended development of the will and concentration. The technique for gaining efficiency requires controlling energy and diverting it to a purpose. Our energy is frittered away. We must get hold of some of the energy and direct to a purpose. If you do it for some time and you develop the capacity of doing it you will have a tremendous mind. That is the basic reason for cultivating the power of concentration. An average mind is frittered away or is spread out on too many things. By the technique of concentration what you do is get a part of that energy and by daily practice make it so strong that you can achieve things. It is dependent upon a very simple principle. You have seen children burn papers with the help of a convex lens. What is the principle behind that? So much of solar energy is being wasted, because it is spread out on a larger area, diffused. With a contrivance you collect some of those energies, collect them to a focal point and being collected they become so strong that they can burn a paper. Similarly so much of our mental energies are being

frittered away. By this technique of concentration we try
to collect a part of this energy and focus it on a particular
goal, and as a result mind becomes tremendously strong.
And if that goal is God, it is meditation, opening the path
of the final realization of life's goal.

So this is the idea, the development of the body,
development of the intellect, development of self mastery
and self control, and then the development of the spiritual
ideal of one's own real nature. These are the four covetable
goals and the method he has propounded for attaining them
is most scientific and effective. - He was a monk through
and through. Naturally he stressed the simplicity of life.
Build the body, but practice a little simplicity, because too
much complexity of life deprives the soul of its fulfillment.
As is the experience of all people, especially in the West, too
much of machine has come, and machine has a tendency of
killing the soul of man. And too much of conformity, too
much of organization has a tendency of cutting man to its
own size. So as is the common charge against any type of big
organization, it does not give much scope for the individual
to flourish. The creativity of the individual is choked.

In the machine age of the last three hundred years, the
area of man's freedom has been very much limited; but
freedom is the cry of the soul. Vedanta has identified the
ultimate salvation as freedom. Freedom is the term used
for the definition of God. What is God? Vivekananda was
once asked this. He said freedom. But freedom in the
absolute sense. And as a corollary of the absolute sense

we could say even this social and individual freedom is
desirable. Freedom is our real nature, the Spirit, pervading
the entire universe and beyond. We are one with that Spirit,
and being one with the Spirit there is no limitation for us.
Unless that aspect is recognized and man's attention is no
longer directed only on the finite aspect of nature, there is
going to be dissatisfaction. All the wherewithals of life, all
the luxuries of life can be poured on a man or on a particular
society, but unless this real nature of man is discovered
dissatisfaction is inevitable. And that is the reason, we find
that men in the economically advanced countries in the
world are dissatisfied, they have not found their true nature.
As the Chandogya Upanishad puts it, *in the finite there is no
joy. Abiding satisfaction comes through the Infinite alone.*

But man has all the time been directing his energies to
the finite. As a result even when he gets those finite things,
he feels dissatisfied Real satisfaction can come only when
he directs his energy towards the spiritual realization of
his real nature. His real nature is Sat-chit-ananda. It is
satisfaction. Man's real nature is Spirit in which there is no
want. So until he realizes that condition, however much
social improvement is done, however much individual
conveniences are provided, man is not going to be happy.
And it is a good sign from the standpoint of the spiritual
ideal that unless and until that stage is realized man cannot
be fully satisfied.

This idea has to be discovered by every individual.
Those who are suffering from the lack of wherewithals

of life, provide them with that. That is what Vivekananda wanted. In the economically depressed countries, let them enjoy a little, but then when they have solved the economic problems, the food problem, the higher ideas must be brought before them. And that is why he said when you go to raise the masses, especially in India, don't kill their religion, because by giving some of the wherewithals of life or the luxuries of life, you will take away something which is grander, something which will bring solace, succor, and permanent satisfaction to life. And that is the spiritual realization of his real nature, the nature of the self or the Atman. So that is the message of Swami Vivekananda. It is basically the spiritual message, but put in such a forceful language that we should read it in his own words. We have his words in nine volumes. Read especially his letters. And you will find how inspiring they are. And from that you will feel that you are also inspired to do something, and practice something so that you can realize the ideal of life.

PART I

Chapter 8

THE UNIVERSAL MESSAGE OF SWAMI VIVEKANANDA

Swami Vivekananda was a great spiritual master and prophet. Many of his ideas are of universal import. While introducing the four yogas he said that "Our problem is to be free." In the preamble *to Raja Yoga* he proclaimed:

Each soul is potentially divine. The goal is to manifest this divinity within, by controlling nature, external and internal. Do this either by work, or worship, or psychic control, or philosophy, by one, or more, or all of these-and be free.

Whether discussing the problems of India or the world, maya or Brahman, he continued to emphasize the purpose of our lives-to realize our own divinity. In a letter to Miss Noble (later known as Sister Nivedita) Swamiji wrote that his ideal was "to preach unto mankind its divinity, and how to make it manifest in every moment of life." This is the most universal message of Swami Vivekananda. to realize this, one must pay as much attention to the means as to the end. Through the practice of the yogas, by serving God in man, and with the practice of strength and fearlessness, we are sure to realize the goal. In the progress of spiritual life the real test and requisite is strength and fearlessness.

Divinity of Man

The search for unity has been the one passion of all mankind. The Vedantic philosophy points out that the unity of existence is a logical necessity, and this truth has been asserted by saints and sages and recorded in the Upanishads. The visible universe, the individual, and the Ultimate Reality are one and the same. Sri Ramakrishna realized this unity. His foremost disciple, Vivekananda, experienced this truth and realized the real nature of man as transcending the body and the mind. It is the spirit-the undying, unchanging nature of man, in which there is no weakness, no defect. This realization impressed him so much that he declared at the Parliament of Religions in 1893:

Ye divinities on Earth - sinners! It is a sin to call a man so; it is a standing libel on human nature. Come up, O lions, and shake off the delusion that you are sheep; you are souls immortal, spirits free, blest and eternal: ye are not matter, ye are not bodies; matter is your servant, not you the servant of matter.

This grand message of the divinity of man was thus forcefully presented by Vivekananda to the world. Universal in scope, it stresses the positive, basic aspect of man's nature. By being familiar with this message, man everywhere will be free from superstition and will realize his divinity. The swami declared:

No books, no scriptures, no science can even imagine the glory of the Self that appears as man, the most glorious God that ever was, the only God that ever existed, exists or ever will exist.

Based on this idea of the divinity of soul and the innate perfection of man, he gave the two famous definitions: "Religion is the manifestation of the divinity already in man," and, "Education is the manifestation of the perfection already in man."

In the West especially, Vivekananda comes out in bold relief as the messenger of the glory of the Atman and its infinite possibilities. His message was very much appreciated in America. Being on a new continent, infinite opportunities opened up before the immigrants from Europe. In their old countries they experienced the limitations of life and often faced starvation and persecution. In this new land they felt the glory of the person. So Vivekananda's message of the majesty of the soul immediately appealed to them. Even today, this message has a tremendous appeal. It is a universal message, which people everywhere need to hear in order to recognize the divinity of man and his infinite possibilities in spite of immediate limitations. This will create zeal, which is essential for man everywhere, but especially for man struggling for better opportunities, a higher standard of life and a more equitable society.

Concept of Service

A corollary of the idea of the divinity of man and the unity of existence is the concept of service. Swami Vivekananda specially stressed this idea. He said, "Ethics is unity," and often pointed out that knowledge was the finding of unity in diversity, and that the highest point in every science was reached when it found the one unity underlying all variety. This was as true in physical science as in the spiritual realm. Thus, according to him, the whole field of moral science was based on the unity of existence, and all types of service had this idea of unity as their philosophical basis.

In India, Swami Vivekananda is often looked upon as a great patriot who exhorted the youth to engage themselves in the service of the suffering of millions of their motherland. In his own words: "Doing good to others out of compassion is good, but service of all beings in the spirit of the Lord is better." And again he said:

This is the gist of all worship-to be pure and to do good to others. He who sees Shiva in the poor, in the weak, and in the diseased, really worships Shiva; and if he sees Shiva only in the image, his worship is but preliminary. He who has served and helped one poor man seeing Shiva in him, without thinking of his caste, or creed, or race, or anything, with him Shiva is more pleased than with the man who sees Him only in temples.

This idea of service as interpreted by Vivekananda originated initially from the famous statement of Sri Ramakrishna, who in an ecstatic mood one day said that we puny creatures cannot really show pity to others, who are God incarnate; we can only *serve* these veritable gods. The young Narendranath came out of Sri Ramakrishna's room that day and said, "I have learned something unique today. If I live, the world will hear about it." After the passing away of his master, while traveling by foot across

India, Vivekananda's heart was filled with compassion for his fellow-man and he recognized the tremendous importance in the statement he heard that day. When Swamiji first went to America, his initial idea was to find money for the poor people in India. But soon he emphasized the universal aspect of his message. In a letter to Diwan Haridas Viharidas in 1894 he wrote:

Yet I believed and still believe that without my giving up the world, the real mission which Ramakrishna Paramahamsa, my great Master, came to preach would not see the light, and where would these young men be who have stood as bulwarks against the surging waves of materialism and luxury of the day? These have done a great amount of good to India, especially to Bengal, and this is only the beginning. With the Lord's help they will do things for which the whole world will bless them for ages....I was born to organize these young men; nay hundreds more in every city are ready to join me; and I want to send them rolling like irresistible waves over India, bringing comfort, morality, religion, education to the doors of the meanest and most downtrodden. And this I will do or die.

Vivekananda's vision of organizing the young men of India is seen today in the work of the Ramakrishna Math and Mission and among many other individuals and groups who are following his dictum to serve God in man.

Harmony of the Yogas

Vivekananda recognized that there are different roads leading to the same center - God. He said each one of these yogas - the yoga of work, wisdom, concentration, and devotion - is capable of serving as a direct and independent means for the attainment of freedom. He spoke of four paths of realization: jnana yoga - the realization of man's own divinity through knowledge and understanding; bhakti yoga - the realization through love of a personal God; karma yoga - realization through detached action and selfless service; and raja yoga - realization through mind control and meditation.

Vivekananda visualized an ideal character as a blend of these different disciplines. He felt that development of man is at its best-in other words, Self-realization is at its perfection-when human nature finds a many-sided expression in which bhakti, jnana, yoga, and karma all discover their respective possibilities and limits. He felt that by their combination it was possible to produce a balanced character, free from the possible defects of each of these exclusive paths-the heartlessness of the intellectuals, the bigotry of the emotionals, the aloofness of the meditative and the arrogance of the active. Swamiji found the perfect blending of the four yogas in the "ideal" character of Sri Ramakrishna, and said:

Such a unique personality, such a synthesis of the utmost of philosophy, mysticism, emotion, and work, has never before appeared among mankind. The life of Sri Ramakrishna proves that the greatest breadth, the highest catholicity, and the utmost intensity can exist side by side in the same individual, and that society also can be constructed like that, for society is nothing but an aggregate of individuals. The formation of such a perfect character is the ideal of this age.

Swamiji stressed the idea of the harmony of the yogas. Man thinks, feels and acts. When these three functions are not very active it is the yogic condition. When we relax, and the mind is having no particular emotion, thought or activity, it is experiencing the condition similar to the mystic mood. These yogas represent the four possible states of the mind. During different times of the day we may be in these different moods. Sometimes we like to be reflective, sometimes active, sometimes contemplative, and sometimes under the spell of the emotions. So a combination of the four yogas, or cultivation of the four methods will be productive of the best results. With the practice of one, however, the others are also indirectly practiced. When a mother loves her child intensely she likes to learn about child-rearing, and a part of her mind is always with the child. And of course she will always be working for the child. So it is clear that love gives her knowledge, concentration, and service, and this combination produces a better character. Similarly, if a businessman loves his work, knows the various forces operating in the field, has the capacity of concentration and also spends hours in his business, he is sure to fare better, especially if he consciously utilizes these four faculties. It is not that by following one method no result will be achieved; rather that by striving for a blend a more balanced character develops.

Strength and Fearlessness

A bold attitude toward life is what Vivekananda wanted, and that is what we read in the Upanishads and other scriptures also. As he said:

It is only in our scriptures that this adjective is given to the Lord-Abhih, Abhih. We have to become fearless and our task will be done.

Swamiji exhorted men to shed all their nervousness and cowardice and fight the battle of life boldly, but calmly. So it is strength that is necessary, and to bring in strength we must *think* of strength. Swamiji often stressed this idea. In one context he said:

Thinking all the time that we are diseased will not cure us; medicine is necessary. Being reminded of weakness does not help much. Give strength, and strength does not come by thinking of weakness all the time. The remedy for weakness is not brooding over weakness but thinking of strength.

Through faith we get clarity of vision, peace of mind and vitality of life. Our happiness and effectiveness depend upon the thoughts we think. Hence the urgency of changing our thought patterns. We must think such thoughts as create happiness, fearlessness, and joy.

It is through the practice of strength and fearlessness, the cultivation of a cheerful, positive attitude, that we will be able to understand and realize Vivekananda's universal message of divinity of the soul, the harmony of the yogas, and the concept of service.

PART I

Chapter 9

THE INSPIRATION THAT IS VIVEKANANDA

Swami Vivekananda's ideas have been seen through various eyes, and new light has been thrown upon these ideas. In one sense, Swamiji is inexhaustible. It can be argued that Swamiji's core message is that man is the Atman, Atman is perfection, and perfection defies all types of limitations.

'I Shall Not Cease to Inspire'

The first thing about Swamiji that strikes us is his importance in inspiring us. His teachings are there of course, but his *life* is also there. He has left behind a sangha, an organization, a circle of devotees, to put into practice the ideas he gave. And a great man is more a principle than a person. But still, to my mind, his most important contribution is the inspiration he creates.

I remember — and this is the experience of many people — that when we were young, there was a Bengali volume, a second volume of Swamiji's letters, which was very inspiring. Now it has been included in the larger compilation, *Letters of Swami Vivekananda. The* letters written between 1890 and 1902 are of a more inspiring type, when Swamiji was trying to energize people to do things. Romain Rolland has described Swamiji as 'energy personified, and action was his message to man'. So when you read his books, you get thrilled, as do some of the famous writers and thinkers and singers, but you also feel that inspiration comes in your own life. I was in Madras for more than twelve years in the 1950s and 60s. The president of the Tamil Writers' Association became my friend. And being inspired by us, he began to read the *Complete Works of Swami Vivekananda*. Early one morning, he came to the Math to meet me. That was not the time sadhus met people, but still I had to come out. He said, 'Swami, I could not contain myself. Last night I was reading Swamiji till twelve o'clock; then suddenly the inspiration came, by reading his works, that I must *do* something. But what to do at midnight? So I settled with my pen and wrote two stories in one night.' The reason he was so impressed was that for the previous two years he could not write a book or any stories for that matter, because he was constructing a building. That building took up all his energies, all his attention. There was no creativity left in him to write anything. So that is the important idea, that is in whatever way you are going, Swamiji's inspiration can help you in that particular way. Not that you will necessarily turn traditionally spiritual overnight, but you will be inspired, and when inspired things will happen. And that, according to Swamiji, is the real fulfillment of life: to manifest the perfection we have in us. How it is manifested and how much it is manifested, only by that, will it be judged whether our life is successful or not.

So the major idea is, Swamiji is an inspirer of people, especially the young people. When we remember his inspiring words, we feel energized, enthused; all the blood boils, as it were, to do something. What things will come? Much will be determined by the composition of our mind. Inspiration doesn't always express itself in the same way. We have the classical example of the *Ramayana* stories. Three brothers, Ravana, Kumbhakarna and Vibhishana, practiced hard austerities. That was considered to be the major method by which strength, power and wisdom were acquired. Because Ravana was of the rajasic type, his mental composition was of rajo-guna. He became a king and wielded power in the three worlds, but he also became a tyrant. Kumbhakarna was a lazy man, so by his tapasya his laziness increased, though it was probably a covetable laziness to some extent. He could alternately sleep for six months and eat for six months! We may smile at this, but remember, eighty per cent of our activities centre around these two: having good sleep and good food — to attain our security in these two. Twenty per cent of our activities may involve something more than these two things. Vibhishana was of the sattvic type and had spiritual attainment, realization of God. The idea is that spirituality can give you inspiration, but your mental composition must be all right.

Need for Purification of Mind

Swamiji's major prescription is service. He used to say that renunciation and service are the national ideals of India. Why *national* ideals, these are the ideals of the whole world. I was at one time the editor of the *Vedanta Kesari* in Madras. My predecessor was Swami Budhananda, who was a good thinker. At one time he filled up the

journal with quotations he had collected for two years —
from the *Mahabharata* and other books — to prove that a
householder is a greater renouncer than a sannyasin. Why?
If I am a monk and I have got a headache, I can go to sleep.
I need not care for the world. But if I am a mother and my
child comes home, in spite of my headache, in spite of my
illness, I shall have to get up and look after the child. Now,
unconsciously that mother has acquired the quality of a
yogi - self-control, control of the emotions and demands
of the body, by working for the child.

Along with receiving inspiration, it is very important
to purify our minds as much as possible. The method of
achieving purification is contemplation of the pure. The
lives of Ramakrishna, Holy Mother, Swamiji and others
can purify us, but it is also important to do some unselfish
action.

True Worship

Swamiji's prescription is to purify yourself, and then,
to be useful to society, to work for others. Spiritual
work is all right, but if you work for others, at least
something substantial will remain. When Swamiji went to
Rameswaram, he said in his lecture in the Shiva temple that
if we go to the temple with fruits and flowers but forget
that God is there, the whole thing is a waste. Of course,
some result will be there inasmuch as it is a discipline; it
is not a hundred per cent waste, but still a waste. But if
we go to a sick man and give a little medicine, or go to an
ignorant man and give a little knowledge, if we remember
God is in him, we get the full benefit of worship. But

even if we forget the god in him, still, our action has a social benefit. It involves the practice of unselfishness. The more unselfishness increases, the more purity will come. Impurity is self-consideration. In all our affairs we normally equate things from our own standpoint. Unselfishness is ignoring oneself.

I remember one thinker's very beautiful definition of humility. We know what humility is, but his was a very unique way of explaining it. Humility is the capacity to praise your adversary. Very difficult indeed! To praise one's adversary, to say that he has got good qualities, is wonderful. It requires us to think a little deeper. When we can do this, it means that complete egolessness has come. We are then able to appreciate goodness elsewhere, or find goodness in somebody else.

Atma-vikasa

Swamiji's idea is that we will be much more successful if we can purify ourselves, make the mind ready for results, ready for the manifestation of our hidden powers. As Vedantists we should believe that nothing comes from outside. All the capacities are already within. They are to be brought out. Instead of self-development, our word is *atma-vikasa,* self-manifestation. The Atman is all perfect, it manifests itself in a limited way. Unknown areas are there in human nature in which the Spirit can manifest. In the world's oldest book, the *Rig Veda,* it is said that God covered the entire universe, but transcended it by ten fingers more, meaning that He is not finished with the universe, He is something more also. This means that a puny creature

like a man or a woman has the same perfection God has;
it is a question of difference of manifestation. And in
innumerable ways we can manifest the Spirit in ourselves.
When I first came to America, years ago, two women had
been declared Generals of the US Army, for the first time
in history. There had been queens and fighters, but not
Generals. That means that an ordinary creature like a man or
woman has unknown, undiscovered, unmanifested areas.
So that is why Swamiji advised us to every day think of
ourselves as the Atman and manifest the power of the Spirit.

Assert Yourself

One writer spoke of 'prayer without tears'. Prayer,
normally, is asking. Vedanta says, instead of weeping and
crying, *assert*. You have got the power within you. Assert
it. The theistic idea is that God has got the power, and that
we ask God, 'Please, God, give me something.' But instead
of that, assert. Assertion is a better psychological technique.
If we say, 'I have got a headache, I have got a headache;
O Lord, do something for me', the subconscious absorbs
the idea — headache, headache, headache. So instead of
producing health, more unhealthiness will be produced. On
the other hand, Vedanta will ask you to say, *'Suddho'ham,
buddho'ham, niramayo'ham;* I am pure, I am illumined, I am
healthy.' You may argue, 'I am not healthy; I have a headache.' But, really speaking, you don't have a headache.
Vedanta pushes you to the question, 'Who are *you?'* That is
one of the inquiries Vedanta asks us to make. Some groups
don't go into philosophy, religion, pujas and bhajans — they
use straight questioning.

Who are you? Analyze, analyze, analyze. Vedanta asserts, 'I am not the body, not the mind, but the Spirit.' The moment you say, 'I am healthy, I am healthy', you are identifying with your Spirit nature. When you say, 'I have got a headache, I have got a headache', *who* has got the headache? The body, of course. Or, you may feel bad mentally, but you have already argued that you are not the body, not the mind, so *you* are not suffering. When you say 'I am healthy', you are telling the greater truth, the higher truth, the more enduring truth. Truth that is more enduring is real truth. Temporary truth is no truth.

The materialists came forward and said, 'No, we don't accept this. How do you know that this is so? Our studies don't reveal the Spirit.' The Vedantists explained, 'We don't know your method of physical analysis or logical process, but we can realize the Truth by our special method of inspiration, or intuition, by what is called *anubhuti,* or *Bodhi,* experience, realization. These are the different terms used by different schools to describe the ultimate understanding of one's real nature. This method may not be accepted by the materialists but that does not matter, for according to them it cannot be known by their methods. As you know, it is one of the limitations of the Sciences that they cannot know the Infinite. This is not evident to ordinary people, but the ultimate nature of everything is revealed to the realized soul.

Swamiji asserted that man is Divinity in human form. When he went to America, he told the people, 'You are not sinners. It is a sin to call you so.' Very dramatic words! And by the by, it would be a very good idea, especially for you young people, to memorize fifty of these inspiring sayings of Swamiji. Through your whole life they will be useful.

Swamiji's method was to bring out the positive side. If somebody denounces me and then gives me advice, half the time I am not going to accept it even if he is right.

So when Swamiji said this, he was speaking to Americans, who were immigrants or descendants of immigrants from Europe, who had either been persecuted religiously or went to America because of famine or for a better livelihood. They found that the country was theirs for the taking. Soon there were ranches and fields, ten, twenty miles long. To such a person, if you say, 'You are a sinner; you are hopeless', he is not going to believe it. For religion's sake he may grudgingly agree, but he is not going to really accept it. Swamiji said, 'No, you are the all-powerful Spirit.' That appealed to the pioneering Americans. That is one reason why Swamiji became so successful. He inspired. He touched the real core of the people's lives. He told them, 'You are something grand, something infinite, something unlimited.' That is the special idea Swamiji tried to inject in the Western context.

Serving the Manifested Atman

Normally, commentators translate the word *atmarama* as 'one who finds bliss in the Self'. But is it bliss in the Self with closed eyes or open eyes? Sri Ramakrishna is seen in both ways. In his commentary on the *Narada Bhakti Sutras*, Swami Tyagishananda explains that the effect of seeing the

Atman everywhere is service of men and other creatures. So a man of illumination can do both: he may go within or serve the manifested Atman. Once you have realized, you are free; what do you want to do? The scholarly swami is telling us that the normal, natural course of a man of illumination will be to serve others. It is a very beautiful way of putting Swamiji's idea.

This is an important idea in the Indian context. Swamiji stressed this idea of service, because India needs service. Even after more than fifty years of independence, people are starving, they are ignorant, there has not been much improvement. Of course, they say forty per cent of Indians belong to the middle class, and that is why America has got interested in India. But, still, in the larger community, people are not free from hunger and insecurity, so some manifestation of energy is necessary. The Ramakrishna Mission immediately attracted the attention of society because of pinpointing this idea of serving society and doing it.

Nowadays, the question of relevance is often brought up. In what way, as a person or as a principle manifesting ideas, is Swamiji relevant? He is significantly relevant in two ways. Man must continually be made aware that he has got infinite possibilities. If he knows and believes that he has got possibilities, new avenues will open up. The method will be to serve others. That way, society will be benefited, the individual will be benefited. Thus, stage by stage a practitioner will go towards higher realization, which is the ultimate goal of life.

Everything Positive, Nothing Negative

Swamiji's special prescription is that all of us should have an ideal. His famous saying is, 'If a man with an ideal makes a thousand mistakes, I am sure, the man without an ideal will make fifty thousand. Therefore, it is better to have an ideal.' Swamiji always tried to improve people, not by showing their defects, but by showing their merits. In one of his famous letters he says, 'No negative, all positive, affirmative. I *am*, God *is*, everything is in me. I *will* manifest health, purity, knowledge, whatever I want.' (6.276) But that has to be done by asserting the positive aspect of ourselves, by thinking of our divine nature. If I lack strength, I think of the Atman as full of strength. If I lack courage, I think of the Atman as full of courage. That is the method. There is another famous saying of his:

But, says the Vedantin, being reminded of weakness does not help much; give strength, and strength does not come by thinking of weakness all the time. The remedy for weakness is not brooding over weakness, but thinking of strength. Teach men of the strength that is already within them. (2.300)

That is why, even for India his prescription is to think of strength, not weakness. In one context Swamiji denounces India, but his major thrust is, 'Love India, honor India, respect India.' The idea is that you must develop that love for your own country. Not only for your country — ultimately you will have to embrace the whole world, but not by ignoring your country. Now the present world is being ruled by nationalism, and everywhere the nationalistic states are lionized. But, transcending nationalism, we must also recognize the universal idea — to make the entire world our own.

These are a few ideas from Swamiji. We can take up Swamiji from any angle and try to show that a particular idea of his is useful for the betterment of the individual, of society and of the world at large. That is the special purpose of a religious teacher, a teacher who is an inspirer. 'Awakener of souls' is the term often used for Swamiji. Let us be inspired by him; let us try to build our lives and also dedicate them for the good of others.

PART II
Vedanta

PART II

Chapter 1

VEDANTA FOR MODERN MAN

Vedanta means the end of the Vedas. The Upanishads embodying the philosophical ideas are the last literary products of the Vedic period, which were studied after the Samhitas and the Brahmanas. The Vedantic literature is vast, but the Upanishads, Brahmasutras and the Gita are its principal books. The commentaries of Acharya Shankara on these are the main guides, though Vishishtadvaita, Dvaita and other views of the devotional schools are also included in Vedanta. Vedanta is both a view and a way of life. It is a living philosophy and not mere speculation, for thousands of people have been shaping their lives according to its teachings. There are some points of difference among the different schools in their ideas about God and His relation with man and the world. Swami Vivekananda tried to synthesize the different views following Sri Ramakrishna's realizations about them. The main ideas of Vedanta are the unity of existence, non-duality of the Godhead, divinity of the soul and harmony of religions.

Vedanta carries the essentials of all religions. It has been described as the Perennial Philosophy, the lowest common denominator of all religious beliefs, requiring the 'minimum working hypothesis', as Aldous Huxley puts it. Essentially speaking, it gives us three propositions: (1) that man's real nature is divine, (2) that the aim of life is to realize the divinity of man and (3) that all religions are in agreement regarding this. This working hypothesis is necessary, for without it 'there cannot be any motive for research or experiment or any way of bringing sense or order into the observed facts.'

The modern spirit has been defined as utilitarian and rationalistic or scientific. Vedanta appeals to modern man because it answers both these requirements to a great extent. Vedanta is the science of religion. It supplies us with a philosophical basis for all the religions. It collates all spiritual data available from the different traditions of different countries, sifts them and weaves them into a coherent whole. Moreover, it takes into consideration other experiences too, and then by logical inference formulates an explanatory theory and finally recommends a way of action for the realization of the goal propounded by the theory. From this point of view it is purely scientific and rational. It gives scope for research and experiment and does not present the truth only from a dogmatic stand-point, though in the ultimate analysis it also depends on the Shruti or revelation. But this revelation, says the Vedanta, is not unique. It has been realized down the centuries throughout the world and can be experienced now too. It also points out that the experiences of saints and sages, mystics and devotees are part of the observed facts of at least a section of humanity and so they can never be left out, as is often done by some thinkers, while giving a world view. Science, said Swami Vivekananda, is the search for truth in the external world whereas religion is the search for truth in the internal world. Both are grand, both are noble. But the discoveries of science are more tangible and spectacular. They can be shown objectively too and are not confined to a privileged class. Religions are often esoteric and their results are not so spectacular. But Vedanta does not believe in secrecy and privilege. It is open to all for observation and experiment, experience and realization. As such it is very logical too.

We find that modern science has outgrown the stage of mechanistic materialism and in a sense has come nearer to Vedanta. The universe according to Vedanta is not what it seems, for at the core of all this there is one substance. Modern science too says that different objects are different arrangements of identical units and that these are in a perpetual flux. Now if there is an essential Reality in the universe, it must be omnipresent and so must be within every object. Science stops with matter and has no means of pushing its enquiry further. Vedanta adopts the discoveries of the spirit of man and finds a higher reality behind matter which it calls Atman. The Vedanta recognizes the transcendent and calls it Brahman. It also realizes the immanent Self or Soul and at the final stage it identifies these two — Brahman and Atman. The modern ideas of human unity and the dignity of the individual get a tremendous support from this view of Vedanta.

To realize our essential nature is the goal of our life, says Vedanta. The necessity of it is felt only when we find ourselves dissatisfied with our immediate objectives and achievements. And this dissatisfaction is bound to come since man's nature is infinite and cannot be satisfied with the small gains of the world or its limited gifts. Says the *Chandogya Upanishad*, 'There is no bliss in the limited, the infinite alone is bliss.'

Karma and reincarnation are two of the theories accepted by Vedanta. They try to explain the difference in equipment and achievement seen among men. We may consider this difference to be due to lack of justice in the world-scheme or we may say that it is justice that makes the difference, giving punishment and reward according to the nature of one's action and Karma. The working of justice does not cover this life alone but also other lives lived by the soul before it. Man has to answer for his Karma, and by doing better Karma, can improve his lot on this earth and in future lives.

A question has been raised: Why don't we remember our past lives? Vedanta says that we don't remember even our actions and thoughts of a few years ago. Moreover it claims that by yogic practices we can remember the past.

Now let us for a few moments think of the modern man. Who is the modern man? What are his aspirations? What are his problems? The modern man has been described as rational, as scientific, as pragmatic. He lives in the present. He does not take things for granted, but wants to test everything with available knowledge. He is not willing to be a creature of circumstances. He has a will to improve materially, individually and collectively. He is ambitious and is a lover of freedom. Modernism has been described as 'views or methods, especially the tendency

in matters of religious beliefs, to subordinate tradition to
harmony with modern thoughts'. Vedanta has nothing to
fear from reason or scientific thoughts. It is true it believes
in the oneness of the creation, the realization of which is,
according to it, the supreme goal of life, but, as I have said
before, it depends on experimental data available from
the scriptures and records of mystics. Once this material is
accepted, Vedanta becomes relentlessly rational. Acharya
Shankara, the great propounder of Vedanta, said that
thousands of scriptural texts will not make fire cold. This
shows his stern devotion to logic.

The modern man with his pragmatic outlook can make
much use of Vedanta, for the latter is nothing if not practical. Swami Vivekananda has pointed out in his remarkable
lectures known as 'Practical Vedanta', how the Vedantic
principles can be applied to personal and social situations.
Vedanta does not believe in putting off all the ultimate
knowledge to an afterlife. A man must realize the truth
here and now. It does not take things for granted, but
gives scope for experiment and research. The available
knowledge through the sciences is still on shifting grounds,
but even then its major trends are often not antagonistic to
Vedantic findings. Moreover, Vedanta supports all types
of knowledge as steps to higher knowledge.

Vedanta says that freedom is our essential nature and
hence any striving towards more and more freedom is
commendable. It goes a step further and makes our idea of
freedom broader. Modern man is very ambitious. Vedanta
provides a goal to the ambitious and the adventurous.

That goal, being a non-material one, is free from the defect of unhealthy competition.

The modern temper is to avoid rituals. Vedanta stresses the essentials of religion and says that a man can realize the highest goal even without rituals. But those who want can have them, as Vedanta looks upon them as symbols reminding us of the Ultimate.

Modern life is complex. It has several outstanding problems too. The Vedantic idea of the purpose and scheme of life and the different ways of realizing the goal can help in the solution of some of the problems, as a sort of byproduct. They can be directly applied for specific problems too, For example, in this age man has to live a life of tension. Sometimes drugs are used to bring calmness and composure to the mind. But tranquillizers are found to have only temporary efficacy. Vedanta through its philosophical tenets as well as yogic practices offers a much better substitute. For one thing, it takes away the minds of men from the conflicts of competition and hunger after pleasure by placing a non-material aim before them. For another, by its practical technique of meditation and yoga it produces mental calmness and spiritual poise.

The fear of failing to keep up the pace or one's place in life results in worrying and brooding, in many of the modern people. While this result can be tackled by the yogic technique, fear itself can be uprooted or neutralized if we have a glimpse of the Vedantic idea of oneness of all life. The *Brihadaranyaka Upanishad* says that fear is born when we see a second. Vedanta knows only one and no second. The idea that ultimately there is only one spirit indwelling everything can cut at the root of all fear. Even if partially practiced, it will help a man to be partially free from fear. More, it will help him to cultivate all the higher virtues which are the basis of any social order. Ethics is oneness, said Swami Vivekananda. This idea of oneness is the ultimate reason why man should love his neighbor and not cut his throat. In modern life we have relativized all values. By stressing this basic reason, Vedanta can help ethics in bringing about a more stable social order. Vedanta while provisionally accepting these values leads us beyond them to the Ultimate.

Leisure is becoming a problem in some of the economically advanced countries. The development of science and technology, syndicates and corporations, is slowly lessening the area of physical freedom of modern man. So he, as Arnold Toynbee says, must find a new realm of freedom, which can only be in the reaches of thought. A modern man must shift his energies, his love of freedom to a non-material region. And Vedanta provides such a field which is the inner world of man. Moreover, man requires a challenge. We often erroneously think that when our standard of life is high, we will be free from all problems. But the experience of materially advanced countries proves otherwise. For instance, Sweden, the foremost country in providing social security has the largest number of suicides. This shows man requires challenges to fight against and conquer. Such challenges, if located in the material field, will produce competition and dissensions, ultimately landing us in war. The realm of the spirit provides a better challenge, for the effect is better. Vedanta takes up the challenge as one coming from human ignorance and delusion and engages itself in fighting these by bringing the mind of man into vital contact with Reality. When this has been done, unity and not separatism, peace and not war, bliss and not suffering, hold the ground. This is where Vedanta scores its triumph. This is how Truth alone conquers — *Satyameva Jayate.*

PART II

Chapter 2

THE ROLE OF VEDANTA IN SHAPING OUR NATION

With the dawn of independence and the integration of the States India has become a well-knit country in spite of its sad partition. Though it has as many as fourteen major languages India is one, having one Constitution, one Parliament and one President. Politically its integrity is unquestionable. The cultural pattern and the outlook on life and the aspirations are so similar in different parts of the country that India can be called as real a nation as any other nation however much the purists or academicians might doubt. Though the emergence of a common State is a new phenomenon, the cultural unity was achieved long ago due to the common outlook on life and common aspirations. And that stupendous task was performed by the grand philosophy and religion of Vedanta exerting its synthesizing influence on the different groups of people following diverse faiths. The saints and holy men in all faiths developed that synthetic vision because of their unitive mystic experience. Truth is one though the masters call it by various names, was the guiding principle for all sects and groups. That is why we find that different sects, while following their own path as the best, were at the same time catholic enough to pay homage to the other paths or their deities.

With the coming of Islam and Christianity, the two extra-territorial forms of faith, the balance of Indian society was upset. India with its genius for assimilation accepted in earlier days the Sakas, the Huns and others *en bloc* in her body politic with her peculiar method of reinterpretation and assigned each group a place providing for it particular work of the society. But owing to the loss of independence and quick changes of life, her energy was spent in keeping her own house in order. As a result India failed to effect complete fusion and integration of the exotic groups with the local ones. Another reason possibly was that the new groups belonged to the faith of the rulers and not only owed their allegiance to an alien and exclusive system of life and philosophy but maintained their contact also with their centers of origin thus remaining the least affected by the harmonizing influence of Hinduism. But that they were at least partially liberalized could be seen even the other day before the communalistic politics was introduced in the Indian arena by vested interests. Now with the emergence of India as a full-blooded nation, the fusion should be easier. But the different groups in the country, being still conscious of their separate entities, and willing to maintain their peculiarities, a wider basis of harmony is necessary to fuse them all into one group, integrated in their aspirations and behavior. This task can be performed even now by Hinduism. Possibly the scheme of life and professions, which got encrusted through the accretions of ages, will have to be liberalized or removed even for its own society and only the essentials of it put forward to embrace all others. Hinduism can assimilate alien cultures and religious ideals and social units by emphasizing the essentials of spirituality, minimizing ritualism and thus producing internal and external liberalism.

The essentials of all religions are the same: And Vedanta embodies those essentials. It can free Hinduism from the apotheosized hereditary caste and plethora of rituals, in accordance with the taste of the modern people. It can supply a generalized background to other faiths, an all-encompassing system for intellectual basis. If the followers of dogmatic, doctrinaire theologies find the Vedantic theory of all paths leading to the same Godhead difficult to incorporate in their own systems, they can at least recognize that in a land of many faiths they can accept the theory of unity in variety. This recognition will change the mental climate and pave the way for better understanding. After all, the days of dreaming of a world religious empire are gone and if the religions are to fight the onslaught of aggressive secularism and anti-religious systems, they must unite to preserve the faith, not for political or material advantages but for the deepening of the spiritual sense itself.

What is the core of all religions? Is it not the consciousness of oneself as Spirit and having faith in a Higher Reality and in higher values? Religions are worth the name when they foster faith in God and in the higher virtues. The true Muslims, the true Christians join the true Hindus in their faith in God, in devotion, wisdom, sacrifice and detachment. It is not that a man can be a good follower of any of these systems without changing his life, remaining earth-bound. He must lift up his mind and attune it to the Divine. Every religion says that. Vedanta, of course, proclaims this more emphatically and unequivocally. That is why we like to invoke the name of Vedanta or essential Hinduism, instead of Hinduism in general which has a doctrinaire side also like other religions. Vedanta represents the essence, the core, the cream of all the faiths and it is free from all coloring by limitations of any country or society. It points out the truth lying in every religion, unnoticed, unexplored, undeveloped. Let the different religions take the clue from Vedanta, rediscover the truth in their own systems and express it in tune with their own genius. Mutual understanding is the urgent necessity of the times. Let the best minds of every faith come forward and persuade the society to accept the conceptions of unitive experience, of unity in variety, of the synthesis of religions. As Swami Vivekananda declared, Vedanta does not try to convert anyone, it seeks to make a Hindu a better Hindu, a Mussalman a better Mussalman, and a Christian a better Christian. Will not the leaders of religions hear this liberal message of Vedanta for deepening the spiritual lives of their followers, for the survival of religions in this age of materialism at least out of expediency, if not out of religious conviction? Politics alone cannot bring about this mutual understanding, for it seeks to acquire rights, whereas religion endeavors to sacrifice them for the good of the people. This spiritual principle of self-sacrifice is fortunately still the basic idea of our society.

The political democracy in our country is still a new venture. It cannot withstand the onslaught of unrest caused by differing groups as possibly a stable system could. So it is the duty of all groups of people, political or cultural, to discover and stress the common features they have. They should on no account arouse the passions of the people on the grounds of religion and language, or manners and customs. Unless they want to make capital out of the hatred, there is no justification. Even then they should beware of the after effects. Our neighboring country, separated because of jealousy and hatred, and still its masters are being dogged by these two vices. Even in India the hatred we had for the old Government has been partially transferred in the form of apathy to our own one, though it is slowly melting away.

Another thing we can learn from Vedanta. The democratic system raises a man today to the skies and drops him down tomorrow. The heart-break that the process causes may be eliminated or minimized if the sufferers develop the virtues of detachment and sacrifice. Love of country alone may be able, in rare cases of developed individuals, to sustain them but in the vast majority of cases failure will damp the enthusiasm and energy, for mere patriotism is too mixed up with desire for larger work and resultant power. They can remain satisfied with less spectacular work if only they are imbued with high idealism or are temperamentally optimistic. They can do unostentatious work better if they are suffused with the religious idea that any work done in a spirit of dedication is good enough for the development of the inner life of man.

If the spiritual outlook is good for the unostentatious

workers, it is imperative for the people at the helm of big affairs. The power or position of a high rank often breeds pride and arrogance. It is necessary for those in power to be imbued with a spirit of humility, not a mask but a genuine feeling, and that is possible only when they are aware of a higher Power and a Divine scheme of things.

With the coming of independence a peculiar trait of shirking duties and of endeavoring to rise up in life by other means is evident in the cases of many employees. It is a sad state of affairs. As the element of fear of the foreign masters is gone, of course happily, it is necessary to provide for common workers an incentive to create devotion for their work either by infusing love of the country or enlightened self-interest or the Vedantic attitude of looking upon all work as Divine service. While the first two may be of immediate appeal, the last one is more enduring. Vedanta proclaims the unity of existence of all creatures and Swami Vivekananda pointed out its implication, that service to man, therefore, is service to the Divine. Thus our ordinary duties become a way to self-realization. This, as Sri Krishna pointed out, will attract the maximum of devotion to duty and at the same time make the worker unattached and remove his feeling of frustration whenever such an occasion arises. As the work will be a service to the Divine, all dubious means also will be given up. We are, of course, sadly aware that it is difficult for a common man to be really honest in a dishonest environment. It will be the duty of the Government and society to narrow down the necessity, allurement and scope for such dishonesty. Mere idealism possibly will not do for common man, some modicum of amenities, laws and other deterrents also will be necessary. But a spiritual outlook will give a zest in work even to the average man and surely it will enhance the sustained enthusiasm of idealistic people.

The foundations of a democracy as against those of a totalitarian system lie in the recognition of the dignity of the human personality. The Vedantic idea of Divinity in man will supply the necessary philosophical basis. According to this view politics or an efficient system of administration is required for providing man with the normal amenities of life and sufficient leisure and scope for spiritual and cultural self-realization. Swami Vivekananda believed that the potentialities of a man can be best brought out by making him conscious of the immense potentialities of the Self. Preach the glories of Atman, was his advice. In innumerable cases we have also found that this awareness has created a tremendous confidence and enthusiasm in men, expressing itself in various types of creative activity according to their innate tendencies and aptitudes. It is essential, of course, .that a group of people should know of the Atman for a purely spiritual motive also. They will be the beacon-lights for guiding the people in doubt and confusion Attuning one's life to the Divine, which is the source of all strength, is like a tributary's merging in a mighty river, thereby getting the capacity to make an entire area fertile. Nowadays political leaders revel in denouncing the ideal of renunciation. People do not know that they have some social or political groups in mind when they condemn in general terms, sometimes even the ideal itself. As a result the susceptible people get hardened and the very sap of the roots of sacrifice dries up and its effects are felt in other national spheres.

Whole-souled and sustained devotion to a cause comes through, spirituality. Vedanta tries to eliminate the difference between sacred and secular by suffusing the latter with spiritual ideas. The spiritual quest itself brought Gandhiji and many others to politics. Thus it was the motive power of Indian nationalism. So attempts have been made here to spiritualize politics and social activities. Spiritualizing all our efforts is congenial to our national temperament and will make the system more enduring. But it is possible only when a large number of individuals or at least the topmost ones take up the spiritual attitude and thus develop a national character. This will require a spiritual reform according to the Vedantic gospel of service preached by Swami Vivekananda. There is no fear of fanaticism being developed, for Vedanta is free from mere conventions and creeds which are the roots of religious bigotry. Even if there is some fear because of India's recent experience we must give a trial to the coordination of the different spheres of life of the nation which is a united whole. By evolving a synthetic consciousness, the idea of a common ideal, common endeavor and common feeling must be created among the different constituents of the society. That indeed will give India an ideal nationhood.

The message of India to the world is the idea of oneness of the universe. With the imprinting of this idea on his consciousness a man will discover peace within himself and will be at peace with all. India must preach this idea of oneness to save the world from a major catastrophe. Even for her own sake, if she is to remain a neutral and idealistic nation, she must create a climate among the nations of the world for genuine love of peace, amity and idealism. Absolute standards of morality may not be possible to keep up in the beginning, but a time may come when it will be possible. Even if it is a vision, it is prompted by lofty idealism and optimism and is sure to be a great motive force for unselfish, whole-hearted endeavor. People engaged in some national service, such as politics, business or the military, may find their profession stained with unspiritual acts of diplomacy, exploitation or violence. Their moral conflict may be neutralized if they perform their duty for duty's sake and are perfectly non-attached. This psychological sanction is possibly necessary to keep a man active. It must be admitted, however, that it falls short of the highest standard, which possibly is unavoidable in an uncongenial social and world atmosphere. The Karma theory, that their accumulated bad innate tendencies are thus being worked out and as a result they will ascend to the consummation of purity, may hearten them and slowly lead them to the ideal standard.

Our life is the most mysterious of all problems. It is not merely a mechanical and purposeless chance product of blind matter's evolution. Faith in the highest unity and a higher destiny for man may not solve all the moral problems in the language of reason but it will provide the soul of man with a perennial fountain of vigor and progressive enlightenment.

If Indian nationalism takes as its basis with firm faith the ideal of realizing the higher consciousness, it will transcend narrow nationalism and will pave the way for the emergence of a world community which is the dream of the best minds all over the world. India must translate this trans-social and trans-national ideal in her life in tune with her genius. The role of Vedanta is to help her ascend to this ideal of unitive experience from which human unity will flow as a by-product. This may be done by Vedanta through spiritualizing life, and through stressing on harmony of religions, unity in multiplicity, Divinity of all creation and eliminating the dichotomy between sacred and secular. And this is the real Indian way.

PART II

Chapter 3

VEDANTA AND THE DEMOCRATIC SPIRIT

Indian culture down the ages has been influenced so much by Vedantic ideas that it has become synonymous with Vedanta. Vedanta has some unique ideas. Democracy too, specially during the last two and a half centuries, has developed some peculiar ideas and approaches to life. Democracy has two aspects, political and philosophical. Rousseau spoke about the General Will of the people. Thomas Paine spoke about the Rights of Man. Abraham Lincoln popularized the idea of the Government of the people, for the people and by the people. They all spoke the tongue of politics. Based on these ideas democracy developed its economic and political theories. Politically democracy gives to every person the right of being an equally important entity in the social context. Philosophically, it is more or less dependent, originally at least it was, on the religious thinking, on the spiritual nature of man.

Vedanta in all these aspects has got a definite message to give and we do feel that Vedanta can be the philosophical basis of political democracy. Here democratic idea is a creed, but the most important thing is to create a temper, a mental climate, a mood in the average man of society to react to a particular situation with an attitude. That is what democracy as a way of life does. It is not at all foreign to the nature of Indians. In the olden days, the Vedic Aryans were a community of elders having equal share in conducting the work of the society. Later there were the *sanghas* and the *sabhas*. The *Mahabhasya* as well as Panini's *Ashtadhyayi* bear witness to it. These have also been referred to by the Greek travelers in their travelogues. We read of them in the Buddhist literature too. The Lichhavis, in which tribe Lord Buddha was born, and other tribes were small Republics.

The equality of man, in the sense of equality of voice of every man in society, in running the Government is possible only in very small communities, as in Swiss Cantons. Democracy has, therefore, in modern times taken a turn to a sort of representative democracy, a limited democracy. A vast body of people select a group of people in legislatures and, probably, also the top executives in some countries. Every man is equal, politically speaking, in giving his opinion. It is true that there is a difference between man and man. The contribution of an ordinary individual eking out a precarious existence may not be the same as the contribution of a highly gifted individual — a scientist, a social engineer, a man having special skill, for instance. Still, before the eyes of democracy, every man is equal and has one vote. So a sort of equality is practiced.

Now, this particular type of political system, if it is to succeed in practice, in any particular given context, the society must be permeated with a democratic spirit. Otherwise, the path for totalitarian or autocratic Governments will be paved, as we have seen in various countries. So, unless the majority of the people are imbued with this particular idea, particular view of life, it is not possible for democracy to thrive in its real sense. To cultivate this temper is the duty of the thinkers of society and the propagators of ideals.

We find in most of the developing countries the hunger for the good things of life so great and the fall from the ideal so steep, that it has led to the formation of some type of totalitarian Governments. In India alone, among the newly freed countries, democracy is still struggling. It is necessary that we strengthen this spirit, because the alternative in the modern context is totalitarianism; and totalitarianism believes, as one great thinker said, in the atomization of man. What totalitarianism wants is the total control by the State of all the affairs of individuals, even their thinking. Free thinking and expression are obstructions in its path. Hence they insist on the atomization of man.

Sorokin, the great sociologist, in 'The Reconstruction of Humanity' makes a very significant remark that the modern scientific and technological development in Europe and America, has ushered in the big corporations. Huge societies or corporations or business houses control the lives of millions of their employees and their dependents. These big corporations, he says, are the harbingers of totalitarian Government. Now his argument is that if there are big corporations, then, the smaller ones gradually get merged in them. Thereby you get better efficiency no doubt, and for the sake of better efficiency, you go on merging the small units in the bigger units. As a result time may come when 10 or 15 corporations may control the economy of the entire country. Now, if there is a conflict of interests among these groups, there is civil war. Or these big corporations also will be compelled to merge themselves or be fully controlled by a totalitarian form of Government. So Sorokin says, it is very peculiar that America, the most advanced democratic country of the world, is at the same time, fostering the forces which will ultimately nullify its idea of democracy. Any way, all thinkers agree that the assurance of continuance of democracy is in the temper of the people. If the vast majority of people are temperamentally democratic in their outlook and behavior, democracy cannot be wiped out.

Political democracy is guided by people because everybody has got a vote. Government is a summation of individuals. When the majority of people want a particular type of Government, they can have it. So it is necessary, and it is accepted in democratic thinking, that a good amount of discussion should be there. Democracy has been defined by some thinkers as Government by discussion. People start with initial doubts, they discuss the problems and come to a conclusion. So this openness of mind is a characteristic of democracy.

Now, this type of mental climate, attitude or approach towards problems is more or less normal in Indian thinking. But it can be fostered more and more by popularizing the Vedantic teachings. For on five or six counts Vedanta is definitely superior to any of the political theories in its capacity to impart this democratic spirit: of sharing, of discussion, of free thinking, of taking into consideration the view of the other man. India has been guided by this idea, throughout its history. India gave great freedom in thinking, though not so much freedom in doing. As Swami Vivekananda says: India did not give freedom to society. As a result, Indian society did not develop much and could not have a variety of experiments in the social context. But it gave freedom to thought. As a result India excelled in wonderful efflorescence of thought-patterns evolved here. India gave freedom of discussion and that is why, to our astonishment we could see atheists even in old days preaching their philosophy right at the gates of temples. This shows how much freedom was allowed to thought, though there was no freedom for anybody to choose any way of life. There society came in and it controlled the pattern of life; it laid down the social habits and customs and manners and all had to conform to it. But in their thinking, they could have any type of thought they liked and they had perfect freedom to preach that idea as well. This freedom of discussion and patience to hear the other man's points of view is a prerequisite for all democratic development. The Indian thinkers never stifled independent thinking. Whenever a Vedantic teacher tried to expound his theory he began by quoting the views of other people and then tried to answer the objections and establish his own view. There was always an attitude of readiness to understand the other man's viewpoint and an attempt to accommodate his views as far as possible. That is why the Vedantic theory, as developed by Acharya Shankara, could draw upon some of the concepts of Saikhya, Yoga and other philosophies.

Liberalism and the spirit of synthesis was the effect of Vedanta. If Vedanta tried to harmonize the different religions, it was because of its Indian temper. Many people find it difficult to define Hinduism; it is a conglomeration of faiths like Vaishnavism, Shaivism, Shaktism, and the like which were really speaking, different religions in the same way as Islam and Christianity are different. But they were all harmonized because of the synthesizing power of Vedanta, a power which came from its democratic spirit of recognizing the truth, no matter where it lay.

Vedanta said that the Ultimate Reality, in the final analysis, is formless, but then, by some mysterious means It can take any form It likes because It is all-powerful. So It can take the form of Shiva, of Krishna, of Devi, in short whatever form a devotee wants to see. So there should be no question of quarrels among the votaries of the different religions. The particular form you are worshipping is the same as the other form being worshipped by the other man and both are the same Ultimate Principle. Every one can have his own 'Ishta', 'the chosen deity', but at the same time, each should know that all the different Ishtas are really the manifestations of the one God who can be either formless or with form. With that one theory, Vedanta harmonized the different religions and changed them into different sects within Hinduism. The same principle could apply to other religions also.

Vedantic ideas were gradually being absorbed by other religions. The evidence is seen in the coming up of the Sufis, an Islamic sect. It absorbed so much of Vedantic idea of oneness of beings that it was becoming one with Hinduism in its fundamental aspects. That is why in the Indian context you do not find any struggle in the mind of a Hindu to go to a Muslim fakir, if he is an advanced soul, or a Muslim does not find it uncomfortable to go to a Hindu saint for inspiration. Akbar's Dinilahi was a sort of piecing together of the best things in different religions and an attempt to create a new religion. In later days, the Brahmo Samaj and others also tried to find out the best things from different religions and produce a new synthesis, free from all defects. But a vital religion cannot be created in this way. It requires a saint of enormous magnitude and great realizations to create it. Vedanta worked out a synthesis by a better method than the eclectics. It pointed out that all the accepted Ishtas are really reducible to the One. And it gave Hinduism the sense to recognize the truth in an opponent's views and its capacity to harmonize various views.

It will be a matter of not a little astonishment if it is said that this same idea of toleration was at the root of the much decried system of 'Varnas', which in later days came to be called the caste system. It is this principle of harmonization that played not a small part in developing it. It might seem strange; all the same, it is true. For look into the history of mankind, the moral standard of early days of man's life was such that when a particular City State conquered another, though equally cultured and having an equally sensible type of religion, customs, manners etc., still after the conquest, all the male folk of the vanquished City State were either butchered or made slaves. Such was the moral standard then in Greece. We need not apply our moral standard of the twentieth century to the people of bygone days, almost 3,000 years ago. The same thing was practiced even later in other parts of the world, where the original tribes were practically exterminated. As against this, look at the great humaneness of the Aryans. They came here, it is said, from outside India and conquered its original inhabitants. Yet they did not exterminate the conquered people, did not even make them their slaves, but gave them only an inferior position and at the same time accepted them in their society.

Even in the twentieth century, if a country conquers another, naturally the conquering people will consider themselves superior and the conquered not worth any respect. This is the norm even now. If, therefore, thousands of years ago the Aryans treated the conquered race better, does it not speak for the nobility of the Aryans? Then originated the concept of the Brahmins, Kshatriyas, Vaishyas and Shudras—different groups doing different functions of the society. All of them are equally important. It is not that the Shudras really issued from the legs of the Creator, as conceived in the image of the Virat Purusha. The statement was just symbolic. Without legs man cannot move. So the Virat Purusha, the Indian society, could not function without legs, without the people who would be producing wealth. Therefore they should be given recognition: that was the concept. I would repeat, the stress, at that time, was on the positive aspect of the concept, on recognition.

The inferior position was rationalized by the conquered people's lack of power or initiative or incentive but that did not prevent their absorption in the larger body politic. This absorption was effected by a theory called re-interpretation. They said: You need not be completely absorbed in our society beyond recognition. Form a society of your own and take part in the bigger society. Retain your manners, customs, deities, food and everything else. At the same time, find out finer and higher meanings for them. If it is your habit to worship a tree, do it by all means. If it is your habit to worship the stone, do it by all means. But just think that you are worshipping not the tree nor the stone but the God who is behind the tree, the God behind the stone, i.e., re-interpret your object of worship.

In this way gradually the Aryanisation took place, giving a higher and higher interpretation to ordinary things of worship, ordinary manners and customs.

In this way also, gradually, higher and higher standards of morals were brought into the society and the absorption took place. That was the origin of caste: separate groups of people retaining all their characteristics and yet remaining part and parcel of a single society.

In a way it looks peculiar, but it will not if I give an analogy. In India we have people speaking, say, 13 or 14 major languages. Everybody is allowed to have his own. Still we form a body, the greater Indian society. We do not find any disharmony in that, no peculiarity in that. Similarly, in those days, these Aryans said to the others:

Have your own manners and customs, your own food habits, own deities, own method of worship, but still you are part and parcel of our society. If today, the existence of linguistic groups as parts of a bigger society is possible, the caste groups of the ancient days need not possibly be denounced, more so because the standards of the castes in the lower positions were being raised and they were being increasingly absorbed in the larger body politic.

Vedanta played a very important part in this absorption of people of different groups. It declares, that there is the One Spirit in everybody; that there is God in every human being, God whose manifestations can be various. There can be various forms and names. That is why creation means varieties of names and forms, although intrinsically there is oneness. In all these thousands of varieties you find out a common point also. This is the unity of existence, which means, everybody is basically divine.

The Vedantic idea of tolerance was extended to all tastes and expressions' of dress, of food and the like. Variety is the spice of life. Even now, we have got this temperament of consideration for the other man's view. For Vedanta has prepared our mind for it. You can move in any dress you like in the Indian streets. But, even a few years ago, you could not move in many foreign countries without being jeered at, if you went in a dress unfamiliar to them. Even now, that is by and large the case. That means they lack catholicity in regard to other people's tastes. That means they are not able to put into practice the spirit of freedom that democracy assures to every man even when this freedom does not disturb the general social order.

Variety is necessary in life. Unless there is variation in temperature there will be no storms, no rains, no grains, and therefore no life. So there must be variety; it is, in fact, in nature itself. But does that mean that there will be complete dissociation between one variety and another? No. Then also, there will be complete chaos. So, the search for unity is also necessary.

As we allow for varieties, we must try to find out unity also. And this unity was provided for by Vedanta through its theory of unity of consciousness, of the One Spirit indwelling all. With this idea, Vedanta fostered the basis for this great ideal of unity in variety. In democracy you require this ideal. Unity must be there, so that all the people of the different groups, in a country, can feel some common bond. Somewhere one must feel a common aspiration, common ideals and the like. But at the same time a variety in culture, in expression, in food habits and clothes etc. has to be allowed.

In the political context also varieties of manners and customs and varieties of group loyalties can be allowed provided there is national consciousness. But if you allow only variety without unity, without cohesion at the social, temperamental and ethical levels, there will be fragmentation of society and total atomization of man: every man will be directly related to the State and unity will be sought only at the political level, which is the goal of some of the politicians.

In the Indian society people are accused of being much attached to their families. They are not easily transferable from one place to another. This is not good from the point of view of economic development. But there is another side to it. It shows cohesion within the family, unity within the environment. In some countries, thousands of people have been overnight sent to outlying areas, completely cut off from their families. Thus the politicians have in a sense brought about absolute mobility: they can take one group of people at a moment's notice to another part of the country for quick economic development and quick material achievement. It is quite good so far as economic efficiency is concerned. But the goal of a Government is not merely economic efficiency and turning people into automatons but also finding out ways of development of the heart. People shorn of all sentiments and emotional bonds will be turned into automatons, or demons or reduced to atoms in the process of atomization. A thinker has nicely put it as the 'insectification of man'. Like insects men are conducted to any part of the world without consideration of any of their human sentiments.

It was against this insectification that Vedanta fostered liberalism in the Indian thinking itself. And this liberalism is the basis of all democratic concepts. What was the important idea which Vedanta, or the spiritual conception of the universe, gave? Vedanta said that there is a moral order of the universe, that the entire universe is guided by a divine scheme, which is called Rita, Satya or Dharma. Its liberalism consisted in its recognition of different values of life. So in Hinduism we have a four-fold ideal of life, four legitimate goals of man: Dharma, Artha, Kama, Moksha. It is said that the search for the pleasures of life — physical, aesthetic, artistic and intellectual — is a legitimate goal. Now to enjoy these pleasures, we require wealth. So search for wealth is also a legitimate goal. But both must be controlled by the concept of dharma, by a moral law so that in trying to acquire money for the sake of pleasures we do not flout the rights of other individuals. Man must, whenever he tries to get these pleasures and wealth, give an equal consideration to the other man. He must not adopt immoral means. An individual should not behave in a way that disturbs the social fabric. If the social fabric is disturbed he himself, as a part of the society, will be disturbed today or tomorrow. When the vast majority of people in a society do not observe moral laws, that society collapses.

The question is asked: Is religion necessary? The necessity of religion can be explained from various standpoints. One of them is its social necessity, which hardly anybody can doubt, because religions, down the ages, have fostered the development of higher virtues. Speaking the truth is one such virtue. It is very difficult to speak the truth nowadays, they say, and that we cannot manage without telling lies. They may or may not be right in the context of a particular situation, but it cannot be a social ideal. If all the members of a particular society subsist on lies, then that society cannot go on for long. As they say, even dacoits have a norm: they have got a standard of mutual regard. People say, truth is not possible in business. But even then there is a standard of truth. Otherwise things cannot go on. So also with other higher virtues. In a family if everyone is selfish, and each pulls in his or her own way, how long will that family keep together? Similar is the case with society. Of course, the impact is not felt immediately as in a family. If the vast majority of people in a society become selfish a limit will be reached, which, if crossed, will bring about a total collapse of that society, as it happened in the case of the Roman Empire.

It was a complete collapse of character of the Roman people that was the cause of the decline and fall of the Roman Empire, though it had the vigor to rule for a thousand years. So it is necessary that some values are recognized and constantly kept up before our eyes. And these are generally provided by religion.

The Vedic thinkers believed that there is a spiritual scheme of the universe and most of us also normally, if not definitely, believe that there must be some purpose. There are two major theories in the field. In the materialistic theory, there is no purpose in life: you are only a link in the larger chain and your function is to pass on the racial characteristics to later generations. Your duty is finished there and if you want to live at all, live in your progeny. The idealist conception is that there is a divine scheme of the universe and a spiritual purpose in life. It is not meaningless, not 'a way to an abyss'. Whatever may be the approach, this idea gives us much consolation, great strength and energy to fight the battle of life. Life is not all smoothness. So if you come to know that there is a goal, a purpose in life, you will hesitate to resort to questionable means to acquire the things of the world and thereby disturb the whole social fabric. If I know my whole life is finished within 25 years, naturally I would be anxious to get all I can in a short time and I would not discriminate between the means. The result would be disastrous for society.

When Aristotle was asked this question: What is the use of philosophy — philosophy in the sense of thinking, Aristotle said: It enables you to do things, without being commanded, which other people do by being commanded. Some people think of doing things without being commanded because they are convinced that it is intrinsically good to do good; naturally these people become good. Other people become good by the fear of law. Now, society gives some latitude; it allows people to tell some lies. But if this latitude is turned into license and if thieves become numerous, the police force will have to be made larger; if law-breakers are more, the military will have to be increased. Society directs through law and enforces its authority in a particular way, and the individuals follow this norm willingly or unwillingly. But unwilling action is no ethical action. When you are goaded and compelled by a situation to follow a particular path, there is no morality involved in it, although you may do it out of fear. So it is said in ethics that if you conscientiously think of the pros and cons, you have got a free will to do either a right or a wrong thing and if you do the right thing, then you are a good man. When, however, compelled by the situation, you do a good thing, you are neither good nor bad. So, willingly we should follow the higher ideal.

As already said, Vedanta provides us with a philosophy of life and a scheme of the universe. If you believe in this you naturally try to behave in such a way that in your progress in life, in getting good things of life, you do not become a source of tyranny. Of course, Vedanta does not say that all people can be simultaneously and equally happy with material possessions. It is an impossibility. Affluence somewhere means poverty and penury somewhere else. Swami Vivekananda was once asked: Is it possible to do good to the world? Swamiji said: 'In an absolute sense, no; in a relative sense, yes.'

He further said that this world is like a dog's curly tail, and people have been striving to straighten it out for hundreds of years; but when they let it go, it curls up again. As long as you hold it, it is kept straightened. Much improvement is there, social and other progress and much happiness too. As soon as you leave it, it goes down. Thus a particular part of the world will be prosperous, but another part will be less prosperous. But then much of this inequality can be removed by proper distribution. Vedanta can foster a mood for distribution of wealth. A favorable climate of opinion, a mental disposition to share wealth with others is a necessary condition for that. In Vedantic thinking, the idea of sharing is predominant. Vedanta does not believe in any privilege. Swami Vivekananda speaking about 'Vedanta and Privilege' says that Vedanta does not believe in any privilege — whether it is privilege of birth, or wealth or any other. Complete equality is the ideal, but variety is allowed because it is in the nature of things. The ideal is to strive for equality in the full knowledge that disparity is in the very nature of things—a knowledge which must not, however, deter efforts to mitigate as far as possible the sufferings of people. Vedanta tried to foster this idea in the people by the idea of Dana. If you read the *Gita*, which is an important Vedantic classic, you find three important ideas— *Yajna, Dana* and *Tapas*. Every now and then Sri Krishna speaks about these. Acharya Shankara defines *Dana* as 'sharing'. We are already convinced that there must be fair distribution of the good things of life, that we must have a socialistic type of society. At least the means of production must be socialized, so that the equal distribution also can be more efficiently organized.

An example of how the idea of sharing had taken hold of Indian people may be cited here. When the Zamindari Abolition Act was being passed in the State of West Bengal, a great foreign dignitary who was in Calcutta was astonished that there was no rioting, no bloodshed. Land reforms meant hundreds of people were being deprived of privileges which they were enjoying for a long time. Their main means of livelihood were being taken away by legislative acts. Yet there was no bloodshed. He asked the then Chief Minister of West Bengal about it. The reply was that it was the idea of the Indians to consider accumulation of wealth as a kind of cheating. If you procure too much wealth, it is as if you have deprived the other man. That idea is so much in the Indian consciousness that even the rich feel their wealth is not so legitimately theirs.

There is a verse in the *Bhagavata* which says you should have just enough property to maintain yourself. If you

have more than that, it is equivalent to stealing others'
property. As a result of constant repetition, this idea is
deeply imprinted in the minds of the Indian people. And
that is why, as Tagore said, Indian philosophy taught the
kings of India to relinquish their kingdoms at the approach
of old age.

Swamiji says, the Europeans take pride in feeling that
they are the descendants of the robber barons, whereas
Indians try to trace their ancestry to the Rishis. That shows
the temper of our people. Wherever there was sacrifice, we
have given respect. An Indian does not spurn enjoyment;
so he requires wealth. But at the same time he knows a man
who renounces his wealth is a greater man than himself.
That is why in Indian thinking, the Brahmin was given the
highest prestige. He did not have enough to eat; his was
a life of sacrifice for the benefit of the society; at the same
time he was the brain of the society. He gave the laws. If
he had wealth, a vested interest would have been created
in him, as a result he would have tried to frame laws in a
way that safeguarded his interests. It would then not have
been a good law. So the first condition for earning the right
to be the lawgiver was that you did not have any property.
You renounced all your rights and courted poverty. If you
opted for poverty, it is true that you would not get the good
things of life like other men, but the society said: We would
give you the compensation. This compensation was in the
form of prestige, honor.

Honor is a great incentive to work. Why men should
work if there is no personal property, it is often asked. But

then, prestige is an equally potent force. Up to a certain extent, you want property, security, wealth, but a time comes when wealth does not satisfy. Then man begins to give away wealth, because he wants honor. Otherwise, how can you account for the benevolence of some of the capitalists? Their whole life is spent in amassing wealth. All the joys of life they have practically denied themselves only to acquire money. Yet, at the fag end of their lives, or at the height of their money-power, they give in charity, found schools or colleges. Why? For name and fame. Name is a great motive force in guiding man.

Vedanta created awareness that there is a higher goal and that a stage must come in everybody's life when he must transcend the hungers for these pleasures, and be dedicated to higher and higher causes. This mood has been created by constant preaching, over thousands of years. Man knows by instinct that it is good to be of a sacrificing type, but it is also necessary that he must be able to feed himself first. I am sure, no type of totalitarian society that stresses material prosperity to the exclusion of human values can gain ground in India if only the basic needs of man are provided.

Vedanta has thus created in us what can be rightly termed a democratic temperament, of sharing, of discussion, of seeing the other man's viewpoint, of finding a unity in all these varieties of manifestations. And all this is important to make a political experiment with democracy a success. So, if we clearly know the demands democracy makes on the society for its success, and how Vedanta has been of service in creating that particular mood, we will find that Vedanta has already done a great service. It can do still better service if we popularize these ideas, preach them to the masses of India, and let the masses know these basic ideas of Indian philosophy, religion and life.

PART II

Chapter 4

NATIONAL EMOTIONAL INTEGRATION AND VEDANTA

After independence we often hear talks of unity of India. The cause of our anxiety is the sad experience of partition of the country and the resulting suffering of a large section of humanity. Other centrifugal forces are also active due to disparities in language, region, religion, economic status or political belief. So it is necessary to think about this problem and find out ways and means to check the divisive tendencies and foster unity. Whatever leads to unity must be availed of; and this effort must be made on all fronts. Recently the University Grants Commission organized a seminar on national integration. Rapid economic development, equality of opportunity, reduction of inequalities of income and wealth, extension lectures on unity, teaching of other Indian languages, translation of literatures, simplification of grammar, lessening of scripts, observing of national days and of course, discouragement of communalism, casteism and linguistics, were mentioned as some of its recommendations.

All these efforts, no doubt, will go a long way to inculcate the desired idea of unity among people. But it will be fortified if an intellectual basis is provided for unity itself. Professor H. Kabir Humayun wrote: "This risk of fragmentation is greater where there is no intellectual basis for the cohesion among the different groups. A sense of unity based on emotion alone cannot stand the test of time, as emotions are on the whole less stable than intellectual attitudes. This has been proved in Indian history both positively and negatively. The cohesion of Hindu society in spite of the innumerable sub-groups into which it has always been divided was possible because the philosophical basis of such cohesion had been worked out. One may or may not accept the doctrine, reinforced by belief in karma has given coherence and unity to Hindu community life. Perhaps the greatest triumph of the Aryan synthesis was the intellectual integration of different ways and outlooks."

The Indian society could not succeed in integrating the Islamic group, which is evident in later development of the latter's animosity. This attitude, however, is inevitable, for minority groups are always afraid of missing their share, and so cultivate an agitational approach. Hinduism affected a synthesis of different races and faiths through its theory of reinterpretation, giving a higher explanation to the existing thoughts and beliefs. The medieval Hinduism might have partly lost its vigorous dynamism. But the more important cause of failure was the extraterritorial affiliation of the Muslims in religious matters and constant replenishment of adventurers from other Muslim countries. The Indian process of synthesis was slow and imperceptible. But it was nevertheless active. This is clear when we look at Sufism and the efforts of Akbar, Nanak, Kabir, Dadu and others. Moreover, unless disparity is lessened in economic and social fields also, dissatisfaction can be created at any time by interested groups. In that sense, no society or nation is absolutely integrated, not to speak of countries where different racial and religious groups inhabit, so absolute uniformity is impossible, especially in a country like India. Moreover, it is not necessary also. Unity of outlook, the feeling of belonging to a nation is what is essential. That basic unity India had, more or less, down the ages. But with the spread of vigorous propaganda for various conflicting economic, political and religious issues, that unity has been disturbed, for there is no time "to affect the synthesis. So a counter-movement in favor of synthesis is necessary. All the different ideas can be synthesized by allowing free, distinctive expressions to different groups with their own manners and customs. It was precisely because of this that ancient India succeeded in the Aryanization of the entire country.

So while trying for the emotional integration of the nation, we must apply this process of least resistance which we have been practicing for centuries. Some people may be tempted to force the emotional integration of the nation by coercive methods. It may be possible through thorough secularization of life and regimentation of ideas. Secularization may help in removing different opposing religious notions and creating a mind free from all ideas and inhibitions, good or bad. To fill up the vacuum, another idea will be necessary but there also there are conflicting theories. One theory can be inculcated only by force and regimentation. The process will not be easy. The result will be worse than the malaise. Moreover, it will go against the democratic aspirations of people. Hundreds of years of religious training and free thinking cannot be set at naught overnight; if at all possible.

So the only way is the way of co-existence, harmony, synthesis. It is just to allow all the expressions of human thought and behavior to remain side by side. Only they will have to be supplied an intellectual basis and harmonized. Thereby, the irksome edges will be rounded off and smooth life will follow. Such a philosophy was applied by the ancient Indians, and was the Vedantic idea of the unity of existence. That one entity is at the root of all creation is a cardinal doctrine of Vedanta. When this is accepted, all causes of friction will vanish. We shall realize that we and our neighbors are basically the same.

Another corollary of Vedanta flowing from this basic idea is the unity in variety. It says that when the same entity is behind all, there may be variety in manifestation. In the religious field the theory of one god taking different divine forms and the method of higher interpretation of religious practices will facilitate unifying the minds of people.

When we say that the Vedantic idea of unity of existence will supply the intellectual basis for all unity and so it must be vigorously preached, we do not ignore the practical steps that are necessary to inculcate that unity, for a mere idea cannot go a long way. But the importance of Vedanta lies in its capacity to liberalize the mind and prepare it for accepting measures which may not be palatable to particular groups.

PART II

Chapter 5

VEDANTA FOR THE GLOBAL VILLAGE

Vedanta is a philosophy based on the Vedas of the Hindus. But its principles have been propounded by Shankara and others in a very rational way, though its practical aspect is considered as a religion. A religion has philosophy, conduct, rituals, mythology, and scriptures. Vedanta is based upon a body of principles and not on a person or a book, but the practical religion has all of these.

The word 'global' connotes more in a physical sense. As for example, Christians often claim that their religion is universal because it is present in every part of the world. So the term 'global' will be more apt than the term 'universal'. 'Global' is more restricted. 'Universal' is applicable especially in the thought world.

The global village gives the idea of the unified world, where all the countries have come together through easy communication, common economic forces, and world commerce. All the countries react when some depression comes in any other part of the world. So the idea of village is quite applicable in the physical sense. But it pre-supposes this idea of unity or oneness of all the countries of the world, as all the villagers are affected if the particular village is affected.

The very fact that the world has shrunk because of

the modern communication, common economy, easy travels, frequent change of locations of people, differences of languages among the neighbors, style of life, various cultures — all these make it imperative to have some proper qualities. The first quality needed is the cultivation of understanding among various peoples. Socially it must be accepted that there must be some type of unity. Since uniformity is not acceptable to all people, diversity will have to be allowed. For this a philosophy is necessary to strengthen the idea, Vedanta, the philosophy; based upon the Vedas but presented in a very non-sectarian, logical, and universal language, can fulfill that purpose. It recognizes the unity of existence based upon the reality of Brahman or oneness. Vedanta also recognizes in creation there will be diversity. In human nature, also, variety and diversity are natural. So unity in diversity being the principle of Vedanta will be of great help in bringing understanding among different peoples of the world.

Vedanta will have a great influence on the political systems also. The two main political theories fighting each other are stressing the importance of the individual or of the totality. The socialistic systems stress the idea of equality and sharing the goods of life more or less equitably. But in practice they are more dependent on force and violence rather than on persuasion. The democratic systems stress the idea of freedom, allow difference of wealth, but recognize the need for some sharing to be determined by discussion. As the one system depends on violence and force, the other system depends more on the selfishness of man. Vedanta recognizes the supreme importance of the individual. So it speaks of the Atman, the essential self of man, to be divine in nature. So each individual must have his freedom. But because the same divine is in every being, there is the same reality in all. Thus all are inter-related, and the solidarity of the universe is an axiom with it. The Gita says that with the consideration of the Atman, all must be viewed and treated equally. That will be a tremendous message for modern man.

Vedanta will have a great contribution to the resolution of the conflicts among religious groups. Religious strife is a major problem at the present time. The doctrinal religions are becoming more and more dogmatic and violent. Other milder groups also are being influenced by this quarrel, more for self-protection. Religions being the organic necessity of man, they are going to stay. They cannot be abolished as the communists tried. So again an understanding is necessary among them. Vedanta provides the connecting link by stressing that it is the same Absolute which is looked upon as different Gods of different religions. Stressing the idea of the same God lying in every being and every religion will lessen the strife. The dogmatic idea of religion must be discouraged. It is a social necessity. Vedanta provides the principle underlying this understanding. Thus the harmony of religions based upon the unity of Godhead will be a natural product. It will lessen the strife, recognizing the essential validity of all religions. As a result, Swami Vivekananda asserted and predicted that henceforward on the banner of every religion will be written, 'Help and not fight, assimilation and not destruction, harmony and peace and not dissension.'

The next world problem is the question of the women and the masses. Vedanta advocates the equality of all beings, as mentioned above. In practice also it must be brought. Absolute equality in manifestation, of course, is not possible. But equality of enjoyment and scope must be achieved to avoid social unrest and providing justice. The political systems will have to strive to make it a reality. The idea of privilege is taboo in Vedanta, and modern men, because of universal education, are uncomfortably conscious about various privileges existing in society. That disparity must be eliminated or at least lessened as far as possible.

Thus we see that Vedanta has a great role to play in this shrunken world which is popularly described as the global village.

PART II
Chapter 6

VEDANTA: PRINCIPLE, PREACHING AND PRACTICE

The subject we have chosen is very peculiar. And I would like to present the subject from a slightly different standpoint. Swami Vivekananda, when he organized the movement in America, he called it 'Vedanta Society'. The first such society was set up in New York in 1895. But when he came back to India and started the spiritual movement, he called it 'Ramakrishna Mission'. He chose to do so because almost all the Hindu sects in India are Vedantic in some way or other. So Swamiji wanted to specify what type of Vedanta will be preached here in the name of his 'Guru'. In America he did not do it; he only described it in very general terms.

Till 1930 Vedanta was more or less preached through lectures at various conferences. It was highly academic and intellectual way of presentation in those days. India was also occasionally talked about here and there, especially the spiritual service that she rendered to the world at large. We know that Swami Abhedananda's *India and Her People* was prescribed in those days to Vedanta enthusiasts in America. The book was then much talked about.

Now things have of course changed as two million Indians have gone to America and another two million to Canada and many of them are highly qualified. So, people in the West are getting more and more familiar with various aspects of India.

When I was in Delhi before going to the United States in the 60s, there was an 'Orientation Course' organized by the Delhi University with the help of the US Embassy. The Course intended to give some idea of India to students who were going to the West. It was Swami Nikhilananda who was the head of a centre in New York and a well-known speaker who took the initiative in this matter. He met Nehru when he came here, and said 'please give some knowledge of Indian religion and other things to young boys and girls who are destined to go to America. This is necessary because, whenever they are asked any question about India, they do not seem to know anything; they do not care for religion at all'. As a result, the Government introduced the two-week Course that covered a wide range of topics — Brahman to Indian hairstyle. I was invited there once.

In America and other Western countries we preach Vedanta mainly as a principle. But prior to the preaching of the Indian Swamis, Buddhism gained currency in European countries. Then, with the appearance of Romain Rolland, Max Mueller and other people books were translated and the Upanishads became gradually known, but mainly in academic circles. Probably Swami Vivekananda was the first Indian who talked about Vedanta in the West in a special way. Of course, *Light of Asia* and other books had already made some good impression on the Western mind and Orientalists were there, who somewhat prepared the way for Vedanta. Carlyle presented a copy of the *Gita* to Emerson. The copy is still preserved in the National Library near Boston. So, some exposures to Vedanta were already there but not too much. Swami Vivekananda made it much popular, not merely the theory but more in the practical experience of things.

In our preaching today in the West, we lay stress on ten principal ideas related to Vedanta. The first idea is the idea of *unity of existence,* i.e Brahman. Brahman and Atman are the two major ideas which are original contributions of the Indian thinkers to the spiritual think-tank of the world.

As regards Brahman, three issues are there. What is the ultimate nature of Man? What is the ultimate nature of Nature? What is the ultimate nature of God? Advaita Vedanta says, all these three are one. But there are two other systems of Vedanta. They *say* there is but one reality, and that is God, a personalized God. He has got a body which is the summation of all bodies. He has got a soul, but it is the summation of all souls. Madhva and others are more dualistic in form and sometimes they are included in the philosophical works and sometimes not because they are more theological. Most of the religious systems are not philosophical systems. They are, in fact, theological systems. Once I had an experience of meeting a big Jewish scholar. We were speaking from the same platform. After our talks, some questions were asked and we had to answer them. What amused me was that whenever an intellectual type of question came, the scholar said, 'Let the Swami answer this question. He is a philosopher, I am a theologian!'

So the Brahman idea, as Swami Vivekananda says, is 'Unique'. Because when you are rooted in this idea, you become moral, sympathetic, philanthropic and ethical as there is a feeling in you of the presence of the same Divine in all. So love becomes a natural concomitant of spiritual life.

The special contribution of Sri Ramakrishna and Swami Vivekananda in this age is that they have made Vedanta dynamic, more useful in our actual day-to-day life. Their teaching and preaching of the Brahman idea theoretically comes very near to scientific and philosophical thoughts. So, people like it.

Divinity of man

The second idea is the idea of divinity of man or the *Atman* idea. The question came: 'What is our nature?' And queries started from things which are known. Where is our *Atman*, if it is a reality? Though scientists and logicians and others dismissed its existence, we know it exists although we cannot demonstrate it physically. Thus we start enquiry from there. Who are you? Are you a body? That question comes first. Of course, the body is there and ordinarily we cannot think of our existence without our body. But if we analyze, we know this body would not last more than a hundred years. Temporary existence cannot be called a reality. At best it is a temporal reality. I put an American dress on an Indian girl. Today it is there, tomorrow it would not be there. So body is like that, it is not a permanent entity.

After the gross body comes the mind which is subtle and therefore difficult to define. Thinkers found it quite difficult to explain. But we know mind is there as it becomes sometimes too much with us. But the question is — are we the mind? No. Why? Because mind also changes all the time. Even the philosophical systems, especially the Indian systems, believe in the transmigration of souls with the mind continuing from birth to birth. But they also visualize a time when this mind will have a stop, when it will be negated.

Is there anything beyond our body and mind? The materialist says, there is nothing beyond. But they are cornered when they are reminded that nothing comes out of nothing. Here is a man hale and hearty. How can you say that he is nothing permanent? Cornered by this simple question, the materialists, except of course the agnostics, had to give up their position. What is agnosticism? 'I do not know if God exists or not' sort of attitude. The agnostics hold that nothing is known beyond material phenomena. So if somebody says 'I do not know', how can you argue with him? But with great confidence the Vedantist says, 'We know'. How? By our special methodology of *anubhuti*, or *bodhi*, or experience. They say, 'We do not accept your methodology.' The Vedantist replies, 'It does not matter. You have already agreed that you do not know the fundamental nature of things'. You know, it is one of the limitations of the sciences that you cannot know the fundamental nature of things because science deals with phenomena and the created things. 'Why it came' or 'How it came' is purely an idea of time and causation. You cannot ask that question regarding something which is not material, which is a transcendental reality.

Anyhow, Vedanta is the mouthpiece of all religions in some form or other. It asserts that man's original nature is not the body, not the mind. His essential nature is that he is the *Spirit*. That is the Vedantic idea. Man's nature is divine which is ever existing. What exists is divine. Man also is divine in this sense. That is the core, the spiritual part of human being. Spiritual means that which is fine, indestructible and imperishable. This second idea very much influenced the American mind in the days of Swami Vivekananda, because in Christian theology the idea of sin was predominant in those days. Now they have toned it down. Higher religion of course talks about love of God and does not make much fuss about sin and all that. Anyhow that old tendency of Christian theologians has somewhat lessened nowadays. But since it is a basic part of their system, it is difficult for them to give it up.

Anyhow, at that time the Americans heard Swami Vivekananda's words that divinity is man's true nature. His famous saying—'Children of immortality! It is a sin to call you a sinner'—thrilled them. For the first time they discovered that they were not 'sinners' but the children of immortality. A tremendous exuberance came out of that discovery.

Secondly, Swami Vivekananda described *freedom* as the goal of spirituality, the goal of religion. But, according to traditional theologians, the goal was *salvation*. The

Americans like the idea of freedom very much, as they do not believe in degradation of human beings. When the Europeans first migrated to America they found America was vast and empty. They found miles after miles one man could own. Thousand acres were nothing. Hundred miles, two hundred miles one man could own. So this is the vastness. And if you tell such people that 'you are nothing', it is psychologically impossible for them to accept that idea. But when they are told that 'you are everything', 'you are the master of the world' they will listen to you. So, when Swamiji uttered that bold Vedantic truth, they immediately gave him a hearing.

In America, when I go to different circles, except our Vedantic groups, normally they do not like to argue with us. They immediately go to theology based upon particular books. In one sense we also depend on the Vedas, but reasoning remains uppermost in our mind.

The idea of One God

The third idea Vedanta has is the idea of One God, the unity of Godhead. Different religions say different things. Hindus say like that, Muslims say like that. But how to reconcile all these? Ordinary people say, either you are right or I am right. And, of course, I am always right. That is the attitude. So the Vedantins say, 'No, all the people can be right at the same time. They give the analogy of a woman. She is mother to somebody, wife to somebody, sister, to somebody. Even she may be the Prime Minister of a big country like India. But what is the total woman? She is the summation of all these descriptions plus something more.

It was difficult previously to put across that idea. But in this nuclear age, that is possible. We can tell them that as energy inherent in an atom can come out if you know how to smash it, similarly, in a tiny personality of a man or a woman, so much of energy is inherent. The possibility of manifesting that energy is there. This idea gradually began to be appreciated with the progress of science and other things, other discoveries.

When a child says, 'My mommy comes', the entire woman comes and transcends that also. In the same way, when Vedanta says that 'God is One', they are saying that there are different aspects or different ways of looking at God. But when a person realizes God, his look is usually partial, but he realizes the same God. Sri Ramakrishna said, 'It is purifying to take bath in the Ganga. But is it necessary to go on taking bath for 1500 miles, the whole course along which the Ganga flows? Anyhow you enter the Ganga, you get the benefit.' Similarly, 'I touch God' means I touch everything. When I touch a human being, I need not touch him from head to foot. So knowing God does not mean knowing God exhaustively. That is why S. Radhakrishnan the former philosopher-President of India, said in one context that tolerance in Hinduism is a homage paid to the inexhaustibility of the Absolute.

Absolute is unlimited. But when It is viewed from different angles, It looks like this, looks like that and so on.

That is why Swami Vivekananda defined very scientifically that God is the Highest reading of the Absolute. Reading does not mean hundred per cent and it is not practicable either. The moment Infinite God is known to a finite mind or thought process, it is no more infinite and finite God is no God. Hinduism frankly says that. Vedanta says there is God's presence everywhere and take God as you like, according to your belief and capacity. But do not stay stuck there. Evolve the idea further and further, discourse its various aspects and go forward. So they said — unity of God.

If one God is there, understanding among religions is natural. Why is the quarrel among religions? God is the same. That is Sri Ramakrishna's contribution. The idea was there in the books, but Sri Ramakrishna recently pointed out through his direct personal experience that it is true. People like Mahatma Gandhi and those who are deeply spiritual, agree with Sri Ramakrishna. Gandhi wrote in one of his forewords that Sri Ramakrishna's life helps us to see God face-to-face. 'Here is a man in our contemporary time who realized God and conversed with God', he said.

So harmony of religions is a very natural thing. But conversion mars this spirit of harmony. All conversions are politically and socially motivated. Those who are coaxed to change their religion are fed with certain theory and belief. But believing something does not mean it is true. The Al-Qaida people believe that by killing people they go to heaven directly. Now the point is, how to control them? They are terrorists. If they are killed, they go to heaven. If

they live, they are successful. How to solve this puzzle?
Everybody is wondering;

Be that as it may, mere believing is not enough. Religion
must produce good people. That is the major idea. So these
are the four major ideas — the idea of oneness, the idea of
divinity of man, the idea of One God, and the harmony of
religions. What is the goal of life? Freedom. How to attain
it? There are four methods which are called the four yogas.
These yogas have scientific explanations. We think, we feel,
we will. These are the three functions of the mind three
faculties of the mind. If these three are in the withdrawal
condition, that is called the yogic or mystic states of the
mind. Based on these states, Swami Vivekananda gave us
the four yogas.

The idea of meditation

The next idea is the idea of meditation. Throughout the
world, there is now a craze for meditation because many
people have found it to be physiologically beneficial. That
is why millions of people are practicing some kind of
meditation. But as they are not sure why they are doing it,
half of them give up the practice after sometime because
nothing dramatic happens.

Then, in Hinduism, there is an idea, and Vedanta
supports it, that God is a woman, or a female. This idea
appeals to people very much. Not only women, but also
many men harbor such a notion. Once some study was
made and it revealed that 70 per cent Americans believe

that God can be a woman. Let me narrate a funny anecdote in this connection. The story runs like this: Three friends were silting in a coffee-house discussing which was the original *profession* of the world. Then some lady told me, 'Swami, do not say profession, because oldest profession means something else. Please say, oldest vocation.' Then, one man said, 'My profession is the oldest'. 'What are you?" 'I am a doctor, a surgeon', he replied. 'How can you say this?' questioned another Man. And the surgeon said, 'Haven't you read in the Bible how the world was created? How could it be possible without surgery?' 'Accepted!', said his friends. The second man was still older. His companions asked, 'Who are you?' 'I'm an engineer and my profession is the oldest.' 'How do you know that?' the companions questioned. And the engineer said, 'The Bible says that out of chaos came the cosmos. Out of the disordered universe came the ordered universe. How it would have been possible, sir, without planning and engineering?' 'Agreed', the friends said. And now the third man was smiling. He said, 'Mine is still older'. The engineer counter-questioned, 'How?' 'Just you have heard,' he said, 'that out of chaos came the cosmos. But who brought in the chaos, sir?'

An idea that appeals very much to the Westerners is the idea of *karma* and rebirth. When some people ask them why they turn to Hinduism, one of the major answers they give is: 'It is more logical in the sense of *karma* and reincarnation'- Indeed, *karma* theory is rooted in reason. Otherwise, how do you explain the discrepancies in life? I am a poor man. I may be also a rich man's son. I may be a boy or a girl Why? If everything is fine with me, I do not ask questions. But if something goes wrong, I say, 'Why me?' In all the religions, philosophies and sciences, everything put together, three answers have been given.

First, thinkers, logicians, scientists and others say, it is a very natural thing that all people cannot be happy at the same time. Or, they say it is our luck, it is a chance. There is no satisfactory answer why I am chosen, I could be in the good group even. Still others say that in society, government, world order, etc., there is no 'how', or 'why'.

The second answer given is that it is God who does everything. That God also is not very good because He has put me in the bad group! So instead of loving God, you will begin to hate God.

The third answer is that: Take it as your own fault, the result of your *karma.* But how is it possible to accept an adverse situation as the result of my *karma?* Suppose I am born blind. I have not done anything wrong. Where then is the role of my *karma.* The answer is, you must have a better sense of time. A girl gets up in the morning, she is spirited. The other girl looks exhausted. Why? God is neither unkind, nor partial. What did you do last night? Actually when the other girl had a good night's rest, you did not take it for some reason or other. So now you pay for it. That is the theory *of karma.* It is a concomitant idea. You cannot explain the present life without admitting the previous life. That is the basis of *karma* theory. So among these three, *karma* theory is not merely the best, it is 'the' theory.

You may now say, we want proof that *karma* theory is
the best theory. Again, this is one paradox of our life that
when we talk about God or *karma* or some such things we
want proof first. Otherwise we do not believe. But if we
ask: 'Does everybody believe that America is very great?'
The answer is 'no'. In fact, nobody believes everything
hundred per cent. Yet life goes on! Why then do you say
'I must have proof. Then I shall believe in God'? Do you
believe in your children? You are poor, still you spend all
your money on children, your wife, your husband. Why?
Half faith moves the world. Why then do you expect proof
only in the case of God?

So these are the points we have discussed briefly —
Brahman, Atman, One God, harmony of religions, freedom
as the goal of life, four methods of attaining freedom,
woman or female form of God, meditation, and, of course,
karma and rebirth.

How do we preach these principles

These are the major principles. Now, how do we preach
these in Western countries? That is a major and somewhat
complex question. To put it simply, we adjust our work
according to the requirements of the group we face. If
we go to academic circles, we put the principles in one
way, elsewhere we present them differently. We are more
combative in academic circles. But in the presence of the
devotees there is no use becoming combative. There our
approach is casual and we try to explain things keeping
in view their levels of understanding. We also talk about

things that appeal to them most. They are average devotees, I am not talking about very highly intellectual people.

I remember one lady who wanted me to give a talk in a university telling me, 'Swami, all the humanities professors are Vedantic in view. But that does not mean they will become members of your society because academicians are always agnostic'. The lady was right in her assessment. Because the moment you take a side, you are out. You are no more an important person. That is the idea. So academic people take Vedanta in one way and the common men and women take it in different ways. So in preaching we stress the basic idea of the divinity of man. It appeals to them very much. There will be arguments for and against. All the same, the idea pulls them because they feel glorified. Swami Vivekananda always projected their good side, not the bad side. You cannot encourage, not only a child, but not even a grown-up person by showing all his/her defects. You have to show their plus points which Swamiji did. Thus the dignity of man as an idea is very interesting and it creates a great impression on the minds of the Western people.

Then of course we preach the idea of harmony of religions. It is a major idea which all thinking people like to accept. Arnold Toynbee once predicted that by the 21st century, the entire world will have to accept the liberal ideas of emperor Ashoka, Gandhi and Ramakrishna. Sri Ramakrishna out of his direct personal experience preached the equal validity of religions. Truth is there in every religion, he said firmly. This second idea is also accepted now by the Western people. Even the Muslims and Christians in this country believe that God is the same. Only theologians come and try to confuse them. But then, by analysis, they come to believe in the same God. So that is another point that God can be in other religions also. Swami Vivekananda said that the theory of 'Ishta' (chosen ideal) can solve much of the religious quarrels of the world. According to your liking you worship and according to my liking I worship my chosen ideal or *Ishta*.

Then the concept of God as a woman. That is a wonderful idea. Not merely women, but men also like the concept. Seventy per cent of Americans believe that God can be a woman. That is an important idea. Patriarchal societies naturally believe that God is a male person. 'Have you got any woman *Avatara* they ask and we are cornered. We try to escape by telling them that 'Holy Mother Sarada Devi is same with Sri Ramakrishna. We do not distinguish one from the other.'

By the by, when people of our circle get initiated, after some time they want Mother. Mother attracts them very much. Why? Because Mother is all-loving, all-forgiving. That is an important point. She does not find faults. A mother loves and praises even her bad child. God is like that. So the Mother aspect, especially Holy Mother satisfies them very much. So we preach to them the life and compassion of the Holy Mother.

Then, as I said, we have to explain the *karma* theory whenever occasion arises. Many mothers come to us when their children turn wayward and become drug addicts or get involved in some unpleasant activities. 'What sin I committed, what mistake I committed that my boy has turned like this!' I try to assure them saying that it is not their fault. According to the *karma* theory everyone has come with its own bundle of *karma*. According to the law of *karma*, I say, it is not the parents who choose their children, it is children who choose their parents. A soul is to be born. So it looks around — 'Where shall I go?' Now if he did some meritorious work before, he should be born perhaps as a rich man's son. But if he did evil actions, he may be born in a rich family but as a sick man's son. That is the theological formulation of the *karma* theory. So this is the type of things we preach generally in America and other Western countries.

Spiritual life is of course rooted in deep thinking. It is an attitude. Work is an expression of thought. But real spirituality, I believe, is thinking. God is everywhere and I must serve God — that is the idea. God is present here and now. Swamiji said, 'Go and serve the poor'. We try to put into practice mainly this attitude, mainly this conviction in different life situations.

But we have the theistic practices also. 'Puja', for example, is a very popular practice. Our great Ashokananda Swami was an Advaitin. But he gave instructions to nuns and some monks that they must worship daily. 'Puja' is a means to develop devotion, develop love for God, develop the feeling of the presence of the Divine. When you do puja daily with that attitude, feeling comes. You feel God is real. Other paths also may give such feeling but not so directly. Meditation, for example, is more difficult. So 'puja' has been introduced now. That gives believers of other religions some idea of what you are doing. So puja has become very popular. Other religious groups, I believe, are more celebration oriented. We are basically not so celebration oriented. But, I am afraid, in America we are gradually succumbing to popular taste. People like celebration which means eating, singing and dancing. Of course, dancing we do not allow. But anyhow by and large these are the things people like. Many people in America think we are serious people and we do not mind. Rather we think it is a compliment. Incidentally, a famous American professor, who subsequently became a devotee of Sri Ramakrishna, approached a swami preaching in America and said, 'I want to realize God. I want to seriously practice spirituality.' Then the swami told him: 'Then you go to Vedanta Society. They talk about serious spiritual life. But they are very dry, no singing, no dancing.' Of course we also try to bring some variety nowadays. That is the idea of practice.

We do not insist in America that everybody should come for 'puja'. If you have not seen puja, we say 'come and sit'. That is an education itself. Then you can try to enter into it and increase your understanding of the philosophy behind puja rituals and all that. Western system or Semitic religions are group oriented, while Eastern religions such as Hinduism and Buddhism are essentially individualistic. I make contact with God quietly. But sometime we must do it together. You may meditate in a group. In a way it is better because you cannot get up so easily. You look around and find that others are sitting quietly. So you cannot jump up as it may not look nice. In a sense, group meditation is better. Of course, you must have willingness. Otherwise you will not go there at all. But even willingness often fails because you do not have the determination.

Group meditation gives a sort of stamina. *Nistha* or dedication comes out of it. Most men and women in the world are moral, not because they want to be moral, but because of social pressure. I am a drunkard. I love drinking. Then my child is born. I am afraid my child will be taking to drinking. So I give up or try to give up the habit. I once enjoyed telling lies, it was all right. But then I reasoned what will my wife think about her husband. So I stop telling lies. That is why it is said that social pressure and social expectations make you moral.

Benjamin Franklin in his autobiography said that nobody can be purely honest without a faith in God. Your real character will be revealed when you are not supervised at all by any authority how you behave. Unless there is faith, it will be difficult to remain honest morally, physically and so on. So these are some of the usual practices. We normally give meditation, *japam* (repetition of *mantra*) and some kind of private worship—minimum things. Even our centers do not do much. Only in our Hollywood centre we do elaborate worship. Our previous Swami introduced it. He believed in it. So we continue this almost like Belur Math. You have 100,000 people here, we may have 150 people there.

So these are the three ideas I have tried to present. Of course, I cannot exhaust them. First, Vedanta presents certain principles and we lay stress on some of them. Some of the principles are there in the background, either it is too intellectual or too difficult to put into practice. But, of course, you will come to discuss them. There is always a scope for discussion. And third, what they have to do. I know these. But why am I to do? The idea is that you do something with feeling. Swami Premananda, a direct disciple of Sri Ramakrishna, used to tell the relief workers of the Math and Mission: 'Government has given the food for distribution among the public. But what are *you* going to give? You must add love to it. With respect you must give, with love you must give. That is your contribution.'

I remember Tagore. In one place someone asked, 'What is art?' He said, 'The table has four legs. To have four legs is a necessity. But the moment you add a creeper on the wood, it is not necessary, but this is art.' Similarly, spirituality, Swami Vivekananda said, giving medicine is social service, helping humanity. But if you bring the idea of God in that person, it becomes spirituality, a spiritual practice. The only thing you add is a little thought, a little feeling. That is all.

Many in the West ask, 'Swami, what is a Guru?' Guru idea is also very prominent there and many groups present the Guru as their ideal. In our system, *'Ishta'* is the ideal, but Guru is also respected. Guru, *Ishta* and *mantra*. We require meditation and meditation requires an object of meditation. Who gives it? A Guru gives it. He gives a

Name, a *mantra* and also a discipline to be followed by the disciple. So these are the three major points I tried to bring to your notice. Every topic can be developed. But all the truth you do not give at the beginning. Holy Mother said, unless you are absolutely free from the clutches of desires, nothing will happen. Sri Ramakrishna said, spirituality without absolute purity is impossible. But that is possible step by step, as we normally do it. That is how we also normally try. But we have got our literature, we cannot escape. Scriptures will decide what we are going to tell. Sometimes it seems too much for them. Then we try to pacify them. We take everything very literally and that creates a problem. For instance, a lawyer, a good devotee, giving free service for many years, once came to me and said, 'Swami, I am in trouble because Ramakrishna's opinion is that doctors and lawyers will not be saved. I find that the only way out is to give up my profession!' Here Holy Mother comes to our help. She says, 'You have money? Share it'. Then some defects of the money will go away, though not hundred per cent. That is a compromise.

We had a Swami in England, Swami Avyaktananda, a disciple of the Holy Mother. An idealistic type. He used to say, 'No one can be honest in the dishonest society'. Society will compel you to come down and all that. Even if you do not want, situation will make you sometimes do something which you should not do. Of course, you may apply your will power. But it is difficult.

Until recently, most of the admirers of the Vedanta societies were whites. But now we have got so many Indians. Many of them are Belur Math devotees, initiated devotees. I started a centre in Washington a few years ago. There were three groups of Indians. So we avoided all the three groups. I put an American Swami there as in-charge. I am the in-charge, but in my absence he is in-charge. But I purposely said, 'I am not going into your groupings. If you believe, you come; if you do not believe, do not come.' Somebody said, 'Unless you put us in a committee, why should we help you?' 'Do not help', I said, and added, 'the city has got millions of people. I am satisfied if I get 200 people. Why should I care whether you come or not?'

Anyway, people gathered there and I found as many as 44 people came in two or three years. 'We are Belur Math devotees', they said. They saw a centre was started and they gathered around it. So, now it is easier to start centers. In those days it took about ten years.

PART II
Chapter 7

THE GLORY OF THE SELF

The Nature of the Self

Two of the most important doctrines of the Vedanta are centered around the two words "Brahman" and "Atman." Or, you can say, even one word, "Oneness." The Vedantic teachers tried to find out the reality behind the universe and the individual. Through their thinking and contemplation they came to the realization of the basic oneness of all creation, the universal spirit that lies behind everything. This is Brahman, and Brahman in connection with the individual is called the Atman. Atman is the word for Self, and Brahman is for universal basic existence. "Atman" literally translated is "self," but "self has various connotations in English. By this Self or Atman, the Vedantic teachers mean the spiritual core within every man. Not the ordinary soul, but the undying I, immortal, ever-existing substance in a person. That is the definition of Atman.

The Upanishads speak about the identity of the Atman and Brahman. This Self is Brahman itself. It is of the same nature. As Sri Ramakrishna points out, there may be various pillow cases, but inside all the pillow cases we find the same cotton. The same cotton is there, but the external forms are varying. There may be men, women, animals, and other creatures, but behind these forms is the same shining Atman. That is the conclusion of the Vedantic teachers.

Now how do they establish this conclusion? Let us examine a few of the points. The real message of Atman is very simple. Man knows in his heart of hearts that he does exist: "I exist." A thousand arguments may be given to explain him away, but he is not going to accept them. A scientist may come, a philosopher may come and explain away the person. They may explain away even his body; but his feeling that he does exist persists. So the Vedantic teachers started their inquiry from here, because all philosophic systems are built upon, ultimately speaking, direct experience. Inferences and so forth are always built upon some form of experience. Now here is a man who is convinced about his own existence, his direct experience that he exists. So he starts his inquiry from here by trying to find out the permanent nature of that which exists.

By existence here we mean that which is existing all the time. If a thing exists now and doesn't exist later, we call its existence temporary, as opposed to a continuing or permanent existence. Our body is constantly changing. So it cannot be a permanent substance. Thus intrinsically speaking I am not the body. Our mind is all the time changing, so, intrinsically speaking I am not the mind, though I identify myself with it. The Vedantic teachers said that the method of knowing the permanent substance within yourself, that is, knowing your Self, is to separate the extraneous thing from the basic thing. So the intrinsic, essential nature of man can be known by sifting, by removing the extraneous substances that have been added. When that has been done by analysis and relegation of what is not permanent, we are left with that which is abiding. Sri Ramakrishna gives the analogy of peeling onion about the nature of Brahman. As you go on peeling a stage will be reached when all names and forms vanish and the ultimate is felt.

Our mind will then assume a condition in which we feel our identity with Brahman. We are always one with it, of course. We say that this is my body. The very fact that we are trying to objectify it is one of the proofs that the body is not the permanent substance. We are not that, because we are able to objectify it. So also we can objectify the mind. We can imagine the Atman to be like the Spirit. But that is only the concept of Atman which is being objectified, not the Atman itself. When we go to the ultimate stage, there is no subject-object dichotomy; we become one with the Atman, the Self. That is the Vedantic method of analysis.

Experiencing The Unity Within

Why is this basic unity hidden from us? Because the Atman, the Vedantic teachers said, is covered with five sheaths; the concealing sheaths. First is the body, then the mind. These two are very apparent to us. I can easily recognize: "I don't know of myself. I know I am happy, I am unhappy; I am this, I am that; always concerned with, identified with these things. I experience certain states of myself, but I never experience myself alone." Beyond these they found out three more coverings, finer and finer sheaths, they called them—first body, then mind, then vital sheath which prompts us to action of various types, then the intelligence sheath, deeper understanding, finer thought, then the farthest, the bliss sheath, as it is called. It is almost like realizing the Atman but it is manifested in the lower forms also. Whenever blissful experience is enjoyed, the bliss sheath is operating. Thus Atman is covered, and has to be known.

The method? The Vedantic teachers said: "If you want to know the immortal, cover your eyes." "Cover your eyes" means control the senses and look within because the Atman is within the inner core of yourself. The senses take you outside to the externally perceivable phenomena, whereas we are trying to know the perceiver, ourselves. So objectifying of the outer things will not do. The mind, the eye, have to be sent inward. That is one of the reasons why you close your eyes when you meditate—so that the external phenomena cause you only minimal disturbance.

Turn the searchlight within. As Ramakrishna in The Gospel very simply says: The sergeant, the night watch, would be roaming about with a lantern. With that lantern he could see everybody's face in turns, but if you wanted to see him, you had to request him, "Sir, please turn the light on yourself." So the method of knowing oneself is to turn the searchlight toward one's self. That is, go within, dive within. That is the idea. The external organs, the sense organs, always go outside, and they generally enjoy or experience the various things from outside. But if the subject to be known is oneself, they have to be turned within.

Now, the contention of some Vedantins is that various disciplines that religions speak of are not necessary. The bliss of the Self, or the Self itself, is all the time existing. You don't recognize the Self because of these various plays of the sense organs. Stop the sense organs. Become calm. When the mind is absolutely calm, automatically you will know the Atman. But to feel the bliss of the Atman, the mind need not be absolutely calm. Even if it is partially calm, you will feel it. Because the real nature of man, the real nature of the Atman is that bliss, so when the obstacles are removed, that blissful nature of the Atman comes out.

Often people wonder, and this question has been raised many times, why when you sit for meditation, (even yogic meditation which does not mix up any emotion), a type of bliss automatically comes when the mind becomes quiet. Devotees think of God, a loved object. If you meditate on a beloved object, a type of joy comes. That is understandable. But yogis don't meditate on a loved object or any thing — just quiet the mind. But still even they, when mind is a little calm and peaceful, enjoy a type of blissfulness. Because the real nature of man, the real nature of the Atman, is that bliss. So when the obstacles are removed, that blissful nature of the Atman comes out.

Various physiological and other arguments are given to explain this blissful experience. They are all true — partially everything is — nothing is completely wrong, but the metaphysical reason why this bliss wells forth is because of the blissful nature of the Atman, the Self. Man's real nature is joyfulness; not of the hilarious type, that is an extraneous thing. All hilarious things will have repercussions later. All enjoyments based upon the external will have an end and will be missed later, and often will have their reactions. But the bliss of the Self, of the Atman, has no reaction. It comes from within. It is your natural joy which is being manifested when you remove all the obstacles. That is how they describe it: "Shanta upasita" 'Be calm and meditate.'

The basic teaching is training to become calm, tranquil in mind. That is all. Atman is the same Absolute from which this universe issues forth and into which it goes back. How to know that basic substance, the Absolute God? They say: "meditate," but first become tranquil. Unless you are tranquil in mind, you can't really meditate. Of course, the word "meditation" nowadays is used very loosely from various angles, and all meditations have some sort of usefulness and validity. But strictly Vedantic meditation is, in the preliminary stage, to become tranquil so that you remove the obstacles to knowing the truth.

If the mind is absolutely calm you need not do anything, but in the early stage of effort, to a great extent you try to quiet the mind and then also focus the mind on the Atman. Atman, of course, in the early stages will be the concept of the Atman as the universal substance, the universal spirit, spirit covering everything. Then a stage will come when the mind will be absolutely calm, and Atman will be known. You will be one with That. Mind will be transcended. That is the idea.

The mind is by definition always in ripples. What is the mind? It is difficult to define, but we define it on the basis of its observable effects, as we would define any conceptual thing, such as electricity, etc. This type of grand definition we try to give. So mind is that which thinks, cogitates. When you stop the cogitation mind ceases to function. Then in one sense it is killed, Manonasa, it has ceased to function. It remains in the seed form, but practically speaking, it is killed. Then a stage comes when Atman is fully known, then you are one with It. So the main job is to make the mind calm. For that, if yoga helps, very good. Meditation helps. Fine.

Identification with the Impermanent

The question is raised, "Why has this confusion and restlessness come in our mind?" Very easily we can understand we are not the mind. But it is difficult to know we are the Spirit. Theoretically we can conceive the Atman, but when a prick comes to the body, immediately we shriek. Any stimulus that comes from outside throws us off balance. So one method of making the mind calm is not to be disturbed by the pairs of opposites, as they are called. If feeling of miserableness comes, say, "I won't succumb; I shall remain calm." If happiness comes, hilarious happiness, still I will remain calm. A blissful type of happiness is another thing. A yogi's type of joy is not so very much up or down because the theory is that if it goes up it will come down. But he has got a calm type of enjoyment. Say you are in good health; your job situation is fine; family situation is fine; wife, children, all are fine.

Then a type of blissfulness you feel. Nothing special you are getting, nothing you are missing; a calm type of joy. Yogic happiness can be compared to that type of joy. It is a calm, serene type of joy.

Now why do we confuse the body with the Self? If something happens to the body we feel uncomfortable, because we identify ourselves with the body. Something has happened to the mind. We identify ourselves with the mind and feel miserable. The sense of identification is the cause. A child falls sick and is writhing in pain. The mother also almost writhes in pain because of the sense of identification. The example is often given of the dress that is on the body. If the dress catches fire, you catch fire. But if the dress is removed and put on the hanger and then it catches fire, you don't catch fire. Of course through identification you may feel pain by the destruction of the dress, if it is costly, or somehow important to you.

The Vedantists have got a humorous story: A man went to the market, higgle-haggled, and bought a cow. He paid the money, bought the cow, and was going back home. In a few minutes there was an accident and the cow died. Who will feel sorry for it, the man who reared it up for three years and sold it, or the man who bought it fifteen minutes ago, by paying the money? He knows, "It is my cow," and so he feels more sorry than the other man. This is the effect of the sense of possession which comes out of the sense of identification.

In all religions, the sense of possession has been

decried. Why? Vedantic explanation is that every sense of possession pre-supposes the sense of identification with the non-eternal, with the non-self. So, in the popular language, it is said if you have money, give the money. Share with other people. That is lessening this idea of identification. Sense of possession has to be given up so that the sense of identification is lessened. That is the reason. The moment it is not there, you may be surrounded by any amount of wealth and other things; that will not affect you.

Again an example is given by analyzing the three states of existence. We are awake; we know that we know things. When we go to sleep, we dream. In the dreaming state also we know various things of the dream world. When we are in deep sleep (sushupti) the mind is almost set at rest, except for the seed form. When we wake up from sleep we say, "Oh, I slept so well I did not know anything." Even there the principle of awareness was present; that "I did not know anything." So the Vedantins said, by analyzing these three states of existence of man; the waking state which is common with everybody, the dreaming state, in which also we know that the mind or some sort of awareness is there, and the deep sleep state in which we do not know anything; that in all three states we have to assume there is a principle of awareness operating behind. The Atman is this principle of awareness which gives validity to all these experiences. There must be a continuing substance which is present in all these states, and that substance is the inner self of man, the Atman. It cognizes all these different conditions, including, "I don't know."

There is a story of a man who was going for his bath. In India one's bath often is taken in the ponds outside. So the man needed a towel with him. Then suddenly some work came, and he was busy for a time with the work. Then again he remembered the towel. He went to his room. The towel was not there. So he and his wife began to search the whole house. "Where is the towel gone? Where is the towel gone?" Suddenly the wife noticed that it was on his shoulder. "Here is the towel. It was all the time there only you did not know it. That is all. After the realization comes, man knows that he has not got anything new. It is eternally with him.

PART II
Chapter 8

VEDANTIC PRACTICE IN EVERYDAY LIFE

If a man knows he is the Self, the Atman, what are the benefits? There <u>are</u> benefits, though the philosophers are not anxious about them. They want to know the truth, the real situation, that is all. "What is my real nature? That is their problem. They are not concerned whether by knowing your real nature you will become happy or unhappy. But the vast majority of humankind wants to get away from the troubles of life; in some form or other neutralize the trouble and, if possible, get a little joy also. Out of them, one or two probably exclusively want to know their real nature. Others also probably want to know, but this desire is mixed with various other things.

Now this very simple but abstruse philosophy of the Atman, how can it help us? We have the concept and we try to make the mind calm and meditate on it. Before meditation we hear about it through the descriptions given in the books, but all descriptions will be approximations, inexact. So we try to understand it, reflect upon it, and then meditate.

The benefit will be you will *know,* or at least finally believe, that you are not the body, nor the mind, you are the spirit, the Atman, limitless, ever free. As sufferings come, you can say, "I am not the body, so the suffering of the body is not mine." The more you can believe, or, rather, the more you are convinced of this, the more you have experienced that condition, the freer you will from the hold of the body. Give up the body consciousness. Whatever makes you more and more body conscious is a bar. So lessen the body consciousness. Through this hold, all the other spiritual disciplines will creep in. Other considerations - how many children I should have, whether I should marry or not, whether I should eat two items or three items, two or three times a day or not, whether I should fast or not, whether I should share with others or not, all these questions are detail work but may be accommodated within this idea. The purpose of all these is to lessen the body consciousness, that is all. Because we are too much identified with the body, whatever makes us excessively concerned about the body has to be lessened. Even if a man does not care about realizing the truth, his body is a problem with him. The more is he body conscious, the more every pinprick becomes many fold. So for pure convenience he must lessen body consciousness.

Buddha, was the son of a king and was going to inherit a kingdom. He had a well-built body, was an athlete, a great warrior. He had a beautiful wife, a little son, many friends — everything a normal man covets. The first time he came across people suffering, old-aged, dying, he was very much shocked. So what will be our level of shock is difficult to say. The finer the mind, the subtler will be the experience. But Nature has its own method. Vedantins say nature is giving you experiences through which stage by stage you are going toward realization. Gradually you become aware of something, or search begins for something which is beyond the visible world.

If in the mind suffering comes, I negate it; "I am not the mind." Bodily pain comes; I negate; I disidentify myself. Mental pain comes; I disidentify myself. So in these two levels disidentify with the body and the mind. The Vedantic theory or metaphysical truth can help a man even if it is believed partially. The main discipline will be that whenever the unpleasurable experience comes I disidentify myself. I am not the body, nor the mind, so this pain is not mine. "This Atman should be repeatedly heard, reflected upon, and meditated upon", says the Brihadaranyaka Upanishad.

We, of course, mix up a little devotion, yoga, and a little karma. The idea is that we have hypnotized ourselves into thinking that we are limited creatures, identified with the body and the mind, but really we are not and we must be freed from that notion.

This question was asked of Swami Vivekananda, "Daily I go on thinking, 'I am the Spirit; I am the Spirit. I am the Atman; I am the Atman.' And then I become the Atman. Is it not hypnotization?" Swami replied, "No, it is de-hypnotization. Your real nature is the Spirit, but you have hypnotized yourself into thinking you are the puny creature, limited by the body and the mind. You are not." In daily life you do it. You are a teacher, an engineer, a doctor. Ten years ago you were not any of them as you have identified yourself now. In normal life identification is very useful, but identification brings in pain also.

So there must be allotted at least a few minutes every

day, whatever your approach is, to the Divine, for knowing the truth or avoiding the pain? Remember this condition whenever any unpleasant painful experience comes through the body or the mind. If all other normal methods are not useful, but basically that idea is kept, then a great source of succour is there.

The Vedantic teachers said, to know the Self is the purpose of our life. The method of knowing the Self is to remove the ignorance. That is all. And the path is paved by becoming tranquil and reflecting repeatedly, "I am not the body, not the mind, but the Spirit."

PART II

Chapter 9

THE MESSAGE OF VEDANTA

The philosophy of Hinduism is Vedanta, but Vedanta is preached in such a way that it forms the essential part of every religion. Swami Vivekananda in 1890's stressed upon this aspect, and Orientalists earlier popularized the teachings of the Upanishads and Vedanta. The term Vedanta is Veda plus 'anta,' meaning end of the Vedas. Vedas are the holy books of the Hindus. Why is it the end? Because it comes at the last part of the Vedic books. There are four sections called the Samhitas, Brahmanas, Aranyakas and Upanishads. Upanishads are the basic books of the Vedanta; in fact, the Upanishads themselves are called Vedanta. In the Upanishads we get varieties of references of philosophical thinking and ideas, all in germ forms. Later philosophers came and gave a cogent philosophy. The earliest is Gaudapada. His grand-disciple is Acharya Shankara. Shankara is the main philosopher who organized the monistic system of Vedanta philosophy. He was the greatest philosopher India has ever produced. All the later philosophers of India became philosophers either by supporting him or by contradicting him, for all these thousand years. The normally accepted time of Shankara is 788-820 A.D. Some others say a few centuries earlier.

Until now over 180 Upanishads have been discovered. Some of them, of course, are very new. There is an Upanishad called Allah Upanishad. Darashiko got it written, and was responsible for propagation of the Upanishads. He got them translated into Persian, from Persia they went to Germany, and then was known to the western world. Then there is Chaitanya Upanishad, Christa Upanishad. In India, if a system was to be accepted in ancient days as an orthodox system, it must have had support from Upanishads, the Gita and the Brahma Sutras. If these three books support your theory it will be accepted as an orthodox theory.

In the word Upanishad, 'Shad' means to burn out or lessen. So Upanishad is the knowledge which lessens the bondage of the world or takes quickly to knowledge. Some of the Orientalists have translated it as 'sitting near' the teacher, or a secret or sacred doctrine which is taught by the teacher to the student, to be communicated orally. The source is the Veda or Shruti. Why Shruti? In those days there was no writing, so the teacher would convey this knowledge orally, students were to remember it and as it was handed down from person to person through hearing it was called Shruti. Then there are some other books. All other books, Smriti, etc., are secondary in authenticity. The main system of the Vedanta philosophy is Advaita. But then there are various other systems which accepted the theistic aspects, accepted a God deriving from the same Upanishads. So they are also called Vedantic systems, but theistic. There are various teachers teaching the different systems of philosophy. Shankara first, teaching non-dualistic philosophy. Ramanuja is qualified non-dualistic — Vishistadvaita, and Madhva is famous for a dualistic system. Then there are some teachers — Vaishnavite as

well as shaivite teachers — who gave theistic interpretation
of their philosophy, making either Vishnu, Krishna, Shiva,
or Devi as the most important, or the highest deity. Then
we have Vallabha in western India, Chaitanya in the East,
Nimbarka in Vrindavan. Srikantha the Shaivite philosopher
of the Shaiva Siddhanta philosophy. How these different
systems arise? These are all not merely academic systems;
thousands of people live their life by these philosophies.
The knowledge of these systems becomes imperative to
understand the background of the people, the attitudes
with which they accept things.

The questions in philosophical systems are mainly three:
what is the ultimate nature of man, what is the ultimate
nature of the world, and what is the nature of God, the
ultimate reality. There are three major views in Vedanta.
The dualistic says that all these three are different: man,
nature and God are all different, but man and nature are
dependent upon God. The qualified non-dualistic system
of Ramanuja, which is followed by Ramananda and others
in northern India consider the ultimate reality as One,
God, Soul is the summation of all souls. His body is the
summation of all material bodies. There is an in between
position between dualistic and non-dualistic system. The
Advaita, non-dualistic or monistic system believes that all
three are One in their essential nature. That is the position
taken by Shankara, and that is normally known as the
Vedanta philosophy.

There are two methods to arrive at truth. Through
analysis you go to the truth, or you take the truth and

deduce things from that truth. Vedanta takes from the experience of great saints and sages that the ultimate truth is One, and then they become relentless. The alternative position is less capable of explaining the situation. So this is the position that all the things that we see around us are ultimately reducible to one substance—call it background substance—they called it Brahman.

What is the nature of man? He is not the body, not the mind, he is ultimately the Spirit. That which is persistent in man is the spirit and that spirit naturally is the same as the ultimate Spirit or the totality. So Atman is identified with Brahman. There is only one substance. The world reduced to its elemental condition, man reduced to his elemental condition, and the entire situation reduced to elemental condition, meet in Brahman or unity of existence. So the major plank of Vedanta is this oneness—that everything is ultimately One, and from this Oneness flow various other individual and social aspects, impresses so much that the famous pragmatic psychologist William James says, on hearing a lecture by Swami Vivekananda, "An absolute One and I that one - surely we have here a religion which emotionally considered, has a high pragmatic value. It imparts a perfect sumptuosity of security."

Shankara's position is that the Ultimate Reality is the Absolute, but when we look at this universe from our angle, we think of a cosmic mind which rules the world. The world is an ordered universe; there must be some sort of consciousness directing these events. Anyhow, the Ultimate Truth is the impersonal Absolute, which

really speaking doesn't take a part. The basic argument of
Vedanta is given through an oft-quoted example, the rope
and the snake. In darkness, in twilight you are going along
the road: suddenly you see a snake. You jump, "Oh! A
snake!" Then a man brings a light, and you say, "Oh, it's a
rope only." — but the palpitation continues for sometime. So
that is the example used by Shankara to explain his system
called mayavada, vivartavada or Brahmavada. Vivarta
means taking one for the other. Actually it is a rope but
you have taken it as a snake. It is not that Shankara says the
world doesn't exist — the world exists, but its real nature is
Brahman. Brahman here appears differently. How? By an
inscrutable power called maya. And what is maya? Swami
Vivekananda was fond of telling maya is a statement of fact;
we are put in this world to seek certain things, but when
we try to logically establish those things we can't establish
them, so it is a logical necessity to find out the truth behind
them. Logically you can't really establish the real condition,
so they gave this example: rope is mistaken as a snake, if
there is nothing there, you don't confuse, so there must be
something.

Behind this universe, behind this man, there is something
permanent which is confused as something else. That is
the view of vivartavada, taking one thing for the other.
How it happens? Through maya, a special power which is
a statement of fact which cannot be really explained, but
what is its function? Its function is to cover the real nature
of things and superimpose another upon it. This analogy
is very useful for explanation. It covers the nature of the
rope and superimposes the nature of the snake. So that is

how Shankara explains that the nature of the world we see around us is based upon real substance, but that Brahman is mistaken and taken as something else. So if you search for real nature of things, you will have to go to that. This is a major argument he gives.

He says there are three types of reality. One is completely unfounded, like the son of a barren woman or a garden in the sky, without any support—not a hotel garden on the fifth story, it is just an imagination. Then comes our relative universe. It is real, I touch it, I experience it, but when I try to explain it, it goes out of our grip. Our day-to-day life is based upon these relative experiences, this pragmatic world. The real nature is called the third category, the ultimate nature, the thing as it is, that is the other category which is not normally seen in the world. Whatever experience we have in the world is relative, based on the relative experience. The first one is practically a non-entity, but the second one is the different types of truth, and in life we make this type of distinction. We imagine some value for certain things, say, a piece of paper; it comes out of the mint, which the government recognizes, and it becomes a dollar bill or a note. A ten dollar bill is really paper, nothing else. After the war hundreds of these paper bills had to be given for a cup of tea. This is the explanation given by Shankara how one thing is taken as another.

The forms will change. Nama and rupa, name and form, give distinction to things. How to distinguish one man from the other? Because he has got a special form and special name. Eliminate name and form, you get an abstract idea of a human being. Similarly when you remove the name and form, the basic nature of the things comes out and that is the thing which is eternal, persistent. The Chandogya Upanishad gives this example. Women use varieties of gold ornaments, in the nose, in the ears, on the neck and give different names to them and different forms to them. Today's necklace will be tomorrow's bangles. So really necklace and bangles are all changeable, the real substance which is persistent is gold; or clay for various earthen articles. As articles, finished goods they look different, they have different names but the basic substance is the gold or clay. And knowledge means, knowing the eternal, the true nature of things. There are two types of knowledge, para and apara, supreme and relative. Relative knowledge is without, that we acquire through books, experiments, etc., based upon the relative aspect of things. It is a necklace or a bangle, that is called normal knowledge, relative knowledge. Basic knowledge, Supreme Knowledge, will be of the real nature of things, of the gold or the earth. And really speaking, that is the knowledge which matters. Other things also matter but that which is persistent, and will not change, is the abiding knowledge. That is the supreme knowledge or superior knowledge. All other knowledge is secondary. From the very beginning the Upanishads distinguished these two types of knowledge and gave the secondary position to this knowledge. As a result there is no conflict between religion and sciences in India, because it was already accepted that they are different. The superior knowledge need not impose its standard upon the relative knowledge. Brahmavit, a knower of Brahman, becomes all-knowing. How? If all things are really reducible to one substance, and if I know the nature of that elemental condition of the substance, then I know the basic nature of all the different substances. What does it matter whether I know the distinctive aspects of this bangle or necklace? Of course, ordinary life could not go on unless we know the distinction. That is how they went to the basic nature of things, and philosophy is the inquiry into the basic nature of things.

So these are the two important ideas: the idea of oneness and the idea of divinity of the soul. According to Vedanta, or Hinduism, all will be saved today or tomorrow. All the people will realize their ultimate nature. The name of that ultimate substance they gave as Sat, Chit, Ananda — Satchidananda. Why? These are the three fundamental desires of man and these fundamental desires point out to the idea that there must be some condition in which these are achieved. For that we need the world. This point has been looked at from the psychological point of view.

Brahman or Satchidananda, the ultimate reality is the thing which is existence absolute, knowledge absolute, bliss absolute. They define God as the highest reading of the Absolute. All the gods of different religions are really the different readings of the same Absolute. So God is the same. He has got these two aspects, the immanent aspect in the world and transcendental aspect beyond the world. God not only covers the entire world, he transcends it also. In the Rig-Veda we have got a famous saying: "God covered the entire world and surpassed it by ten fingers." A graphic way of telling it. Now if God is completely identified with nature, then it is called pantheism. So some of the philosophers said, no. the Hindu conception is not pantheism, it is pan-entheism; that is, everything is in God — God transcends it, he is not exhausted in it.

PART II
Chapter 10

ONENESS AND ETHICAL VALUES

From Oneness flow all the moral and ethical values. Why should I love my neighbor as myself and not cut his throat? What is the basic argument? Normally the nineteenth century secular political systems have accepted this idea because of the training of hundreds of years of religious systems. Vedanta said it is because the other man is really yourself in another form, so to hate him is really ultimately hating yourself. Loving is really feeling identity, when you love a person, or your child, your parents, your son, daughter, people of your family, people of your neighborhood, people of your country or of the world— some sort of identification you feel and that is how ethics or moral values form. Swami Vivekananda was fond of saying ethics is unity. Whenever you have felt some sort of unity, you feel a sort of identification. The basic reason is the unity of existences. From this can flow all types of egalitarian political systems and other theories. Samyavada is the word used for the socialistic theories in India and Atma-samya, equality through the spirit is the Vedantic position.

So the social implication of unity from two directions can be found, one is this idea of unity percolating in the social field. All types of human understanding are based upon, ultimately speaking, on this sense of unity which is provided by this idea of oneness of the universe. Variety may remain, but you should be able to find out the unity underlying all of them. Through the Gita (7.7), Krishna says, "I am the thread connecting all the jewels." So unity in variety is a special message of the Indian culture, and that has come to India through Vedanta. The variety may remain for variety is the spice of life; without variety you don't enjoy things, but then through them you should be able to find out the unity underlying. Two ways of finding any type of human understanding are either you eliminate all differences and make all the people look alike, move alike, talk alike, or the other method to allow the variety but find out the unity. Vedanta tries the method of unity in variety which is a distinctive aspect of Indian culture. So you have got varieties of languages, etc. which politically speaking sometimes become uncomfortable but that is the only method of bringing in some sort of peace and understanding without destroying the distinctive aspects of things.

The second aspect for the individual flows from the idea of the Atman, the innate divinity of man. When Vedanta says man is divine, it doesn't say man in his changing aspect but man in his real nature. Divinity of man is a cornerstone of Vedanta. Man ultimately is the spirit. To know that real nature of man is the goal of life.

What is the position of prayer, etc. in Vedanta? An average man requires some sort of a superior being to whom in times of trouble he can go for succour, solace — in one word, religion. They said yes, religion can be given recognition by Vedanta. But God is within. So the Vedantic meditation is not asking, but asserting, saying, "I am pure, I am with knowledge, I am free from disease and distress." Asserting the positive aspect is psychologically more valid also.

The harping on suffering may produce a condition of suffering. So the better method will be not to think of suffering, but assert your real nature. It is not hypocrisy it is the real position. When you say you are suffering, really your outer aspect is suffering; you really are not suffering. All this suffering is coming because of your identification with body and mind which are not your real nature. So assertion of the spirit is the Vedantic method of prayer. Christopher Isherwood describes it as prayer without tears. It is prayer in a sense; asserting, suggesting to the mind, but no weeping, no tears, no crying, and he thinks modern men like that type of prayer more than the weeping type of old pattern. The very oft-quoted line of Vivekananda are "Telling all the time, 'I am diseased, I am diseased' will not cure the disease, medicine is necessary. Telling all the time, 'I am weak, I am weak' will not cure the weakness; strength is necessary, and strength doesn't come by thinking of weakness all the time." Strength lies in your deeper self; so assert all the strength, all the enthusiasm, all the courage, all the energy that you require. They are all inherent in the spirit. Spirit is the repository of all the strength, so think of yourself as the Spirit and bring out all these qualities. If you are nervous, think that the Self is the repository of all courage, strength, and confidence, and courage will come, confidence will come, energy will come. Whatever you lack, think that the Spirit is all this. So that is how Vedantic meditation goes on—assertion.

PART II
Chapter 11

THREE STATES

The Advaita Vedanta establishes the ultimate reality by analysis of our different states. We have got our normal practical experience of the waking state, but we have got other experiences also. All our knowledge is based on our waking experience. A group of Vedantins said why should we limit it to our waking experience alone? We have got other experiences. We have got dreams and they are one type of reality. We have our deeper sleep — another type of reality. But what is the persistent reality in all the three states? When I am awake I know that I am aware of things, when I dream then also I feel that I am dreaming something — not dreaming but having experiences, so consciousness is there. When I am in deep sleep I don't experience anything, but when I am awake, then I say, "Ah! I slept well. I did not know anything." That also shows awareness. That consciousness is the persistent factor in all these three conditions: waking, dreaming, and deep sleep. The scientific systems say that we have got to take experience into consideration. Vedanta says, yes, but take the total experience. Consciousness is the unbroken factor in man's experience and that is ultimately identified with the Self.

A man got heavily drunk. Suddenly he had a desire at midnight to have some sweetmeat. He went to a sweetmeat shop, went on banging the door, the man got up. He said,

"I want some sweetmeat — one rupee worth of sweetmeat." The man found that to drive the man off is more difficult than to oblige so he gave him the thing, and he brought out a ten rupee note. The shopkeeper said, "I can't give you change at midnight." "It doesn't matter, I shall come tomorrow." He notes that a bull was lying in front of the shop. Next day again he came but the bull was lying in front of a tailor shop. He went in and asked, "Where is my money?" "What money?" "Why last night I bought one rupee worth of sweetmeat, ten rupee note I gave, nine rupees I want." "Don't you see that it is a tailor shop?" "Yes, I see; just to cheat me of these nine rupees, you have changed the shop itself." " How do you say that?" "Why, I have got my proof. This bull was lying in front of the shop yesterday also. Similarly we also wrongly identify the thing, by adventitious aspects.

Vedanta as a philosophy tries to harmonize the different religions, gives the basic position and tries most rigorously and logically to come to the conclusion. The basic position is only hypothesis. But Vedanta says it is not hypothesis, but the experience of saints. They realized this ultimate truth and their realization has been recorded in the scriptures, so scriptures, actual experience of the saints and sages are the basic material with which we try to analyze. How to develop a philosophy? You have certain experiences; while trying to explain these experiences you evolve a philosophy.

Again man has a persistent belief that he will not die; in some form will continue. You know Bertrand

Russell's story: he took his young five-year old son to see the mummies in Egypt, and the boy began the persistent question: "Father, where had I been in the days of the mummies?" And Russell, the great advocate of agnosticism, says in spite of working hard for a few hours, I could not persuade the boy to accept that he did not exist. This persistent, obstinate belief of man that he always existed is one type of proof—not the rational proof in the ordinary sense—but one type of proof that man continues.

Five important doctrines of Vedanta are discussed. The idea of the unity of existence, that all things are ultimately one; as a corollary, the divinity of the soul—that man is ultimately speaking is spiritual in nature, and that is why Vivekananda says each soul is potentially divine, that divinity is to be manifested. Third, unity of godhead. All the gods that we see in different religions are ultimately one God. Fourth, as a corollary comes the idea of harmony of religion, if it is the same god they worship, what is there to quarrel? Fifth, the idea of freedom. Vedanta believes salvation means getting out of this confusion, this illusion, this bondage, and its method is to assert that I am not the body, not the mind, but the spirit. Immortality is an automatic corollary of this system. In the Upanishads they describe God as amritam, abhayam; God is immortality itself, he is fearlessnesses itself. There is the persistent fear of man of losing his identity or fear of other things. This gives him courage and assurance of continuity. These are some of the basic ideas of Vedanta.

Applied in social life absolute equality will be the

goal of Vedanta. Swami Vivekananda has two lectures, the last two lectures of the first volume of the Complete Works of Vivekananda called 'Vedanta and Privilege' and 'Privilege', and he speaks about the extreme type of equality even in social level. Now these are corollaries of the system.

PART III
Religion

PART III
Chapter 1

TRUE RELIGION

Every religion contains certain elements which are peculiar to the culture, time and historical circumstances of its birth. Consequently, the various mythologies, rituals and theological beliefs of each religion will necessarily reflect its unique character and will differ, one from the other. And yet, behind these various manifestations of religious phenomena lie certain universal truths which, because of their subtle and inexpressible nature, are often best expressed in the language of ritual, symbol and myth. It is these universal and eternal truths, which transcend our ordinary powers of comprehension but are immediately grasped by the purified intellect, which we may call 'true religion'.

Swami Vivekananda once remarked that 'Sri Ramakrishna incarnated himself.... to demonstrate what true religion is...'[1] When we examine the life of Sri Ramakrishna, we find that, both in his teachings and in his realizations, he was able to directly experience these universal truths of spiritual life and to explain them to his disciples in the most simple and straightforward manner. This fact is equally true of Holy Mother Sri Sarada Devi and Swami Vivekananda. And yet, if we carefully look at their lives, we find that each laid a special emphasis on and demonstrated a different aspect of spiritual life, so that, taken together, we get a complete picture of true religion and religious life as it manifests itself in the fields of spirit, emotion, and practice.

Perhaps the most basic truth of spiritual life, and the one which Sri Ramakrishna stressed above all others, was that religion is realization. Dogma, ritual, philosophical speculation all have their place and importance only to the extent that they lead the spiritual aspirant along the road to direct experience of truth. The great emphasis placed on God realization in Sri Ramakrishna's own life can be seen in all his actions and teachings. When he was a young priest in the Kali Temple at Dakshineswar, he became consumed with a passion for the vision of Kali, the Divine Mother. His longing for God grew day by day and became so intense that he even gave up food and sleep. Ultimately he felt that life without the vision of God was unbearable; and just as he was about to take his own life, he had the vision of the Divine Mother, 'a limitless, infinite, effulgent Ocean of Consciousness.'[2]

After the vision of the Divine Mother, Sri Ramakrishna felt a desire to verify his experience by practicing spiritual disciplines as prescribed by the scriptures. He felt that by comparing his experiences with those of the past realized souls he could confirm the genuineness of his own realizations. As a result, Sri Ramakrishna began to practice a variety of spiritual paths, one after the other, and was able to confirm the authenticity not only of his own experiences, but also of the different spiritual paths themselves.

One of the earliest proclamations concerning the universality of truth and the oneness of existence, in spite of the different interpretations and names given to it, is that of the *Rig Veda* (1.164.46): "That which exists is one; sages describe it in various ways."[3] Though this truth provides a theoretical ground for the ultimate harmony and unity of all religions, we do not find its full application in the spiritual history of the world until we come to the life of Sri Ramakrishna. From the time of his realization of the Divine Mother to the end of his period of sadhana, Sri Ramakrishna conducted a grand experiment in spiritual life wherein he demonstrated the truth that all religions, when practiced with sincerity and longing, lead to the same goal.

After his initial experience of God-consciousness, Sri Ramakrishna practiced the various attitudes of the Vaishnava schools, from the *dasya bhava* (the attitude of a servant towards his master) to the *madhura bhava* (the attitude of a lover towards her beloved). In each case his sadhanas ended in complete union with his object of worship. He also practiced all the major disciplines of the Tantrik School and attained perfection in each one within a period of a few days. In every instance, again, he lost outer consciousness of the world, and his individuality got merged in the Divine.

Sri Ramakrishna not only practiced the dualistic disciplines of the Vaishnavas and the Tantrik sadhanas of the Saktas, he also underwent the austere exercises of the non-dualistic Vedanta. After being initiated into monastic life by the wandering monk, Tota Puri, Sri Ramakrishna sat for meditation, attempting to realize his perfect oneness with the attributeless Brahman. On the very day of his initiation into sannyasa, he attained the highest state of Nirvikalpa Samadhi in which he directly experienced his identity with the Absolute.

Having thus realized God both in His personal and impersonal forms, through devotional practices as well as non-dualistic disciplines, Sri Ramakrishna realized that one and the same God was being worshiped and realized by the Hindu devotees. And yet, even after attaining such unprecedented heights of spirituality, Sri Ramakrishna was not content to rest. He had a desire to know how devotees of other religions worshiped God and to see if their methods of spiritual practice would also take him to the highest goal of life. Consequently, he practiced the disciplines of Islam under the guidance of a wandering Sufi by the name of Govinda Rai. Living and thinking in all respects like a Muslim, Sri Ramakrishna faithfully practiced the Islamic disciplines and was soon rewarded with a vision of a bearded man, presumably the prophet Muhammad, who approached him and merged in his body. Sri Ramakrishna then had the vision of God in His personal aspect, and finally of the impersonal Absolute. Several years later, Sri Ramakrishna had a similar experience of Christ, and thus realized the truth of both Christianity and Islam, the two great Semitic religions then current in India. This vision of Christ and the ultimate merging in the Absolute represented the final stage of Sri Ramakrishna's grand experiment with the various religions of the world known to him at that time.

Sri Ramakrishna reached certain conclusions based on his experiences with the different faiths of the world. He said:

'I have practiced all religions- Hinduism, Islam, Christianity- and I have also followed the paths of the different Hindu sects. I have found that it is the same God toward whom all are directing their steps, though along different paths. You must try all beliefs and traverse all the different ways once. Wherever I look, I see men quarreling in the name of religion- Hindus, Muslims, Brahmos, Vaishnavas, and the rest. But they never reflect that he who is called Krishna, is also called Siva, and bears the name of Shakti, Jesus and Allah as well- the same Rama with a thousand names. A lake has several bathing areas. At one, the Hindus take water in pitchers and call it 'jal'; at another the Muslims take water in leather bags and call it 'pani'. At a third, the Christians call it 'water'. Can we imagine that it is not 'jal', but only 'pani' or 'water'? How ridiculous! The substance is One under different names, and everyone is seeking the same substance; only climate, temperament, and name create differences. Let each follow his own path. If he sincerely and ardently wishes to know God, peace be unto him. He will surely realize Him'.[4]

Sri Ramakrishna thus realized that all religions are true in the sense that all represent valid paths to God-realization. All are striving for the same divine essence, whether it be conceived of as personal, impersonal, or even as the void. The differences found in the various traditions are based not on the essential and eternal truths of religion, but on the particulars, which are the result of often complex historical forces.

Sri Ramakrishna also felt that the variety found in religions was a positive and necessary fact of life. He used to say that the different spiritual paths were created to suit aspirants of different temperaments just as a mother prepares different dishes for her children, based on their taste and power of digestion. For those with a devotional nature, the path of bhakti is best suited and the object of their worship will be a personal God of love. The jnani needs an impersonal Absolute to satisfy the demands of his intellect, and so on. But it is one and the same Reality, cloaked in different names that is propitiated, worshiped, or meditated upon in each case.

Another conclusion which Sri Ramakrishna reached was that there was a natural progression from dualistic worship to non-dualistic experience, whether described as union with God, in devotional language, or the realization of one's identity with the Absolute, in philosophical terms. This truth can be clearly seen in Sri Ramakrishna's own experiences, for in each case, his sadhana culminated in the loss of his individual identity and the merging of his mind in the object of his worship or meditation. Sri Ramakrishna often said that non-dualism was the final word in spirituality and that all paths find their consummation there, although a devotee of God may prefer to keep a slight sense of separation in order to enjoy the bliss of union with God.

Another conviction of Sri Ramakrishna's was that one must develop unswerving devotion to one's own spiritual ideal. Despite the fact that he considered all paths to be valid means for realization of God, he also saw the need to choose the path best suited to one and to stick to it with great determination. This *nishtha* or steadfast devotion to one's spiritual ideal, was one of the dominant characteristics of Sri Ramakrishna's spiritual practices; whichever path he was following at the time, he did so to the exclusion of all others. When he practiced Islam, he removed his mind from all traces of his devotion to the Divine Mother until he had realized the truth of that path. The same is true for all of his other spiritual practices as well. However, he also cautioned against being one-sided and feeling that one's own path alone was valid. For this reason, he recommended that his disciples practice other religious disciplines to a certain extent, all the while remaining steadfast in their own path.

Sri Ramakrishna believed that nothing could be achieved in spiritual life without great yearning for realization. Whatever be one's path, crooked or straight, yearning was the one ingredient which could compensate for all other shortcomings. Sri Ramakrishna further taught that in order to develop yearning and passionate love of God (*anuraga*) one also had to cultivate dispassion (*viraga*) and the renunciation of lust and greed. Whether the formal renunciation of the monk or the mental renunciation of the householder, dispassion had to go hand in hand with the passion for God-realization in order to carry one to the highest goal.

Once one has realized the indwelling divinity of his own nature, he automatically sees the same divinity dwelling equally within all beings and all things. As a result, the God-realized soul attains a state of same sightedness, universal compassion, and a feeling that all beings are part and parcel of oneself. This truth was embodied in the person of Holy Mother to a degree rarely seen in the history of the world. One has only to look at her final message to mankind to understand this fact: '*Let me tell you something, my child, if you want peace, then do not look into anybody's faults. Look into your own faults. Learn to make the world your own. No one is a stranger, my child; the whole world is your own*'.[5]

Holy Mother's love, based on her spiritual vision of the oneness of all beings, was a universal love which knew no distinction of high or low, good or evil. It was a mother's love, devoid of even the slightest taint of selfishness or partiality. The truth of this can be clearly seen in an incident regarding a poor Muslim robber by the name of Amjad. One day Holy mother invited Amjad for a meal after he had helped build the wall for her new house. Since he was a Muslim and of questionable character, Holy Mother's niece, Nalini, served him food in a disrespectful manner. Mother scolded Nalini for this and served him herself, even cleaning the place after he had finished. Nalini was horrified, and declared Holy Mother had lost her caste! But Mother told her to keep quiet and said, 'Just as Sarat (Swami Saradananda, one of the highly respected monks of the Order and Holy Mother's chief attendant) is my son, exactly so is Amjad'.[6]

While Holy Mother demonstrated that the highest spiritual truths manifest themselves in the heart as well as the head, Vivekananda showed that these same truths must also manifest themselves in the field of action. Swamiji's emphasis on 'practical Vedanta' ushered in a new era in the spiritual history of the world, wherein old distinctions regarding spiritual life and practice no longer held true. As Sister Nivedita wrote, '*If the many and the One be indeed the same reality, then it is not all modes of worship alone, but equally all modes of work, all modes of struggle, all modes of creation, which are paths of realization. No distinctions, henceforth, between sacred and secular. To labor is to pray. To conquer is to renounce. Life is itself religion. To have and to hold is as stern a trust as to quit and to avoid*'.[7]

Vivekananda's 'practical Vedanta' and his belief that service to living beings was tantamount to worship of God came as the result of a particular experience he had one day while listening to Sri Ramakrishna explain the tenets of the Vaishnava faith to the devotees. In the course of conversation he mentioned *jive daya*, compassion to living beings, as one of the pillars of their faith. But hardly had he uttered the words than he went into a spiritual mood and said, "Talk of compassion for beings! Will you, little creatures, bestow compassion for beings? You fellows, who are you to bestow it? No, no; not compassion to Jivas but service to them as Siva'.[8]

The future Vivekananda was deeply moved by these words and the depth of feeling behind them. Coming out of the room he exclaimed:

Ah, what a wonderful light have I got today from the Master's words! In synthesizing the Vedantic knowledge, which was generally regarded as dry, austere and even cruel, with sweet devotion to the Lord, what a new mellowed means of experiencing the Truth has he revealed today! In order to attain the non-dual knowledge, one, we have been told so long, should have to renounce the world and the company of men altogether and retire to the forest and mercilessly uproot and throw away love, devotion and other soft and tender emotions from the heart..... But from what the Master in ecstasy said today, it is gathered that the Vedanta of the forest can be brought to human habitation and that it can be brought to human habitation and that it can be applied in practice to the work-a-day world... If the Divine Lord ever grants me an opportunity, I'll proclaim everywhere in the world this wonderful truth I have heard today.[9]

Swamiji not only proclaimed this truth throughout the world, he also established a new monastic tradition in which service to the poor and suffering represents worship of 'the living God' and a new form of spiritual sadhana.

We can thus see that the great truths of spirituality regarding the oneness of existence and the divinity of man find their unique expression in the lives of these spiritual luminaries: Sri Ramakrishna, Holy Mother, and Swamiji. From Sri Ramakrishna we learn that through great longing and renunciation we can have the direct experience of God. In Holy Mother we see this realization of oneness manifest itself in an all-embracing, impartial love for all beings. And from Swamiji we understand that by serving the divine dwelling within each and every person, we can attain to the same state of realization that the saint, immersed in meditation, attains through his spiritual practices.

References:

(1) C.W. 6 p. 83.
(2) M., The Gospel of Sri Ramakrishna, p.14.
(3) *ekam sad vipra bahudha vadanti*
(4) The Gospel, p. 35.
(5) Swami Nikhilananda, *Holy Mother*, p. 319.
(6) Ibid., p. 134.
(7) The Complete Works of Sister Nivedita, 1 p.9
(8) Swami Saradananda, Sri Ramakrishna The Great Master, p. 817.
(9) Ibid., p. 817-18.

PART III
Chapter 2

THE ROLE OF RELIGION NOW

As the world rapidly approaches the twenty-first century it faces a variety of challenges, some new and some old. How it handles these will determine to a large extent whether the upcoming century will represent a bright, new chapter in the history of mankind, or a failure of the inhabitants of our planet to live harmoniously with one another and with their environment.

When we examine the particular problems awaiting us in the century to come, it becomes abundantly clear how many of them is the result of actual misconceptions regarding certain basic truths about God, mankind, and the universe. And although all religions manifest these same truths to a greater or lesser degree, perhaps none has developed them in as rational and systematic a fashion as Hinduism. Consequently, the extent to which these universal doctrines of Hinduism, or more properly, Vedanta, are put into practice in the future century, the brighter will be our prospects for peaceful coexistence and prosperity.

There are certain specific areas which seem critical for the future of the planet, three of which are the political, the religious and the economic. In each of these three arenas we find dialectic at work, two forces apparently moving in opposite directions. This is clearly seen in the area of world politics in the very distinct cases of Western Europe and the Soviet Union. In the former we find a tendency towards breaking down barriers and borders, and a real indication, in spite of opposite trends, that the twenty-first century will usher in a new and long-awaited "one-world community" or "global village". On the other hand we find ethnic and religious communities in the Soviet Union and many parts of Africa and Asia asserting their separate identities and individual freedoms. We find a similar dichotomy within all of the major religions of the world; on the one hand there is an unprecedented movement towards mutual understanding and brotherhood, and on the other a tendency towards fanatical fundamentalism and hatred.

It is here where the Vedantic technique regarding unity and diversity, the oneness of existence, and the divinity of the soul, so prophetically proclaimed by Swami Vivekananda at the dawn of the twentieth century, can play a critical role in resolving such dilemmas. According to the ancient Hindu teachings of Vedanta, both unity, in the form of an underlying spiritual reality, and diversity, as the manifestation of that oneness represent fundamental facts of existence which must find expression in the social realm as well as the cosmic. Thus, a basic brotherhood and identity exist at the core of all individuals and communities, which are not disturbed by the very real need for the expression of individuality. Any attempt to form world community which disregards the different religious and ethnic needs of its members is bound to fail, as is the equally improbable scenario of distinct national, ethnic, and religious communities living in harmony without first understanding their essential brotherhood and spiritual oneness.

A similar dichotomy exists in the economic area as well, wherein both extremes of consideration for the individual and the community have failed to live up to expectations. The praiseworthy ideal of socialism to treat each individual equally and supply all of his basic needs recognized the essential oneness and inter-relatedness of all beings but failed to acknowledge the very basic principle of freedom which forms the essential nature of the soul. Capitalism, on the other hand, has given great scope to the ideal of freedom, but at the expense of justice and equity. It is only when such economic systems base themselves on the spiritual principles of both freedom and equality, as expressed in the Vedantic philosophy, that a just and productive system may be constructed harmonizing the virtues found in both capitalism and socialism. Such a system, if at all possible would eliminate exploitation and privilege, while at the same time allow free expression of the individual to manifest his true and essential freedom.

It is somewhat difficult to say how major a role Hinduism, and specifically the universal and liberal teachings of Vedanta, will play in the direction which the world takes in the century to come. Even in this century we can see the subtle and often unperceived influence of Vedanta in the ecumenical movements of the day and in changing views regarding the compatibility of science and religion. With new advancements in communications and the unprecedented influx of Asian nationals to the West, many thinkers assume that the ideals of Eastern philosophy, and Hinduism in particular, will find their way more readily into the though currents of the world and will continue to exert their silent influence on the way we think and live. We can only hope that the Vedantic truths of unity in diversity, oneness of existence, and divinity of mankind will play a prominent role in both the individual and national life of the twenty-first century, ushering in an era of peace and prosperity.

The quiet influence of India had always been there as Vivekananda said:

Like the gentle dew that falls unseen and unheard, and yet brings into blossom the fairest of roses, has been the contribution of India to the thought of the world. Silent, unperceived, yet omnipotent in its effect, it has revolutionized the thought of the world, yet nobody knows when it did so. C.W. 2:274.

Much more prominently this influence will be there in the coming century. Arnold Toynbee, Sorokin and other Western thinkers predicted this. In Russia, a Vivekananda Society has sprung up in Moscow. Many other aggressive religious groups are also going there. Along with desire for worldly goods, there is a great urge no doubt for spiritual experience. The leaders of society there realize this and want to encourage the socially beneficial aspects of religion rather than mere emotionalism. Communistic countries tried to banish religion but found that it is impossible. People require faith for sustenance and inspiration. But religions in their turn bring quarrels and dissension as is very clear in the Soviet republics. In spite of seventy years of schooling in atheism fight has started on religious grounds between Azerbaijan and Armenia. What is the way out? Hinduism can play a definite role in this field. The tolerance in Hinduism is well-known though some groups are taking advantage of it and making us feel bad about our spirit of accommodation. As a result, in India it may have a more limited part to play. But throughout the world if religions are to be forces of amity and understanding and not forces of destruction, they will have to take the lesson from Hinduism. That is the most important role that India and Hinduism can play in the twenty-first century in the theater of the world, over and above providing, as a religion, consolation and strength to the people.

But the preachers of religion must be active. The exhortation of Ramakrishna is to go forward. Bhaga Caraiveti, move on, is a popular saying of the scriptures. It is not in the Upanishads but in the Aitareya Brahmana (adhyaya 33, Khandas 1-6) informs Swami Nischalananda. The story is called Shunahkshepa Upakhyana. Bhaga Caraiveti has been repeated seven times there to show the importance of the message.

Sister Nivedita advocated 'Aggressive Hinduism' to encourage the nation to be active. For solving the world's problems, 'Aggressive goodness' must be the message, says Swami Nikhilananda. Let this be our motto.

PART III

Chapter 3

SOCIAL SERVICE - PERSONAL AND IMPERSONAL

After Indian independence social service institutions, as well as different institutions of the Government, are multiplying. There was a national awareness even earlier; but now it has acquired a tempo which deserves genuine commendation. Service in India was more or less decentralized. Down the ages people served the poor and the sick in an individual way. Every householder was expected daily to offer food to the needy. It was considered to be one of his five main duties. As a result, as Swami Vivekananda once remarked, there was rarely any death due to starvation during normal times. But times have changed. The Indian society is changing its character. The purely agricultural society is fast being replaced and urban civilization is having its impact on society. Because of the aftermath of War and inflation, private charity of almost every householder is coming to an end. With the rise of the standard of living in one section and utter lack of it in the other, the gulf between people has widened. So in modern times as one section finds it more and more difficult to help others, the other finds itself more and more stranded. With the break up of the joint family system and increase of taxes more people are now open to uncertainties of life. The agricultural reforms have given succor to some people, but it has created problems for others. That is the nature of the modern complex society. Because of all this, private charity is lessening day by day. The problems are often so vast, that they require planned and coordinated effort. Many institutions are coming up for the purpose and they are very useful. On the necessity of united effort, Swami Vivekananda once said:

"Give up jealousy and conceit; learn to work united for others. That is the great need of our country. Have patience and be faithful unto death. Do not fight among yourselves. Be perfectly pure in money dealings. So long as you have faith and honesty and devotion, everything will prosper. So long as there is no feeling of disunion amongst you, through the grace of the Lord, I assure, there is no danger for you."

But no effort is free from defects. The danger of institutionalizing charities is always there. It may dry up the springs of voluntary charity and leave the workers entirely dependent on the Government which collects money through taxation, direct or indirect. It is said about larger social organizations that they should guard against service becoming impersonal in these social welfare institutions. It is an important point to be taken note of. A tie of love is natural when a man gives something directly to a sufferer out of sympathy. In institutionalized services, he misses the spiritual joy of giving and at the same time seeing the effect of his gift immediately or in course of time. This is from the giver's side. The middle man, the social worker Borough whom the money is given, may not always feel uplifted, for the candidates may be too many and the receivers often 'demand' things as their right. These are enough to damp the enthusiasm and sympathy of the worker. The sight of abject poverty and suffering day in and day out along with the darker side of human nature might make him indifferent to suffering itself. Institutionalization requires definite rules to prevent misuse, but too much of it may kill the initiative and zeal. The desire to do spectacular things also may crop up, which will drain away much of the resources.

When all these factors are taken into consideration the note of warning will acquire some meaning. The remedy, however, lies in awareness and more sympathy built up on the philosophical attitude supplied by Vedanta that God dwells in every being and by serving others we are ourselves benefited.

Mr. K. M. Munshi once said emphasizing the need for depending on institutional social service, the whole fabric of society which persisted in this country a few centuries ago was breaking up. At one time, it was found that the joint family system was insurance against poverty and against women and children being rendered helpless. That could not exist under the present conditions. Various factors, including the Income-tax, were working against that system. Automatically the people or the families were divided and the result was that in the various parts of the country, they saw many helpless members of such families struggling. They were driven to reorient their whole social services concept, particularly in view of the fact that large industrial cities were springing up. Naturally, therefore, they must go to institutional service to give succor to the poor people either with the help of the Government or with the assistance of philanthropists. (The Hindu, November 9, 1958.)

Nowadays, many old and infirm people are being left to their fate. Some attention must be given to such people. Of course, the problem is acquiring vast proportions and may be difficult for voluntary groups to tackle it, and so the Government must come forward. A welcome measure was introduced by the Government in giving pension to needy people above 70 but it got a rude shock after the Chinese attack for the money is being drained away to defense. It should be revived. It is time that some institutions come up to give shelter to old people, not only to those who have been reduced to beggars but also to people who have some means of living but nobody to look after them. It has been done in some of the advanced countries. We are aware that some Vanaprastha Ashramas have been organized for well-to-do people. If productive work according to the physical capacity of the people concerned is organized, many other people can be given security. Happily, there are some societies working for children. But till now no organized effort has been made for the old people excepting the beggar homes. It is an urgent necessity, specially for the women section of it. It cannot be done by poor old people themselves. But it can surely be organized by some well-to-do people who are retired and healthy and might be commanding the necessary drive, skill and prestige. Very poor people have no constituency of their own, so religious and well-to-do people will have to take up the work specially when the state looking after people is lessened. Bankim Chandra advocated that retired people should spend their Vanaprastha period in social service. We hope some unselfish elders will come forward to shoulder this responsibility.

PART III
Chapter 4

SERVICE AND POWER

Everywhere in the world one witnesses an almost mad rash for political power. Every nation except the monolithic totalitarian States -- in such States power remains frozen in the iron grip of dictatorship of diverse ilk — is divided into fighting and often hating groups of people, known as 'parties' with various names. Fighting, wrestling, jostling and all sorts of things go on among them for securing power. They have varied philosophies, views, programs, slogans and ready criticisms against one another. Election time is the devil's hour in any country! In election campaign they openly talk of 'giving the hell' to the other party. At one point, however, and on this point alone, all the fighting men are at one. If you ask them what for they are after power, all of them will tell you with glowing fervor that they only seek to serve their fellowmen for their good; as doing good is not possible without power, they seek power. By and large, power has come to be accepted as the condition precedent of service with the vast majority of mankind. But does this too popular an equation of power and service stand any serious scrutiny from the standpoint of human welfare?

The question that immediately crops up before we take up any work is whether it pays or not. On analysis, we find that the question of 'paying' is generally related to the interest of the speaker. If we probe a little deeper we find that love of power is at the bottom of all this cant. 'Will to power' has been considered by philosophers like Nietzsche as the prime motive force for all human activity. While this may be admitted in general as true, we must remember that this tendency belongs to man's lower nature. Our effort should be to transcend this desire of self-aggrandizement.

No man can enter the portals of true greatness until and unless he has succeeded in subordinating his will to power, to will to dedication and service. In the realm of spirituality every single authentic teacher has warned seekers against the temptations of power. Power-seekers are those who have lost sight of the goal having gone astray. Those who stick to seeking power can never attain the *summum bonum* of spiritual life.

In affairs secular it must be admitted, however, that power is necessary and when correctly handled much good to the people can be accomplished with its help. It is especially essential when we think in terms of changing the structure of the whole society in a spectacularly short time. But the desire to thrust one's own plan and ideology without preparing the society for them is not praiseworthy, for it is not conducive to the permanent good of society. Moreover, great risk is involved in investing all powers in a group of people, for often a group is reduced to a man. That was the case with Germany, Italy and Russia in recent past. Though much technological improvement and economic advancement were effected by these countries, through the concentration of all powers in dictatorships, eventually the wielders of such power came to prove themselves as direst enemies of abiding human welfare. The lives of Hitler, Mussolini and Stalin of recent past proclaim a powerful and urgent lesson of history. It is obvious that the type of power which these dictators wielded is positively harmful to the free growth of the society. Even for individuals concerned, such power has proved ruinous. 'The desire of power in excess caused the angels to fall,' said Bacon. Sooner or later the mighty autocrats are thrown down from the high pedestal and they suffer humiliation and ignominy even if they are dead.

But there is another kind of power which is benign, beneficent and enduring. This power comes to one as a result of devoted selfless service. This is the power that all the great religious teachers had. The root of this power is the love for and dedication to the service of the fellow-beings. Because of this only, Gandhiji could move the whole nation. There is the lean man, Vinoba Bhave, who goes about in loin-cloth from village to village begging land for the landless of India. He has no temporal power. But when this begging parivrajaka falls ill and lies down somewhere in a wayside shade, the President or Prime Minister of India, who is the repository of the temporal power of the Republic, rushes to his bedside to enquire about his health. Such is the superior power of selfless service. In India at least the stature of a man grows in proportion to his personal strivings and sacrifice for the welfare of others.

Power is an instrumental value. It should not be divorced from the ideal of unselfish service. The ideal situation is that in which temporal power rests in the keeping of the dedicated servants of humanity. India has been fortunate in having a few such men to handle power after the coming of Independence. Not a little of India's recent material progress can be attributed to the leadership of a band of selfless men of sterling character. If India's neighbor could not turn independence to as good an account, it is because power there came to men who were not actuated by the motive of selfless service. Even India cannot be complacent on that score. For the spirit of selfless service seems to be fast dying out even in this country.

Nowadays we hear much about the welfare state ideal. The ideal of state or of economics has evolved into the welfare of the people due to the moral and religious influence exerted by the lovers of common men, and the inherent sense of justice in man. Basically the welfare ideal is only a variant of the ideal of dedicated service to fellow-beings. This is why the welfare state ideal cannot stand strong and sturdy except on a spiritual conception of life.

To work for the welfare of others without any selfish motive, it is necessary to conquer the love of power. Herein is the best test of our love for service. Those who in effect go by the motto 'no power, no service' are mere self-seekers. The question of compromise between service and power may arise only when our minds oscillates between the two; for a compromise is nothing but a mean found between two opposite desires. We must have an all-devouring passion for service and all other extraneous considerations must be ruled out. Every step in social progress, every advance in human knowledge, throughout the history of humanity, has been gained by those who had the sole idea of laboring for others out of love and who had given up all the ideas of profit for themselves. This attitude has been described as 'the social application of sannyasa' by Sister Nivedita. Activity becomes easy and quick if it is socialized. But in organized efforts, power cannot generally be equally distributed. The West in spite of its loud assertions of self-interest and individuality has been highly successful in all cooperative efforts. Those who want to serve others, especially in a planned and corporate manner, must be free from power-consciousness. We must consider the scope of service as a responsibility, a privilege, a trust and we must keep our minds always awakened, refreshed and alert. To do this it is essential to cultivate a spirit if renunciation. If we multiply our wants daily, we will be busy in meeting our needs, and in that case where will be the required time and mood for doing service to others? That is why the cult of simple life, of reducing desires, has been so vigorously advocated by men like Tolstoy and others. The Indian ideals of titiksha and aparigraha (austerity and non-acceptance of gifts) would make a man fully fit for dedicated service. There were no greater workers than Buddha and Christ. And what was the secret of their tremendous success in work?

'Only a great monk can be a great worker; for he is without attachments,' said Vivekananda. Vitoba cites cites the example of Buddha's renunciation of all powers in the Sangha. The same example was followed by Gandhiji. He was the soul of the Congress. But he was not even a four-anna member, hi every age social reformers without any political power have affected many social changes — all by their enthusiasm for the work, singleness of purpose and love for people. So service and power need not be bracketed together. We must take to service with a sense of dedication. This attitude to work as worship will give us enduring enthusiasm in spite of admitting that mixing of self interest for average men, the higher ideal must be before the society. As much energy must be thrown into our renunciation of power into our dedication to service, as into most men's preservation of selfish interest. *As the ignorant perform action being attached to it, even so, descendent of Bharata, should the wise perform action, unattached, desiring the welfare of the world,* says the Gita (3.25). The future of humanity depends on the earnestness with which we apply ourselves to working out this significant but neglected teaching of Sri Krishna. If wisdom remains static, virtue passive, goodness defensive, virile, active and aggressive ignorance will continue to dominate the world with all its consequences.

PART III
Chapter 5

SIGNIFICANCE OF THE SHANTI MANTRA

Every Upanishad has a Peace Invocation which ends with the words: 'Shanti! Shanti! Shanti! The commentators explain that whatever the obstacles that may come to a person from unknown forces, or elements, or from men and other creatures, or from his body and mind are driven away by repeating 'Peace' thrice. Apart from spiritual realization, religion helps us psychologically too and gives some immediate return. Everybody wants peace. When daily necessities are met, the immediate thing that is necessary is mental peace. By mere repetition of the word 'Shanti' calmly, silently, peacefully, a sort of poise comes. So whenever a person feels very restless, let him not give way to all these excitements, but repeat, 'Shanti, Shanti.' This will give a soothing effect. Just let him coolly sit for meditation, which will bring the mind from external things to thought, and ultimately he will be able to soak the mind with the idea of peace.

Steadiness of the body is a great help. Mastery of the body is necessary for pursuing any serious thinking. That is why in Raja-yoga so much stress is given to steady posture so that the mind does not become distracted by the body. As a person goes on practicing any particular type of physical discipline he gets used to it, and does not become restless. Physical control is the first step towards mental control. Physical peace is the first step towards mental peace, so one must first try to gain control over the body.

Next, one should try to throw out all the disturbing, exciting, anxious, and evil thoughts. All thoughts have some sort of influence on the mind. So one method is to bring up those thoughts and then throw them out. Those who are familiar with our puja method know well that there is a system of Bhuta Shuddhi (purification of the elements). Tranquility of mind is only possible when the mind is free from disturbing thoughts. Those thoughts must be given up first before we sit for prayer. Ordinary thoughts will not be so disturbing for normal meditation; it is enough if we can remove thoughts that are too distracting. In Bhuta Shuddhi, all the dross is first thought of as dried up and then burnt up. Then think that yogic nectar flows through every limb of the body, purifying it and making it whole. After that meditation is begun on the deity. Sri Ramakrishna actually saw the papa-purusha (the personification of defects) being burnt up. This method is now being applied by many psychiatrists. When you go to bed, some psychiatrists say that you should write your disturbing thoughts on bits of paper and throw them away. This is a psychological method of getting rid of uncomfortable thoughts when you go to sleep. The spiritual method is to connect your mind with the thought of the Lord.

Sri Ramakrishna again suggested another method. When you sit for meditation, first of all wash your mind. When the mind is full of dross, you wash it and feel yourself pure, and then sit for meditation on the Lord or the Divine Mother, or on the Infinite Atman. This is both for a psychological purpose and for spiritual development. When you sit quietly and calmly, try to think, 'Om Shanti! Shanti! Shanti!' The repetition of Shanti has a great soothing effect on the mind. Then you will be prepared and in a receptive mood to sit for a deeper study of the scriptures. This is why the Upanishads ask us to recite the Shanti Mantra before beginning any study.

PART III
Chapter 6

THE GITA

Throughout the religious history of India, no single scripture has captured the hearts and minds, or so well represented the spiritual aspirations of the people of India as the Gita. Of all the holy books of Hinduism, the most popular is the *Bhagavad Gita*, "The Song of God," or "The Song Celestial." In Hinduism, a religion characterized as much for its diversity as for its unity, no single text has been more universally relied upon for daily inspiration. Countless editions, commentaries and translations of the Gita have been published, and its influence on the world at large has steadily grown since its first English translation was made in the 18th century.

The Gita is composed of eighteen chapters and is found in the *Bhishma Parva* of the *Mahabharata*, the world's longest epic poem. It deals with the descendants of King Bharata, particularly the Kauravas and their cousins the Pandavas, and their struggle for control of the kingdom. Various opinions exist regarding the date of composition of the Gita, and it is difficult to settle the question conclusively. For one thing, works such as the Mahabharata are often written over a period of centuries, with later portions added on to the original body. Some scholars are of the opinion that the Gita was composed relatively recently and later interpolated into the text. Others take the opposite stand and claim that the Gita was much earlier than the Mahabharata, perhaps pre-Buddhistic, and later incorporated into the text. However, the consensus is that, since the philosophical ideas of the Gita are consistent with those of the Mahabharata, the Gita was probably composed around 200 B.C., along with a large part of the Mahabharata. The traditional view is that the Gita is an integral part of the Mahabharata and is a few thousand years old.

Next to the Bible, the Gita is the most translated book in the world. There are several reasons for this popularity: literary, historical, and philosophical. For one thing, the stories of the Mahabharata - as also those of the Ramayana, India's other great epic poem - have captivated the imagination of the Indian people for centuries and have become an integral part of their culture. Sri Krishna, friend of the Pandava brothers and Arjuna's charioteer, is the deliverer of the message of the Gita and is one of the most beloved figures in the religious history of India, worshipped by millions as God incarnate. Dramatically speaking, the setting of the Gita cannot be rivaled: Arjuna on the battlefield requesting Sri Krishna to position his chariot between the two armies about to make war. There he sees his own kinsmen, his cousins, his uncles, grandfathers, teachers and friends. Overcome by grief, he throws down his bow and arrow and refuses to fight, thus evoking from Sri Krishna one of the world's most inspired spiritual talks, delivered with unparalleled eloquence and power.

Another fact contributing to the Gita's popularity

is that, as an epic *(itihasa),* it falls within the category of traditional knowledge *(smriti,* in its widest sense) as opposed to revealed knowledge *(sruti).* Thus, whereas the Vedas and Upanishads were traditionally restricted to a certain caste, the epics, such as the Mahabharata, as well as the Puranas, legal texts, *sutra* texts, etc., were open to all, giving the highest spiritual truths. And, indeed we find many verses in the Puranas referring to the Mahabharata as the "fifth Veda," which is attributed to Vyasa, the legendary compiler and arranger of the Vedas. Consistent with its popular nature, the Mahabharata presents its teachings not as a dry philosophy but interspersed with, and by means of, varieties of fascinating stories. The Gita not only represents the most sublime teachings of the Mahabharata, it also occurs at the most climactic moment of the story.

Though not considered a revealed text, the Gita occupies a special place in the school of Vedanta, representing one of the three authoritative works on Vedanta, technically known as the *prasthana-traya,* the other works being the *Upanishads* and the *Brahma-sutras.* The individual most responsible for helping to elevate the Gita to its present position is probably the great Vedantic sage, Sankaracarya. We know from his Gita commentary that earlier commentaries had been written and were known to him; and it seems clear that he wrote his own, partly as a refutation of an earlier view advocating the dual practice of ritual and knowledge. But Sankara's commentary is the earliest known to us and certainly the first of any real importance. Since his time, it has become incumbent on any Vedantic thinker wishing to establish a particular philosophical position to write a commentary on the Gita, as well as on the Brahmasutras and the Upanishads. Thus, at least partly because of Sankara's high esteem for the Gita, its status has been raised above other works of its kind, including the Mahabharata itself, and it occupies a position of authority within the Vedanta school second only to that of the Upanishads.

Aside from the literary merits of the Mahabharata, its accessibility to all, and its position of respect within the school of Vedanta, there is a further, more basic explanation for the longevity and popularity of the Gita - the sublime and universal nature of its teachings. Much has been written about the teachings of the Gita, and even a cursory study of the various commentaries reveals how open to diverse interpretations much of the Gita is, and how much difference of opinion exists as to its true meaning. But the variety of commentaries that the Gita has attracted, only further elevates its stature as a true spiritual classic. This is because of its broad teachings, which have influenced many philosophical schools and religious sects, and its personal appeal of practical spiritual advice, which crosses the parameters of political boundaries, socio-religious customs, and centuries of time. The Gita passages are charged with special power, since they are the words of the Lord Himself. Therefore spiritual aspirants through the ages have been inspired to memorize Sri Krishna's teachings and thereby soak and strengthen their minds with the revelations of God incarnate. There is no end to the creative force of a powerful idea. By holding a Gita imperative in the mind, an indelible impression is made on the unconscious, which in turn creates an atmosphere of success in the aspirant's spiritual life. How many people have been comforted by Gita passages like, "Arjuna, know it for certain, My devotee never perishes." It works like a tonic to a despondent soul.

In day to day life, we strive for clarity of mind, since that is when the thinking faculty is at its best. The Gita tells us, "Fight, being free from mental fever." (7.30) Sri Krishna gives order and balance in his method, so that the aspirant need not plunge into spiritual life in a haphazard way: *"Yogah karmasu kausalam."* (2.50) and *"Samatvam yoga ucyate."* (2.48):

"Being steadfast in yoga, O Dhananjaya, perform actions, abandoning attainment, remaining unconcerned as regards success and failure. This evenness of mind is known as yoga."

This verse gives three requirements for perfect work. First, perform work as yoga; second, don't choose the nature of your work; and third, don't be anxious for the result. If we develop the habit of liking our work, discontent will melt away, and our lives will be sweeter.

As a spiritual aspirant strives for the goal of God realization, he realizes the importance of strengthening character. Jealousy is a great weakness and obstacle to spiritual life. How can one overcome a trait so ingrained in human nature? Sri Krishna gives us a philosophy that enables us to transcend our pettiness:

"Whatever being there is great, prosperous or powerful, know that to be a product of a part of my splendor". (10.41)

Practically applied, the Gita imperatives have immense personal value. They have the power to elevate and broaden our narrow, finite ego-consciousness into the grandeur of our true nature which is one with the Universal Consciousness.

There is a traditional belief that the Gita represents a summary of the essential teachings of the Upanishads, or that it functions as a commentary on the Upanishads. This idea is explicitly stated in the introduction to Sankara's Gita commentary, where he calls the Gita "a summary of the essential ideas of all the Vedas." We also find this belief embodied in a famous verse found in the *"Gita-dhyana,"* or "Meditation on the Gita." This verse compares the Upanishads to a herd of cows. Krishna is the milker of the cows; Arjuna is the calf; and the Gita is the milk. The affinity of the Gita to the Upanishads is also seen in the number of the verses from the Gita that seem to quote, or at least echo, certain Upanishads, notably the *Katha, Mundaka, Isa,* and *Svetasvatara.* One can easily imagine Yama uttering the very words to Nachiketa in the Katha Upanishad that Krishna does to Arjuna in chapter 2 (11-30) of the Gita on the immortality of the Self. Furthermore, as if to emphasize the Gita's Upanishadic nature, we find the Gita referring to itself as an Upanishad in the colophon at the end of each chapter.

The Gita stresses the philosophy of detached and dedicated action as well as a harmony of all the yogas in

one's approach to spiritual life. Sri Krishna's battle cry
to Arjuna to conquer his enemies and regain his rightful
kingdom is symbolic of the dominant theme of the Gita:
to perform one's duties on the battlefield of the world,
free from attachment to the fruits, and to thereby attain
the highest goal of life. Taken literally, Sri Krishna's
emphasis on action can be interpreted as a necessity of
historical circumstance, namely, Arjuna's need to go to war.
However, in an allegorical sense, Kurukshetra symbolizes
the battlefield of the mind, where passions must be
conquered before one can attain Selfhood. Consequently,
the duties we are exhorted to perform are understood to be
a blend of spiritual practices - not only *karma yoga* (selfless
action), but also *raja yoga* (meditation and *japa*), *jnana yoga*
(discrimination and dispassion), and *bhakti yoga* (devotion
to the Chosen Ideal).

However, the teaching of karma yoga is thought by many
to be Sri Krishna's special message and the very heart of
the Gita's teachings; and the Kurukshetra battlefield on the
eve of battle is the most appropriate time and place for him
to deliver that message.

The emphasis on karma yoga represents a departure
from the Upanishadic preference for the path of knowledge
or discrimination. It is true that we often find Janaka and
other royal figures in the Upanishads, teaching the highest
truths while at the same time ruling over kingdoms, but
for the most part there is very little emphasis on action or
the performance of duties. Perhaps the reason is that the
Upanishads were geared specifically to those already free

from social obligations - the forest-dwellers and hermits - while the epics and the Puranas were intended for society at large. Still, this distinction cannot solely explain Sri Krishna's persistent return to the theme of karma yoga which, as taught in the Gita, is relevant to the householder as well as the monastic.

The Gita's presentation of the secret of work does not discard earlier Upanishadic teachings. Rather a rigorous attempt is made to revitalize concepts from their old, and sometimes petrified forms into fuller meanings, more suited to the needs of the times. Terms are redefined and old distinctions are challenged. We find such questions asked as, "Who is the true sannyasin?" "What are action and inaction?" "Is there any real distinction between the paths of action and knowledge?" etc. The answers given in the Gita are in all cases perfectly consistent with the spirit of the Upanishads, though often at variance with traditional interpretations. For example, Sri Krishna maintains throughout the Gita that the "true" renunciate is one who understands the real meaning of renunciation, namely the renunciation of the lower self, the ego with its desires, attachments and aversions. Thus he terms the real sannyasin as one "who neither hates nor desires," (5.13) "Who performs his duties without attachment, not he who merely gives up his obligatory rites and the keeping of the sacred fire." (6.1) The Upanishads take for granted the fact that one should have this understanding before renouncing the world. However, they do not go so far as to say that a householder with such a frame of mind is more deserving of the title "sannyasin" than the hermit without such an understanding. Sri Krishna further explains (4.18) that what appears to be action or the renunciation of action from the ordinary point of view may, in fact, be its opposite. Thus the sannyasin who secretly feels in his heart that he is the doer while performing austerities, will only create further karma for himself even though he appears to be actionless in meditation; while the person who knows himself to be an instrument, free from the sense of "I" and "mine," though hard at work in the middle of a busy marketplace, will experience the same tranquility as if he were in a secluded forest. It is the second person who is truly "actionless" because he is without any feeling of agency.

All this does not imply that the Gita has any bias against renunciation - only against a hypocritical renunciation (3.6) brought about as a result of an aversion to duty, as was the case with Arjuna. Sri Krishna concedes that "one who delights in the Self alone has no more duties to perform" (3.17) and that "for one who has reached the state of yoga, quietude or abstinence from action is the proper path." (6.3) And yet, Sri Krishna reminds us that even the genuine renunciate must perform some action, if only to maintain his body (3.8) and thus must also practice karma yoga.

Another example of the Gita's technique of reinterpretation is the concept of *yajna* or sacrifice. One of the characteristics of the Upanishads is a distinct antipathy towards the extreme ritualism of the Vedic period, where elaborate sacrifices were performed for the attainment of such desires as heaven, progeny, cattle, etc. The Gita, without endorsing rituals for the fulfillment of desires *(kamya-karma)* nevertheless utilizes the concept of yajna as standing for sacrifice in the larger sense, and builds an entire ethical framework around it. In chapter 3 (9-16) and chapter 4 (23-33), we find that virtually any action can be transformed into yajna if it is done in the spirit of sacrifice, or as an offering to God. Furthermore, Sri Krishna explains that every action we perform, including inhalation and exhalation, is to be performed as yajna. With this revitalized understanding, even the old Vedic rituals can be performed without an eye on the results, but with a desire for the social and cosmic good. (3.11-12) Sri Krishna gives the final word on yajna when he claims that by seeing all elements of the act of offering (including the offerer himself) as nothing but Brahman, he attains Brahman.

While the Gita no doubt embodies many distinctly Upanishadic teachings, we also find a realistic strain, probably the result of the comingling of the Sankhya teachings with those of the Upanishads. One of the most important teachings of the Gita is bhakti yoga, the path of devotion to a personal God. This heralds the very beginnings of the theory of the divine incarnation, or avatara, which we find elaborated upon in the Puranas. What results is a philosophy of harmony, in which varieties of paths and attitudes are all recommended for leading to the highest goal. However, if we must look for one unifying element in all these diverse paths, it would be the insistence on selfless action, karma yoga - whether performed out of a sense of duty, for purification of the mind, as an offering to the Lord, or based on the Vedantic teachings regarding the Self.

The spirit of acceptance and liberality, the many-sidedness of its teachings, and the urgency of its message delivered on the battlefield, have given the Gita a timeless and universal relevance not often found in religious scriptures. Its distinctly democratic air, its emphasis on same-sightedness and equality make it especially suited to the present age.

The Gita has long been a source of inspiration for both householders and monastics, for world-movers such as Swami Vivekananda and Mahatma Gandhi, for unknown hermits and simple villagers, faithfully performing their duties. And it seems certain that its timeless message of hope and practical spirituality will continue to inspire future spiritual aspirants of all faiths.

PART III
Chapter 7

SPIRITUAL DISCIPLINE

All achievements are made through disciplines. When discussing spiritual discipline, sometimes the word spiritual *practice* is used, because modern man has distaste for the word discipline. Discipline implies a little compulsion; a methodology is followed day after day with a particular doggedness. We learn certain things, pass through rigorous practice for some time, and become adept. Spiritual practice is whatever you do with the idea of pleasing the Lord. But when the word discipline is used, it implies a conscious, methodical, purposeful reaching for a goal, using a particular method.

For example, if you think of God while sitting like a yogi, in a particular posture, at a particular time, with particular preparation, and you do it regularly, methodically, it will be called a discipline. But when you are doing garden work, or you are walking, or cooking, and in between you think of God, that may also be called a spiritual practice.

There is a mystic tradition in every religion, which, as it were, jumps into realization. Mystics may not always follow normal methods, but intense desire, intense love for God somehow or other arises in them, and that gives them various types of spiritual experiences. In Vedanta it is recognized that if you want to achieve anything, strong desire is necessary. Mumuksha it is called-strong desire for liberation. When do you want to be liberated? When you feel that you are bound by the senses, bound by the world, bound by various things in life. When you feel the bondage, then only do you want to get out of it. If you don't feel the bondage, there is no question of getting out of it. So Mumuksha, desire for liberation, comes to a person who feels that he is bound in every direction.

There are various theories of how religion originated. Some say it comes from man's sense of wonder, some say it is one's underlying nature that causes it, or a sort of a fear But Swami Vivekananda said that the origin of religion is the desire of man to transcend the limitations of the senses. I cannot see far, so I use scientific instruments to see far off. I cannot hear far, so science develops various instruments to enable me to hear more. This is more or less at the sense level. But religion of the unknown, of the beyond, comes in when I feel that I am bound by my senses. So trying to transcend the limitations of the senses is an important idea. Vedanta says transcendence occurs stage by stage. Every religion has some method for transcending thought, but Vedanta codifies it, systematizes it.

Every religion has got four aspects. One is a philosophy. That is the core of a religion. Another is a body of rituals by the help of which you try to retain the ideas. Rituals have been described as concretized philosophy. Philosophy when put into practice, and in a more complete form-that will be ritual. Then, a body of mythology, with tales of saints and sages, and the deities and others who give a sort of support for the spiritual ideas that we uphold. There is also a body of conduct-how to behave in life, a body of moral principles. Most of the religions have a book also. All religions which originated later have a book for their propagation.

The body of practices may include forms of conduct for social needs, or rituals for bringing in the feeling. For example, a mother loves her child, so naturally she goes on slaving for the child, feeding the child, and not merely saying, "I love you." She must work for the child also. So ritual is a way in which we give our feelings a sort of a physical expression or external expression. After some time these expressions become systematic, methodical, and often traditional. Say, for example, saluting or shaking hands. In India we pranam. Here, you shake hands. In some places they show the tongue. These are all customs. A new custom is gradually systematized and it becomes normal. All disciplines start like a discipline but they become a part of one's nature. For example, if everyday you had to think about how to dress, how much time would be wasted? So after some time you get used to dressing and then do it in a mechanical way. First you learn how to do it, but once you have learned, you do it more or less without thinking.

When I first came to this country, I heard that a Swami had once commented that after 20 years he knew which tie went with what type of suit. I then decided that I was not going to try to learn this, because I did not have twenty years of previous time here. Of course I had ladies around me - secretaries and so forth - and I would tell them, "Don't buy me anything which doesn't match, so that I need not think too much - and don't give me alternatives." That would involve too much thinking. Now much comes at the habit level, otherwise so much time would be wasted. It is so with everything in which you acquire efficiency; so much energy has gone behind in practicing it.

So Discipline leads to the formation of habit. Of course in this case the discipline is for a purpose, a spiritual goal, but discipline is useful, is necessary, in every walk of life. Swami Vivekananda used to say that Character is repeated habits? Daily you behave in a certain way; that is how your character is formed. If you are a nice person that means today you are nice, tomorrow nice, and the day after tomorrow also nice. If today you are nice, tomorrow violent, and the day after tomorrow angry, you will not be called a nice person. This means it is a question of day to day practice. Unconsciously you react to certain situations.

Sometimes a distinction is made. What is moral or ethical action? The moral philosophers said that every decision must have a conflict. This is right, this is wrong. This is good, this is bad, and I choose the right, the good. Their point is that unless there is a conflict involved, one's action it is not a moral action, it is instinctive. But, some thinkers argued the other way-that discipline is a method of conscious action, it is not instinctive. When a discipline is consciously followed it becomes a habit, and then one's actions *look* instinctive. But they are the result of an ideal, and previous practice.

For spiritual realization, some disciplines are spoken of, but they all have ramifications in other areas of life. All religious principles have got three dimensions. One is the usefulness for the person, for his day to day life. Second is the social benefit or social consideration. And third is the usefulness for higher spiritual realization. Spiritual realization in the sense of realizing God can wait. But our day to day problems we shall have to face. So all this discipline will be useful in daily life also.

Now when you turn to spiritual life, right and left you hear the teachers saying that you must meditate, you must think of God. To think, I must know what to think about. There is a technique of thinking; the source book which describes this technique, of getting the mastery of the mind, is Patanjali's *Yoga Sutra*. There are hundreds of varieties of meditation now, but that is the source book. Of course, man consciously or unconsciously learns some type of concentration. When you are a child, you learn one type, then as you grow up, the span of attention increases, the capacity for concentration increases, and then you achieve many things in life. Meditation means trying to think of a thing for some time, but that involves two practices: to withdraw the mind, and to focus it. Our minds are roaming about in many things. If you try to sit quietly then you will see how the mind jumps from thing to thing. When you are able to collect a certain amount of energy, and focus the mind at a particular point, it acquires tremendous strength. An analogy is a convex lens. When a certain measure of solar light is collected together and passes through a focal point, it becomes so powerful that it can burn paper. So this is the idea of concentration. A devotee of God develops concentration so that he can think of God without disturbance.

What creates disturbance? First, man has a body. The body doesn't like to sit in one posture too long. Aches are there, pains are there, even if you are young. When you are old, of course, that is part of your life. So first the body must be trained, so that you are able to sit for some time without moving. Second is the mind. These two things are working in a person. We must learn how to control the mind to keep it in one place. Postures, and quieting of the mind are the preliminaries for meditation. Yoga books speak about moral preparation, physical preparation, and then a little posture, so that in one posture you can sit straight. Swami Vivekananda says you should meditate with your spinal column straight, chest forward. Chest slumping is a moody pose. Sri Ramakrishna used to scold young people for stooping. When you have become old, if you have no more strength, what can you do? Then probably instead of being a raja yogi you will have to become a bhakti yogi. "O Lord, I have no more capacity. I shall lie down and meditate, walk and meditate, whatever I can do." Nobody loses the chance; scope is there for everyone. So first is the physical discipline.

Another thing often recommended in the yogic system is breath control. It can cure many diseases, and wrongly done it may bring diseases also. Unless you know the remedies, it is not too safe to do for more than, say, 10 minutes. For those who do it for a longer time, regular watching is necessary. But up to ten minutes is easy; there is no risk. It is like diving. In diving, you hold your breath. That is not going to do any harm unless it is done for too long a time. The yogis have prescribed deep breathing. Modern doctors have started advising deep breathing nowadays. And by rhythmic breathing, if you can do it, the mind will become calm. If you observe your breathing when you are very calm and serene, you will find that your breathing has become slow and rhythmic. So the yogis said, reverse the process. If you reverse the process and *make* your breath slow and rhythmic, concentration will come.

The third stage is actual meditation. (I am not counting *yama* and *niyama* - physical cleanliness and mental cleanliness - they are of course the first things). Actual meditation has got two parts: withdrawing and collecting the mind, and focusing - *Pratyahara* and *dharana* - gathering and fixing. This becomes easier if you focus the mind on something. By fixing, your mind acquires special power. If you are able to hold the mind in one thought for some time it is called *dharana*. So when we say, "I am meditating," we are really trying to bring the mind in. But loosely speaking, it is meditation, withdrawing the mind from surroundings. The practices that help in doing it are control of the posture, and the effort to focus the mind every day. If you practice irregularly, the result will be irregular. You see, if you eat every day at the same time, when that time comes you will feel hungry. Even if you have eaten one hour earlier false hunger will come. That is the benefit of regularity of habits. You must practice regularly. Swami

Vivekananda recommends that you train yourself up-of course, it is best if it is done from childhood. When you were a child, too much conscious effort was not there-your parents wanted you to do something, so you did it. But when you are already grown up, then you will have to be convinced about it, that it is good to do it, and every day do it methodically.

Thousands of people know that exercise is very good for health. But how many people do it? It is because there is no regularity of habits. Unless you are very fanatical about your health, you don't pursue it, but everybody knows it is good. Swamiji says, 'Compel yourself to meditate, and don't rely on an outside agency. Don't eat without first practicing meditation' and says that sheer hunger will drive off your laziness. Half the time we are lazy. Some days you have the mood and you are ready to meditate for three hours, and some days no mood; you don't want to sit. So you must bind yourself with a regular discipline.

The advantage of a habit is that your moods are controlled. We always pass through moods. Good moods are enjoyable, no discipline is necessary. But when a bad mood comes, how to get out of it? Worrying, grieving, feeling sorry for oneself - all these things are moods. Sometime a mood is there, sometimes it is not there. So by practice I want to control the moods so that they don't last for too long a time. Those who live an active life should try to withdraw themselves every three hours. You must find a way to do it, even in your office. Whether you go inside the bathroom, or open a book, the main purpose is meditation. If society accepts it, you can suddenly close your eyes and do these things, if it doesn't look too odd. But every two or three hours, withdraw yourself from your surroundings, especially if you live a very hectic life, a busy life. The nerves will be soothed, the mind will be clearer, thinking will be clearer, and as a result the moods will be controlled. If some day you have got moods, that is the time for taking a bath, or for thinking of God or reading some book. The moods are controlled that way. A mother may have moods, but she cannot remain in an eccentric mood too long. The children are there and they will be pestering her. In half an hour or an hour she will have to conquer the mood and go ahead. That is the advantage of regularity of habits, and of spiritual habits definitely.

We attend lectures and read books, argue and reason about God and soul, religion and salvation. These are not spirituality, because spirituality does not exist in books or in theories or in philosophies. It is not in learning or reasoning, but in actual inner growth. Even parrots can learn things by heart and repeat them. If you become learned, what of it? Asses can carry whole libraries. So when real light will come, there will be no more of this learning from books - no book-learning. The man who cannot write even his own name can be perfectly religious, and the man with all the libraries of the world in his head may fail to be. Learning is not a condition of spiritual growth; scholarship is not a condition. The touch of the guru, the transmittal of spiritual energy, will quicken your heart. Then will begin the growth. That is the real baptism by fire.

Swami Vivekananda

So this is the first part. Now when you practice meditation, you have to decide on what to meditate. I am to fix my mind on something. A personalized aspect of God is presented. A holy name is repeated, but this is often translated as a holy *formula*. Why? Because monistic Vedantins often don't take recourse to a personalized God, so they think about a principle, or an idea. Some Buddhists and Advaita Vedantins do that type of meditation, but they also repeat some word, such as Om. This repetition is called japam, or japa. Round and round you repeat it. Why? Because the mind's tendency is to go away. You try to pull it in, and it goes away, and again you pull it in. So a picture, a photo, or an image of a holy man or a deity may be given. You fix your mind on this, and meditation becomes easier. That's why it is said that God becomes avatar, human, so that people can relate to him, to his form. To think of the divine form or an incarnation of God, is one type of meditation. You try to focus your mind on this visualization - the Lord sitting in your heart, or sitting in front of you. It becomes easier if you repeat the name. Say a mother has a son called Peter. Whenever the word Peter is pronounced, she remembers her son. Similarly, when a devotee says God, God, Rama, Rama, he remembers Rama. This repetition, japa, is a reminder of the person behind the name.

So if I want to meditate on God, God has an expression in the sense of an avatar, a humanized God, or a deity type of God, I repeat a formula, divine name, called a mantra. It is believed that God's name has got special power. Mantras can be picked up from books; nowadays everything is available in books, and if you repeat the mantra some result will be there. Japa means repetition of the mantra, or the divine name. But the mantra becomes more powerful if it comes through a holy man or another devotee who himself practices. It acquires still more power if it comes from a succession of teachers. The person who gives the mantra is called a guru. So there are five items involved in meditation. First, meditation proper, that is, intense thinking and visualizing. To help it, you have a mantra, which you repeat, japa. The mantra is given by a guru, and he gives the mantra of a deity or an avatar. These five items-dhyana, mantra, japa, guru, and avatar, are necessary.

Sri Ramakrishna used to say that of all the spiritual practices, the two most important and easy methods are dhyana and japa, because they don't require external things. Puja, worship, is done in shrines, or you can keep a picture in your room. Salute, meditate, think. Whenever you see the picture you are reminded of God; that also is very good. Then, religious groups have got pilgrimage, fasting, charity-these are all different methods of spiritual practice; they are also very useful. For day to day practice what are you going to do? Spiritual practice should be done every day, normally a minimum of twice a day. At one time it was four times a day, at all the junctions of the day, then it became three times a day. But nowadays, lunchtime also is uncertain. So the minimum times insisted upon are morning and evening. When day changes into night, and night changes into day, a natural change is there, and the mind often becomes reflective. And people throughout the world who are a little religious think of God at these times. This creates a special type of vibration. There is a vibration theory. Every time you have thought something, it has left an impression on the atmosphere. So if you are trying to be good, all the good thoughts will come to you. If you are trying to be bad, all the bad thoughts will come to you. That is why holy association is very much stressed. We must move in a holy place. That is how shrines come up. Vivekananda recommended in Protestant America in the 1890s, reserving a corner of your room, of your house, or a separate room, where you can think only of God and nothing else. Go and unburden yourself when you are sorrowful, thank the Lord when you are happy, or just simply meditate and think of Him. All the time the emotions need not be mixed in; just calmly sit. His theory was, in three months the place will acquire such a vibration that whenever you go there you will feel uplifted. Some people keep a picture of a holy man or the Ishta, the chosen deity, or an avatar, - Ramakrishna, or Jesus, or Buddha. Whenever you look at the picture you are reminded of God.

At one time we had a swami in Philadelphia, Swami Yatiswarananda. Before going there he had been in Holland. And he was instructing people to do japam. One mantra he gave, a short mantra normally. It is not a prayer; a prayer is a prolonged thing. Japa is a short thing. So somebody said, "Swami, it is a little boring, repeating the same thing round and round." But he gave a very ingenious answer: How many times every day do you think that you are the body? Every time you groan because of this pain, or that pain, or every time you beautify yourself, that means you think you are the body. That many times you will have to think that you are the Spirit; many thousands of times you will have to repeat the mantra. The idea is that you have to remind yourself that you are not the body, not the mind, but the Spirit. That is the Vedantic conclusion. The Vedantins will give argument after argument to try to convince you that you are really not the body. The body dies after 100 years. You are not really the mind, because the mind is changing. But there is a Reality behind you, which is the spiritual self of man, Atman it is called. And at times you vaguely feel that life is not finished with this body, that there must be something behind, something beyond. Religion especially speaks of that idea.

Now for day to day practice, all of this should be done. All these five items are one integrated method called dhyana. Every day you must sit quietly, twice a day minimum. If you are too busy at one time you will have to sit more at another time. And if you love it, do more. Sometimes people say, "How long should I sit?" It depends upon your hunger. In the beginning, you discipline yourself, even if you don't like it. But you should not force yourself for too long. Holy Mother says that real japa comes when the mind gets concentrated and quiet. Then shall I wait till the mind gets quiet? The analogy is given of waiting till the waves of the ocean stop before taking a bath. They shall never stop. Both things will go on in the beginning. So every day methodically sit, think of a form of God, think of his qualities, repeat his name, and try to hold the thought as long as possible, with concentration.

Now at the day to day level it must come to the point where you don't get up from bed without repeating the name of God; you do it automatically. Many people have this habit. Think of God first and then get up. If life is too busy as soon as you get up, if you are swallowed by the chores of life, then practice, sitting on the bed itself. Or get up in the early morning and practice, before the other members of the family get up, and then begin the day. The best thing, of course, would be for all the people to do it. They need not be too religious; it is more or less getting a grip over the mind, getting mental quiet. Just to stop the mind from running about is a form of relaxation. Sitting gives physical stamina also. But these are all side effects.

Sri Ramakrishna used to say, "Come and go." I was in Madras at one time as a novice, a brahmachari. The head of the center was a disciple of Mahapurush Maharaj, Swami Shivananda, whom he used to quote. Swami Shivananda used to say that for normal, average people, "Coming and going will do." That means come and go to the center, to the ashram, to the holy place, or to the sadhus, to those who are trying to live the life. Then later I found that Swami Akhandananda said that Sri Ramakrishna himself used to say that. That means by going to a holy place you are reminded of God. So everyday, along with your meditation, you should read something which will remind you of God. Gradually it comes to the habit level; instinctively you do it. When the urge becomes very strong, you will do more. But you must hold on to the minimum. So daily Swami Virajananda often recommend one page of holy reading-reading of spiritual literature, of a "conversations" type of book, as if you are talking to a saint, like the *Gospel of Ramakrishna, Gospel of Holy Mother,* talks of Brahmananda, Shivananda and others in our circle. The *Gita* and others are there, but they are more philosophical. Even Vivekananda is more philosophical. So this is the method; those who are not serious should just do it, those who are serious should read a little extra - the philosophical part. In your daily reading, suddenly you may find, "Oh, this answer is very good, suitable for me." Everything in the scripture you are not to follow. Take whatever appeals to you, whatever applies in your case. That is how spiritual life is built up; it becomes natural. Life becomes enjoyable.

Coming and going, keeping up the habit, and holding on to the thought of God is the method. The immediate result of meditation will be some calmness, some serenity. The test of progress in meditation is that you enjoy doing it. In the beginning every discipline is unpalatable. But after some time you like it, like exercise. It is not very palatable. What is exercise? Giving pain to the body. But you know that if you give pain to the body every day for half an hour you shall have good health for another 30, 40, 50 years. That's why it must be started early in life. Often people say, oh, you are too young to be religious now. That means when you are old and can do nothing else, all right, then become religious. Even that is not bad of course, if some awareness is there that there is a higher purpose of life, a higher goal of life. I remember in the 50s, in *Reader's Digest,* people from all walks of life were asked a question: The world is going to end in 15 minutes. What are you going to do? From ministers down to prisoners, all were asked that question. And they all replied, "We shall kneel down and pray." Of course if they were given 15 years I don't know what they would have done. But for 15 minutes everybody knows life has no other meaning.

So instead of going into varieties of disciplines, I have only taken up one discipline, meditation, which has five disciplines inside it. Posture and other things I am not including, but they are also disciplines. When you think about practicing meditation, you convince yourself that it is good, then you will do it. Otherwise you won't do it. You may do it at first out of enthusiasm for two or three months, and then give it up. Millions of people nowadays try to meditate, because they have heard meditation is wonderful. But because they are not convinced, or because of wayward habits, in three months most of them give it up. Many of us, because of our jobs, do some type of concentrated work, or concentrated study. But the rest of the life is disorganized and filled with desultory habits. We take a book, we read a little, but there is no definite goal. Some part of our lives should be methodical-that is what I am advocating. Learn to master yourself, your moods, your tendencies, your sense organs, by daily practice. The common practice, instead of varieties and tidbits of practice, should be trying to think of God for some time. Discipline gives you some benefit. And devotees believe that God also gives something. The question comes whether God will be partial to me. I am joining his party; he should favor me a little extra. All the devotees of the world feel that they are the chosen people. If I join

God's group, he should look after me. How to save God
from the charge of partiality? Sri Ramakrishna gives an
analogy which explains it. The wind of grace is blowing for
everybody, but one who unfurls his sails will get the benefit;
others will not get it. It will look as if that person is being
favored, but his cooperation is necessary. So if you want to
get any result, any answer from God, or results from your
practices, you must do them willingly. Practice which is
forced or done unwillingly is not very useful.

So this is the prescription. Understand it; try to convince
yourself it is good, and most important, do it. Once you do
it, even without conviction, after some time, gradually you
will get the benefit. And then you will like to do it more
and more. That is the method of developing good habits,
and developing devotion to God. Ultimately that devotion
turns into love of God when you don't expect anything but
the fulfillment of life. That is the goal of life. So we should
all try to meditate. Meditation is an important part of life;
do it every day for some time.

PART III
Chapter 8

SPIRITUAL TRAINING OF THE MIND

Control is necessary. That is the training of all the religions of the world. The mind has to be controlled. The yogis argue that the more mastery you have over yourself, over the vagaries of your own mind, the better you are placed for enjoying even this normal world - even if you don't have any spiritual hankering. Of course, without a little spiritual hankering, it will be difficult to control the mind. If all the time you pursue your desires, to bring the mind to a quiet position is difficult. That is why the mastery of the mind is necessary, for gaining enjoyable experiences from the world, and also the later spiritual experience which is the ultimate goal of life. Many of our problems arise because of a sense of boredom, monotony, pressure, unfulfilled desires. These are some of the basic causes why the mind is often thrown off its balance, even if there is no major external situation, which can be there, but temporary in effect. You are going along the road, somebody comes and insults you, and you become very agitated, become angry. But that is a temporary experience - you recover soon. But if you are a very touchy man, it may take a longer time to recover. There are many people, especially introverts, who go on suffering within. Extroverts are in that way better. For a few minutes they react and then regain the balance. Children are good in that respect. They become upset very easily, but they are also pacified very easily. They don't have the after-effects of the painful experience that they passed through.

A change of attitude is necessary to get a grip over the mind. If the attitude is changed, you get better results. You become angry. Then a friend of his comes up, and indicates that the man is not all right emotionally. Immediately you cool down. That man may go on reviling you, but the moment you know that this is not a normal man, your anger vanishes - you feel pity for him. That effect has happened by your change of attitude.

Suffering cannot be avoided, painful experiences cannot be avoided - even a Buddha can be scolded. Even a Socrates can have enemies. Even if you are a sage, there may be revilers. In an objective situation you cannot expect that there will be no bad experiences in life. So the minimal thing a man has to learn is how not to be too much affected by these experiences. In normal life, any average man will be affected a little. But we are trying to go above the average. We must have a technique available by which we can learn to recover from these experiences as quickly as possible. Ideally speaking, we should be able not to react at all, to possess inner calmness. Now many people say that if you do this you will become inert. Somebody comes and scolds you, or gives you a blow, and you don't do anything. The religious training is there: if you are slapped on one cheek, you are to give the other cheek. Normal people feel that it is too much. True, it is too much. But if you feel that you have to fight for something, fight for it. The yogis have no objection. The *Gita* had no objection - go and fight. If the objective situation requires that you must be angry, that you must fight, then go and fight. But why should you be *internally* angry? You are to control an objective situation, which requires a little harshness, a little firmness, but internally why should you get upset? You know it is the external situation which demands this behavior. You do it as a witness, as an onlooker. Deal with the situation without getting emotionally involved. That is the ideal state - to react without getting emotionally upset. Of course, the modern explanation is there, the physiological explanation: if you get upset, your blood pressure will shoot up, your heart beat will increase; then you will have to go back to your medicines, or to the modern method of meditation - quieting the nerves, creating the alpha waves and all that. But if you have a grip over yourself then none of the bad effects will come. The mind will remain calm, and at the same time you can work.

Swami Brahmananda, a disciple of Sri Ramakrishna, used to say that even activities which require much effort can be done with 25% of our energies. Most of us spend much of our energy in fretting and fuming. To make decisions we take days and days. When we work we have our worries and anxieties. The actual effort that we give for a purpose is very little. Thinking about pros and cons is all right, but uselessly we waste away much of our energy.

So a calm man, once he decides something, can quietly do it without losing his mental poise and balance. And the more poise he has, the better will be his work. A man who is not agitated, a man who is not thrown off his balance easily, and keeps his mind clear, can do a thing more easily. At the same time he is not mentally affected. Many people

feel that unless they have got some special zeal, or special
love for their work, how can they have energy to do the
work? Our work will not be good if we are not dedicated
to our work with great zeal. Swami Vivekananda said that
he also used to think like that when he was young, that
without great excitement and zeal we cannot do things.
But how can we utilize our zeal often when we waste the
major portion of our zeal in unnecessary things? A directed
zeal will produce a much better result. Then he said that
as the days went by, he learned this lesson: that the calmer
a man is, the more turnout there will be of his efforts. A
determined, calm kind of work will come, because he is not
agitated by situations. We are not talking here about detail
work, but there also, lack of planning and other factors can
lead to a waste of time.

For this type of mind, which can control the vagaries
of the moods, which can keep one in a very controlled,
peaceful condition, some practice is necessary. This explains
why the idea of meditation is so popular. Most of the
Indian children, from early age, are given one training,
called *Gayatri japa*. The *Gayatri mantra* is given to them
for recitation, along with certain rituals to do. The mantra
means: "May my intelligence be directed towards the
Good." Which man will object to that type of training?
It is not a doctrinaire method of training. It is the basic
training for making the mind purer, along with sitting
quietly and calmly daily, and trying to think that thought.
Now if a boy learns from his early days how to sit quietly,
compared to a man who has never controlled himself, he
will be much better placed. A certain grip over himself

will automatically come. And that is how a character is formed, by daily practice.

What is character? If a man is good today, and the next day he is bad, he is not a good man. If he is good most of the time, he is a good man. Or if we say he is a very sweet man, then he is sweet most of the time. If most of the time he has an outburst, or even every now and then, we don't call him a sweet man. Swami Vivekananda said that character is known by the continued expression of our behavior. Character is formed by repeated habits. An action is ethical when you opt for the right course. Instinctive behavior doesn't involve moral struggle. All the spiritual teachers have stressed the idea that when a man has progressed spiritually, these troubles fade away. The conscious moral struggle at every turn is the preliminary stage. Then a stage comes when he instinctively behaves in the right way. Somebody comes and asks him something, and a truthful man instinctively replies truthfully. He is not face to face with the problem of whether he ought to tell the truth or not tell the truth. He naturally does it. As they often say that instinctive goodness is there in people who live with nature. And that is why it is said that people in the farmlands are simpler. So all the humane qualities are more germane to the people in agricultural societies compared with people in industrialized societies.

Life will bring varieties of experience - good and bad, pleasant and unpleasant. We want to avoid the unpleasant and the bad experiences. The good and the pleasant experiences don't require any philosophy or training. You just enjoy them. But a bad experience we don't want. Then we can change the external situation, that is best, but it is not easy. The best thing to do is to strengthen the mind itself. By this process external situations cannot throw us off our balance.

Training of the mind is necessary. With what attitude do you take the painful experiences in life? The devotees try to believe that God has given them this suffering. For them, God does everything, good and bad. They say, "God has given me this suffering to test me, to strengthen me." Or, they think, "Better days will be coming later." The devotee tries to put his trust in God, and accept that the experience was necessary for him.

For every bad situation you later find some explanation, some good side. It ceases to be a suffering in comparison with a greater suffering. The spiritual attitude is to find a meaning for every suffering. The moment you have found *some* explanation, some meaning, that suffering becomes less.

Take the example of a person behaving wrongly. You feel uncomfortable, but you analyze his situation. Probably he has got some trouble, physical trouble, or trouble with his family. Immediately you become sympathetic, and know that the way he is behaving is really not his nature, but because of external conditions. You become more sympathetic. As a result, your suffering also lessens. These are varieties of the mental technique in life situations. But the main purpose of the whole training of the mind is to take the person, stage by stage, towards higher realization. For increasing the happiness in the world, there are so many agencies. Religions need not be a particular agency for *that*. Religion's special field is to show man the way towards higher realization, which will give an enduring meaning to his life. Once you have got control over your mind, you can then go into the deeper experiences. But for bringing in that control, and for peace of mind, in which real meditation is possible, practice this: by controlling the vagaries of the moods - by developing certain attitudes, by developing certain techniques of concentration and one-pointedness. And then, if you have a final metaphysical conviction, the best results will be achieved, which will pave the way for your highest realization.

A conviction about the real nature of man, the attempt to find meaning in all experience, the development of certain attitudes, control of the moods, and giving direction to the moods are ways in which to face the problems of the mind. This way, in the earlier stage, we acquire efficiency. A fund of energy is there, and a desire must be there to do a certain thing, a strong will to pursue it and that strong will ought to be a *good* will for the good of society. Along with that, if the spiritual awareness of the divine nature of man is there, he is a well-rounded, practical, efficient, spiritual man. That is the ideal type of person often referred to by Swami Vivekananda.

PART III
Chapter 9

BE AN INSTRUMENT OF GOD

Man is too afraid to surrender. He thinks he will lose something, but one never loses when he gives himself absolutely to God. Only when he is guided by God does he cease to blunder; because God then works through his hands, sees through his eyes, speaks with his tongue - and he becomes a perfect instrument in the hand of God. He is directed by God in everything. - Swami Ramakrishnananda

Throughout the centuries it has been taken for granted by men of spiritual experience that life has a goal, and that goal, according to these religious teachers, is to realize God, or to realize one's own perfect nature. To achieve this goal, four major methods have been given, which are called the yogas -the paths of realization.

Each of these four yogas deals with one of the four aspects of human nature. Man has three faculties - thinking, feeling and willing, and the condition that arises when these three are in abeyance, not functioning actively, is considered to be the fourth state - the *yogic* condition. So these are the four possible states of the mind: the mind *thinking,* the mind *feeling,* the mind *willing,* and the mind in its *quiescent* form. Based on this view, there are four possible yogas: *jnana yoga, bhakti yoga, karma yoga,* and *raja yoga,* respectively. So in one sense, anything that connects you, joins you, to the Lord, to the Ultimate Reality, could be considered yoga.

The first chapter of the *Bhagavad Gita* is entitled "Vishada Yoga", "The Yoga of Dejection." How can dejection be yoga? Dejection pushed Arjuna into a search for the higher reality and into surrender to the Lord. The *Gita* tells the story of the Kurukshetra War, in which two opposing parties were standing against each other to fight. Arjuna was a commanding general of one side, but on the other side were his own relatives and friends. So he was very much taken aback about what to do. Krishna was Arjuna's charioteer, so Arjuna asked him, "I am getting confused. What shall I do?" Then Arjuna continued, "O Lord, I am your disciple. I take refuge in you. Please guide me." In response, Krishna gave the whole teaching of the *Bhagavad Gita*.

The idea here is that anything that pushes a man towards, first, a deeper search, and then, deeper realization, is yoga. You may come across varieties of "yogas", but the *basic* yogas are four. All other yogas can be put under one or another of these four.

Modern man has little patience; half the people don't want to observe too many disciplines. They want to make things simple. The other half, of course, wants details. So what are the *fundamental* ideas behind these four yogas? As we live our day-to-day lives in society, what should be our attitude? These are the questions. Spiritual life, essentially speaking, is only an attitude. The Vedantins say that practices and disciplines are all necessary and useful. They will push the mind forward - they will purify the mind. Rites and ceremonies, prayers and singing, reading and contemplation, social service and morality - all these things are classed under normal religion. The purpose of all these disciplines is to purify the mind, and in the purified mind, knowledge of the Reality dawns automatically.

In theistic language, this is put in a slightly different way. Theism accepts that there is a personal God. The Ultimate Reality may be formless, but when It is viewed from the standpoint of the world, from the standpoint of the individual, It is called *Ishvara*, the Lord. It is the same Reality. Sri Ramakrishna, based on his own experience, used to say that the Ultimate Reality can be both personal and impersonal. The impersonal is the ideal of the philosophers - the Absolute - but in the religious traditions, the mystical traditions of the world, great saints and sages have communed with the Divine, and experienced a sort of personal relationship. Swami Vivekananda, who was a special propounder of the *Advaita* or nondualistic doctrine, said that, "In spite of all this I feel there is a Mother-heart somewhere." He was trying to be as logical and as non-committal as possible. Normally the approach of the intellectual is non-committal - not to get oneself committed to any position, because direct experience is lacking. The only proof of God is experience; all other arguments are *possibilities*. Based on their own experience, the saints and sages say there is a personal aspect of the Reality, which is called *Ishvara,* or *Saguna Brahman* in the Vedanta philosophy - *Brahman* with attributes. *Ishvara* is not something separate from the Totality. It is the same Totality viewed from another angle, that's all. The father is

only a father if he has a child; if he has no child he is not a
father. If we *are* here, and if we *are* real, in *that* relationship
we see the formless Reality as the personal God.

This is the path of *bhakti yoga,* the path of love or devotion,
which takes for granted that there is a higher power behind
this universe, and that the purpose of life is to realize Him.
Vedanta comes forward and says that realizing Him is
realizing the Absolute. So realize Him! By what method?
There is an elaborate method. Most of the religions of the
world are normally theistic, even though their personal
God may have an Absolute aspect. God may be said to
have a form, or He may be said to be without form, but
having "infinite good qualities" that is, He is kind, He is
just, He is loving. And what is the method of realizing
him? The theistic religions say, "Love of the Lord." *Bhakti*
means love of God, devotion to God. The great teacher
Ramanuja defines *bhakti* as meditation coupled with love,
with affection. *"Sneha-purvam anu-dhyanam'* - meditation
but with a little love, a little affection. A yogi may meditate
without mixing in any emotion. If the Absolute is your
objective, where is the scope for emotion? That is one
type of meditation. A *Jnana yogi* stresses meditation on the
Reality - what It is in Its own nature. A *raja yogi* stresses
the meditation *technique* - to give him some grip over the
thing. But a follower of the path of *bhakti yoga* meditates
on God with love.

Then, in *bhakti yoga,* other spiritual practices follow.
How to express your love? The Lord is personal; we
impose human sentiments on Him. So whatever I like

- for instance, good clothing - I offer to the Lord, or His manifestation, or an image. If I like good food, I offer it to the Lord. The devotee's relationship with the Lord is almost like a personal relationship. A normal man has varieties of desires. He tries to connect these desires to the Divine. Then the desires lose their binding quality. The scriptures say that we should live in the Lord all the time, but we know that in normal life that is not possible overnight. How do we bring about such a condition? As one of Sri Ramakrishna's disciples observed, when this condition is attained - that is, when complete surrender to the Lord has come - liberation has already been achieved. The method is to practice - along with other disciplines -connecting the Lord with all our desires, and thus we gradually go *beyond* desires. As we contemplate the Lord, a time will come, gradually, when the desires will drop away. We will learn to assert our spiritual nature more and more. Vedanta's conclusion is that man's real nature is the Spirit, but it is mixed up with the body and mind. Vedanta asserts that to realize the Spirit, purity of the mind is necessary, *and full* purity can come only from a condition of desirelessness. In the early stage of spiritual life, we desire things, and God also. Connect the desires to the Lord, and gradually, the mind goes up.

The major idea in bhakti yoga is love of God. Worship, singing, praying, pilgrimage, reading, hearing about the Lord -all these are methods by which we may attain that love. Various disciplines have been described: moral and ethical disciplines, religious techniques, rites and ceremonies - and they are all useful. These are *tested* methods which help us to keep the mind centered on the Reality. *Bhakti yogis* put stress upon *japa*, the repetition of the name of the Lord. As Latu Maharaj said, we have not seen God, but God's name is available to us. The names of God have been given to us by saints and sages, from their experience, and that is something tangible. If you go on repeating the name, the result will come. Latu Maharaj put it in a very simple way. He was a simple man, but a saint. "If there is a man of some name in the office, you just address your letters to him at the office. If somebody is functioning there, he will reply to you." If you try to repeat His name, the Lord will hear you if He is there. If He is not there, of course, life loses all meaning. Whether you have enjoyed a little more or a little less, if after fifty years everything vanishes, life loses all meaning, all significance. So putting trust in the Lord, repeat His name. This is a very simple direction.

The major emphasis in *all* the practices in the theistic circle is on thinking of the Lord, or on learning how to think of the Lord. But in the ultimate analysis, spiritual life is an *attitude*. What is the proof that you really love God? You remember Him, you think of Him in *every* situation. So the sages said that the ultimate stage, or the essence of the devotional life, is to *surrender* to Him. There is a famous *shloka*, or verse, in the *Gita*, which is considered by the theists to be the most important verse - the verse which *really* matters. In the eighteenth chapter, sixty-sixth shloka, Krishna says: "*Sarva dharman parityajya mam ekam sharanam vraja.*" "Giving up all other *dharmas*, all other duties, take refuge in Me alone." Duties are good things

- duty to this god, to this man, to this society - these are all good things, compared with the concerns of a bullish, animalistic man. Serving the people of society, serving the gods - this constitutes religion. But Krishna says that the *final* religion, the *final* spirituality, will be to transcend even these. This is called *sharanagati,* surrender. Duties are good things, but they are also binding. Because even the *will* to do things, according to the sages, is not under you. It is really God who prompts you. God is really the inner guide sitting in the heart of man. Every action that you do is really being done by Him. Every move that you make is being made by Him. If that attitude could be taken, then right now you would be a free soul. Of course the moral question will come - if you do bad things also, is God doing that? No religion will say that bad things are good, and that God makes you do them, but the saints give their testimony that from the person who takes the attitude that everything is done by God, gradually all the dross falls away. So if something has been done that is immoral in relation to society, in relation to the accepted norms of things, socially you will not be pardoned - you will have to pay the price. But *spiritually* speaking, if from the whole heart - if it is possible, of course -that attitude is taken, right now you can be free. From the Vedantic standpoint, also, it can be supported in this sense: all good and bad things are done by the body and the mind. Realization is to know that you are not the body, not the mind. The moment you know - really know it, you are free from the pressures of the body and mind. That doesn't mean your body will not pay. Your body will have to pay. Your mind will have to pay. That by realization you will escape all suffering - that is not the idea. That is a different idea. Vedanta is not concerned with that. For that you will have to cry and weep to the Lord to pardon you, or go to the *yogis,* and learn to keep your mind under control. The idea of the *bhakti yogi* is that the Lord is sitting in the heart; He is doing everything. But we often mix-in our own ego. So, because we have still got an idea of good and bad, we ought to do whatever is *good.* A stage will come when we will go beyond that. And the saints say that when that stage comes, we *cannot* do any bad things. Sri Ramakrishna gave an example: with a sword you can cut a man. But if the sword is turned into gold, it is no longer useful for all these rough jobs. The ultimate idea behind all this is that the devotee surrenders to the Lord.

There are two major schools among the theists of Ramanuja's sect, called the Sri Vaishnava sect, in South India. One school says, "We must *do* something. Man knows that he has got some freedom - he can do something. As long as we have that feeling, we must act on it! If we know that this is good and that is bad, we must do the good thing." The other school says, "No, everything is done by the Lord. Why should we plan anything? Let Him guide us." This is the old question of free will versus predetermination. A quarrel over this point is always going on. So these two schools, representing these two ideas, arose in the Ramanuja tradition. In *The Gospel of Sri Ramakrishna,* the comparison is made between the baby monkey and the baby cat. The baby monkey holds on to its mother. The mother monkey jumps from tree to tree, and the baby holds on; whereas the baby cat sits somewhere

and goes on mewing and mewing. Wherever the mother
takes it - sometimes, as Sri Ramakrishna says, on the nice
cushioned bed of the master of the house, sometimes in the
gutter - its only language is "Mew, mew." And wherever
the mother puts the kitten, it remains. Similarly, a devotee
surrenders to the Lord and says, "Whatever You do is
alright. Thy will be done." Of course such a devotee has
no right to question every now and then. He may cry and
weep, of course, but still, weeping and crying, he will
have to go back to the Mother, as children sometimes do.
To whom else will the child go? Nowadays parents don't
beat children much. Once in a while, they may give them
a slap. And the child will weep, and go back to the parent
again. So even if some suffering comes to you, you may
cry and weep, but you will have to go back to the Lord.
He is your Father, He is your Mother, He is your inner
guide. In every situation, the devotee must take recourse
to Him. This school of thought goes to the extent of saying
that even for spiritual practice, nothing else is necessary.
Just surrender to Him.

In one system of Vaishnavism given by Vallabhacharya,
it is said that the only discipline necessary is to *choose*
the Lord -"*Varanam eva sadhanam*" - that's all. "O Lord, I
opt for You. Now do whatever You like." Of course, the
implications of this decision will come *later*. If you have
really surrendered, then you cannot take a step without
seeing whether it is the Lord's will or not. When you are
still in the preliminary condition, you have only made the
decision to choose Him, as was the case of Girish Ghosh as
described in *Sri Ramakrishna The Great Master*. Girish Ghosh

was a very brilliant man of those days - the 19th century. He was the first great playwright and stage manager of modern India - one of the most brilliant men Bengal had produced. But in the early stages of his life, he was given much to drinking, and other vices. Drinking was a fashion, especially in that profession, but Girish was a spiritual seeker within. He went to the one extreme, probably took a turn, and then came in touch with Sri Ramakrishna. Somehow or other, he felt that in Sri Ramakrishna, God had incarnated to bless him. And he had tremendous faith - not like our faith - sometimes we doubt, sometimes we have faith - which is not faith at all. Sri Ramakrishna used to say, "Girish's faith is one hundred and twenty - five per cent." *More* than a hundred per cent - so much strength of faith he had. Girish came to Ramakrishna. He *knew* that Ramakrishna could save him. Probably because of his previous *samskaras,* past impressions, the desire for liberation came to Girish - in spite of all his drinking. His mind was not at peace. He went to Ramakrishna, and asked, "What shall I do?" Ramakrishna said, "Think of the Lord twice a day," as religious teachers normally say - even though the definition of *bhakti* is *constant* remembrance of the Lord. These teachers know that thinking of the Lord twice a day is more than enough for most people - that we don't have the capacity for constant remembrance. This doesn't mean that by thinking of the Lord twice a day the person will realize God. He will realize God *in time*. But this practice will prepare the mind, stage by stage, for realization *later*. Sri Ramakrishna told Girish to think of the Lord twice a day. But Girish said, "Oh, I am such a busy man!" Girish was a type of genius. For hours and hours he could think about the topic on which he was writing. He had the capacity for dictating three different books to three writers at a time: he would dictate to one writer for two minutes; to the next, two minutes; to a third, two minutes. And in, say, fifteen days, three books would be finished. That has been recorded - he had that type of capacity. Girish said, "I am so busy a man, I forget myself!" Ramakrishna said, "All right, at least think of the Lord before taking food." He would at least *have* to take food.

Still Girish hesitated, and thought inwardly, "Such a simple thing he is telling me to do. I should do it, but what if by chance I forget?" Girish knew that if he were to forget, he would be in trouble, because he would be giving his word of honor to God incarnate. So Girish kept silent. He was ashamed to tell Ramakrishna that he could not do even that much. But Ramakrishna understood Girish's mind, and said, "Oh, you may say that even that much I cannot do. Then give me the 'power of attorney'." When a child is small, and cannot manage its own property, the court appoints an attorney to look after the child's property. This is called the power of attorney. Grown-up people can also do this, but it is used more often for a child. When Ramakrishna said, "Give me the power of attorney," Girish heaved a sigh of relief and said, "Ah! That is the way out! That suits me very well. I don't have to do anything, just give power of attorney." And he gave it.

In later days Girish used to say to his brother disciples,

the monks and others, "You had a limited period of doing spiritual practices, *sadhana,* but I have no limit. Every step I take, I have to think, 'Oh, you have given the power of attorney to him. Why should you question your fate? He never promised you that he would take you along a smooth path; if he takes you through the thorns you have no right to question it.'" Girish held to this view so much that when his five year old child died, he was weeping on one hand, but, on the other hand, he said that he had no right to weep. So these are the implications of surrendering. The major idea of this surrender is, "Accept the Lord as the guide of your life, and believe that He protects you." Of course if this idea falls in the hands of intellectuals, theologians, and philosophers, they will say that He will protect you *spiritually.* Physically, He may not. But the devotees believe that the Lord protects them all the time, even in the physical plane. There are hundreds of cases where real help came to devotees. Then again, of course, the intellectuals will try to understand how the help came, because they take for granted that there is no God, and try to explain away how the help comes. They will have to say that the mind, or the unknown powers a man has within him, brings the help. Many explanations will be given. But the devotees believe that the Lord is responsible.

Of course, the psychological benefit of surrender to the Lord is automatic. The spiritual explanation is that you have surrendered yourself to Him, so you become an instrument of the Lord. He is sitting here; He is doing everything. Sri Ramakrishna used to say. "I am the machine; You are the operator of the machine." Realistically, it is so, of course. Ultimately, He is there. But that attitude has to be cultivated. Man is very egotistic by nature, so this egotism has to be lessened. All the religions try by some method or another to lessen this feeling of egotism, and later egotism itself. So, as Sri Ramakrishna used to repeat: *"Naham, naham; Tuhu, Tuhu."* "Not I, Not I, but Thou, but Thou." That is the attitude of a devotee, who knows his limitations, who knows his limited nature, who is still identified with his body and mind. This is the attitude of an *instrument*. The instrument does very good things. But the instrument doesn't think, "I have done this." The machine doesn't think that it is the doer. It is the *operator* of the machine to whom the credit goes. The attitude is, "I am the chariot, You are the charioteer. You use my body, as it were". Not "as it were" - "You use it." We add the "as it were" because we have not yet reached that state of mind, because we are still concerned about our ego. As Ramakrishna says, the ego is like the roots of a banyan tree. You cut down the tree, and the next day it shoots back up. Whatever amount of energy you may spend to remove the ego, again it comes up. So Ramakrishna said (he had a village way of talking), "If this rascal ego doesn't go, keep it as a servant, a servant of the Lord." You cannot be very proud as a servant. You can be proud, of course, in *some* sense. Devotion creates two types of emotions in the devotees: some people become calm and humble, and other people become very enthusiastic about doing the work of the Lord. There are stories of Mahavir Hanuman, who was able to manifest much energy, because, as he declared, "I am the servant of Rama, so I must manifest energy. Whatever Rama's will is, I must do that." But the other type of devotee becomes very contemplative. This type of devotee loses all interest in activity. Both attitudes are sanctioned, if these thoughts remain behind them. Society will, of course, give credit to the man who does something, because society understands tangible things. An intangible result is more difficult for normal society to appreciate.

That is how the devotional teachers put it: be an instrument of God. That attitude has to be kept whenever egotism comes. When hard feelings come, remember that it is all really the will of the Lord. If you succeed in a particular venture, don't take the credit to yourself. Give the credit to the Lord. If failure comes, then also you need not take responsibility; it is His responsibility. A servant in a house works and does many good things, but he knows that the credit is not his. The discredit is also not his. The credit and discredit go to the Master. If a good name comes, the good name goes to the master. The servant's idea is, "Whatever I am asked to do, I do." The overall responsibility is the Master's. That is the idea of being an instrument. The instrument does everything, but only to please the Lord, or on being prompted by Him. So Krishna, in the Gita, says, "Whatever you do, offer that to Me." Then you will be free from the bad effects of all *karma* - and also from the good effects. Both are bondage. In the highest condition; you are to go beyond both. Good, of course, prompts you, helps you. The mind is cleaned quicker through good actions. But, according to this attitude, whatever we do, we should offer it to the Lord, though loving devotees do not like to give bad things.

There is a famous song by Ramprasad which Ramakrishna was very fond of singing. "O mind, I ask you to serve the Mother in whatever way you like." So as the individual progresses in spiritual life, he thinks everything he does is for Mother. "When you eat, think that you are offering oblations to the Mother. Whatever you hear, think that it is Mother's name' - because Mother exists in every sound. Then Ramprasad says in great joy that Mother is everywhere present. Even when you go for a walk around the city, think that you are circumambulating the deity. Every action is to be spiritualized. How is it spiritualized? By bringing in the idea that Mother, the Lord, is sitting in the heart, and She prompts us to do everything. And then, whatever work we do, we somehow or other connect it to the Lord - by offering it, or by repeating the Lord's name. Whenever an action is done, the repetition of the name of the Lord is prescribed in these systems. That is one method. There are various methods, but a standardized method is necessary. According to different tastes and temperaments certain methods can be adopted, so that the devotee is reminded constantly that he is really being prompted by the Lord, or that he is surrendering everything to the Lord. In the earlier stage, the devotee says, "I have surrendered. O Lord, I am Thine. I am Your servant, I am Your child, I am Your attendant." Now, being a child can mean two things: an attitude of helplessness - "I am the child. I take refuge in You," and maybe an attitude of courage, also - "I am the son of such and such a big man, so I am not a small man." Both types of devotees are there, but the main idea is: "You are mine, I am Yours". This idea gradually becomes stronger and stronger.

The Advaita Vedantins come forward and say that at the last stage, a feeling of identity with the Divine will come. Strict theists don't accept that idea. They want to *enjoy* God. If you want enjoyment, a little separation is good. Otherwise you become one with the enjoyment. So the theists say, "No, we don't want to *merge* in the Lord; we want to keep a little separation." In the end, what happens, happens. But the Vedantins say that ultimately, a complete merging comes. As Ramakrishna explains it, a master has a servant who has served him very well. The master becomes very pleased and says, "There is no difference between you and me. Come and sit by my side. You and I are the same." So the Lord can also give this unity of consciousness to a devotee. But Ramakrishna used to say that we should take one attitude *strongly* and practice it as a discipline - combining other disciplines *occasionally*. The main attitude of the spiritual aspirant is to be one.

Now, in a real-life situation, how is this attitude of being an instrument of God going to help? In a normal life there are ups and downs, things are good and bad, pleasant and unpleasant - how am I to accept that? How is this practice going to benefit me in day to day living? Of course, stage by stage, *spiritual* progress will come. That is good. That I understand. But does it have any benefit for day to day living? The theists say, "Yes. There *is* a benefit," because much of our suffering is on the mental level. Suffering is only suffering if the mind accepts it. Perhaps 80% of our suffering is really mental. If somebody has said something unpleasant to you, you may feel hurt. But if you happen to be in a good mood, you may not feel hurt. Or, if you are very hungry and want food, in any way a man gives you food, you will take it. But, if you are sure of your meal, you want the food to be given with respect and love - otherwise you won't take it. It means that much of our suffering comes from our attitude. The *yogis* say, "Control the attitude." But the devotee says, "I don't have the strength to control my attitude. I weep to the Lord: O Lord, don't put me into trouble, or, All right, you have put me here - I shall endure it. If it is Your will that I must suffer, I will suffer." This is a type of resignation -*without complaint* - will be better, of course - that shows that you are more established. Holy Mother says that this attitude of resignation is good, even with complaints. Somebody asked her, "I have varieties of desires. Can I pray to the Lord?" Holy Mother said, "Yes, yes. You can pray." But Ramakrishna was against all desires. He was in favor of not asking and said - "You are not a slave. Why should you be cowed down by your desires?" Yet Holy Mother said, "No, no, - ask whatever you want." But the devotee would not leave it at that. She said, "But we have *bad* desires also." Holy Mother replied, "It doesn't matter. God is like our mother, like our father. God knows what is good for you and what is bad." A child asks for so many things from his mother. The mother says, "Yes, yes, I shall give it to you." But while giving, she knows what to give and what not to give. Here Ramakrishna places the stress on the *technique,* or the spirit of dispassion. Holy Mother places the stress on *relationship* - the feeling that God is *my* mother, and of my mother I can ask anything - good or bad. Mother will know best - that is the idea.

When a man goes into life, he strives for advancement.
He makes effort, but he does not know whether he will get
any result or not. Naturally he is anxious and worried, but
if he can cultivate this attitude: "Oh, I am an instrument of
the Lord, I am His child; let Him do whatever He likes,"
his mind is at peace. If he can fully follow this, there is no
problem. Whatever comes, he will take it. If unpalatable
things come, if the mind is not fully at peace, a little
suffering may be there. But still, the major portion of the
suffering has been lessened. There are many situations in
which we go on worrying for nothing. Our worries don't
help us. Our repentance over past mistakes doesn't help
us. One of the studies I read said that forty percent of
our worries are centered around *past* things; fifty percent
around *future* things, and only ten percent around *present*
things. The past is past; you can't do anything about it
- unless you learn a lesson from it. The future is not yet
come. Much of your energy is wasted away in only *thinking*
- making rosy pictures or dismal pictures - and suffering.
This ten percent is the real situation which you have to
actually face. The moment a man surrenders to the Lord,
he feels that there is a higher power behind him, which
is looking after him, which has got a plan of Its own, and
whatever way It takes, good or bad, ultimately it will be
for his spiritual good - and the moment he has accepted
the situation his mind becomes calm, quiet, peaceful. If the
mind accepts any suffering, the suffering loses its sting. At
least fifty percent, let us say, of the feeling of suffering, the
feeling of misery, the feeling of hurt, will be lessened. The
attitude of a devotee is to think of the Lord, to love Him,
and to surrender to Him. If that attitude is kept up, then

life becomes smooth; even daily life becomes smoother. Of course, that doesn't mean that other spiritual disciplines will not be done. Because as they say, if a mother loves a child, will she not feed it? She will feed the child, nurse the child, look after the child. Similarly, if you love God, there must be an *expression* of love. The expression of love will be in contemplating the Lord, repeating His name, and serving fellow men as creatures of God or children of God. These are all social and moral aspects. These will be the automatic effect of the devotee's attitude toward the Lord.

So, be an instrument of God, bearing everything that comes. The *jnana yogis* stress forbearance, *titiksha* it is called, bearing all pains without complaint. But the *bhakti yogi* says that everything is the gift of God; good or bad, I shall accept it. "Not I, Not I, but Thou, O Lord;" and "Whatever action I do is being prompted by You; let me consecrate these actions towards You." Consecration becomes easier if the work done is good work. What are normally called socially good or morally good or spiritually good things, are to be cultivated.

PART III
Chapter 10

BE THE WITNESS

Affix to the Upanishad, the bow incomparable, the sharp arrow of devotional worship; then, with mind absorbed and heart melted in love, draw the arrow and hit the mark - the imperishable Brahman.

OM is the bow, the arrow is the individual being, and Brahman is the target. With a tranquil heart, take aim. Lose thyself in him, even as the arrow is lost in the target.

In him are woven heaven, earth and sky, together with the mind and all the senses. Know him, the Self alone. Give up vain talk. He is the bridge of immortality.

Within the lotus of the heart he dwells, where, like the spokes of a wheel, the nerves meet. Meditate on him as OM. Easily mayest thou cross the sea of darkness.

---Mundaka Upanishad

When the spiritual view of life comes through experience or understanding, man becomes aware of some higher and deeper purpose of his existence. The spiritual view of life says that man's life is not finished with his day to day experiences. The goal of life is posited as something spiritual. According to Vedanta, the goal is the realization of one's own essential nature. The Vedantic system has pointed out that man works in his body and mind, that all his enjoyments and sufferings are in these two areas. But his *persistent* nature is beyond both of these. To realize one's essential and persistent nature as the spirit, as the Atman, is the ultimate purpose of life.

Man has a mind. He has a body. And this psycho-physical being, man, can discover the essential reality *behind* the mind and the body. But he has to find the ways and means of gradually discovering this reality. Spiritual life, after the completion of a preliminary inquiry, consists mostly of living life with a certain attitude. The theoretical position has been arrived at on the basis of the experience of the saints and sages, and doctrines are formulated on the basis of their experience. From the experience comes the philosophy. From the philosophy come the various spiritual methods and disciplines which help us discover our real nature. There are several methods of achieving this goal, but the most direct method, from the Vedantic point of view, is to disidentify oneself, at least for some time each day, from the body and the mind, and to look upon oneself as the "witness self." There are various other disciplines and spiritual practices such as devotion, meditation, and so forth. But here the idea is to assert that the spiritual self is my real nature.

Whenever experiences come in our life, sometimes good, sometimes bad -especially when bad-we naturally try to take the help of a philosophy or an idea to help us face the particular experience. This idea of looking upon oneself as the "witness self" is one attitude. Whenever any experience comes at any time of the day, the attitude is to just look on-not to identify oneself with the experience. The Indian philosophers have the idea that man is covered, as it were, with different encasements. The Atman is there-the basic essential Self, but around it is the mind and the intellect, which are referred to as the subtle body. Then around that is the gross body. According to the ancient system, man has three types of bodies: the causal body, which is the essential core; the subtle body, which migrates from birth to birth; and the gross body which when added to the other two constitutes a full-fledged man. The philosophers tried to analyze these different bodies in man. Sometimes it is put in a different way-that there are five *koshas,* or coverings. Five sheaths. First is the body sheath, then the vital breath sheath, then the mind sheath, then the intellect sheath, then the subtle sheath, called the bliss sheath. And then beyond these, or within these, is the Atman.

In what way is this idea to be applied in our day to day situation? After establishing this position rationally and philosophically, the next question is how to put it into practice. The idea is that all our enjoyments and all our sufferings arise because of our identification. If I have got a robe on my body, and it catches fire, I catch fire. But if I remove the robe and put it on a hangar, if the robe catches fire, I don't catch fire.

Indian preachers often tell an interesting story to illustrate the idea that all enjoyment and suffering come because of our idea of possession. A man was going to a market to buy a cow. So he higgled, haggled, paid the money, and bought the cow. He was going back home but after fifteen minutes there was an accident and the cow died. Now who will be sorry? The man who brought up the cow for two years, or the man who bought it fifteen minutes ago? Naturally, the man who bought it fifteen minutes ago, because it is *his* cow. Because of the idea of possession, the idea of ownership, he feels the pain. A sort of identification has come. If the cow had died sixteen minutes earlier, he would not have felt so bad. So our enjoyment and suffering are based on this idea of identification or the sense of possession-either I am identified with an object, or it belongs to me.

So the philosophers argued that from the philosophical standpoint your real self is not the body, not the mind, but the spirit. Once in a while we will have to assert that idea, especially when life becomes too much for us, or our experiences are not so palatable. There are various ways of practicing this, but one direct method is to disown the experiences. Really speaking, you are not the sufferer, because the things are happening in the body and the mind. From this angle, Acharya Shankara, the great Vedantic philosopher, faced a crucial problem. In the *Gita* (4.19) it is said that as soon as the fire of knowledge is kindled, that is, as soon as knowledge comes, all the karmas are burnt away. Karmas means the accumulated results of action of this life and previous lives, which give birth to this body. On the basis of these karmas I experience enjoyments and suffering, and also, I add new karmas. Now, the argument has been given that if the karmas are burnt away the man must fall dead immediately, because there are no karmas to sustain his body, since the body is the result of the karmas. Philosophers have faced this problem in three ways. Some

said, "The body actually falls away after twenty one days."
Another group said, "Real liberation in life is impossible. It
comes at the fall of the body." But then Acharya Shankara
and Swami Vivekananda, and a great succession of
teachers, believed that liberation in life is possible. So what
happens to the karma? Most of the Vedantic teachers that
came after Shankara accepted the analogy of a hunter with
a quiver full of unused arrows, an arrow which has been
put on the bow, and another arrow which has already
been released. Suddenly the hunter changes his mind
about releasing the arrow on the bow. "No! Killing is bad.
I shall practice non-violence." The quiver full of arrows
immediately becomes neutralized. The arrow that had
been put on the bow also can be stopped. But the arrow
that has gone out of his hand he cannot do anything about.
So, they said, karma is of three types: one type which has
been accumulated; one type which is about to start; and
another type called prarabdha karma, which has already
begun to bear fruit. The first two types of karmas are burnt
away, but prarabdha karma continues. But Shankara was
a great logician. He said that even this is not necessary.
He gave this idea: what is illumination according to the
Advaitic Vedanta? Illumination or realization means to
realize that you are not the limited, changing, body and
mind. And all enjoyments and sufferings take place in
the body and the mind. So really, *you* don't suffer. When
the saint realizes that he is not the body, not the mind,
but the spirit, he is realizing his real self. Even if there
is some suffering in the body and the mind, he doesn't
suffer. At least he shouldn't suffer. If he suffers, it means
that a feeling of identification is still there. How to get

rid of that identification? By repeated assertion. Even an ordinary spiritual practitioner can do this. Our feeling of identification is so strong that the identification has to be neutralized by daily assertion. So meditation according to this method is just to identify oneself with the real Self, and disidentify with the demands of the body and the mind.

This is a potent method which all of us can to some extent practice in our lives. If our conviction is strong, then it is easier. Otherwise we will be shrieking when every little pain comes to the mind or the body. Somehow or other we shall have to learn the technique of disidentifying ourselves, at least temporarily. In normal life if physical pain comes, the doctor will probably put you to sleep with some medicines, give you rest, so that for the time being you are disconnected with the pain. But in this method, by sheer mental effort, by sheer will I disidentify myself. I know, at least theoretically, that though I am suffering it is really not my suffering. Take another grosser analogy, which is easier. I have got many things in a house. If anything happens to them, it happens to me. But still I know that I am slightly separate. As long as nothing happens to my body, really speaking, nothing happens. I may be impoverished, I may be wailing and weeping, but still really nothing happens, because there is a clear disjunction. The idea of possession has to be lessened, that's all. Then the pain will be less. The same idea is to be applied in day to day life. It is a little tough, of course, to accept this idea and put it into practice-but what is the way out? There is no way out. You can pray to a kind God, a responsive God, but He may reply or He may not reply.

If He replies, you say He is a good God; if he doesn't reply, you say, what is the use of believing in that God? But if you are left to yourself, if there is nobody else on whom you can put the blame, if from outside nobody else is coming to help you, you will have to help yourself. So for such people, this idea is much more potent, much stronger. The idea of non-attachment is a subsidiary idea that can be dovetailed into this basic metaphysical position.

So in day to day activity, in our daily work, one method is to consider oneself as the witness, the onlooker. The second method is to practice a little detachment. Now an average man cannot work without definite gain. But the idea of physical gain gradually is replaced by other types of subtler gains, such as aesthetic enjoyment and intellectual pleasure. These are also gains, but of a subtler type. And from this comes the idea of spiritual gain. You give up something physical but still a spiritual gain is there. So here the objective is spiritual gain. If you are a believer in God, you offer the fruits of action to the divine, or else, just remain detached. I have done my part; the results should follow. If they don't follow, let them go to hell; I don't care. That is the idea. Anyhow, nothing else is there in our hands. I have done all the things that should be done. If the results don't follow, there may be other factors involved in that particular situation. So I don't care any more One of these attitudes will *have* to be learned if we are to live in the world with a certain measure of serenity and poise.

You will see that in normal life also, the less the idea of

possession, the less the idea of involvement is there, the more unaffected you are. The source of all enjoyment is involvement. But the source of all pain, also, is involvement. So there must be some period of life, or some period of each day when we practice detachment. You may have noticed sometimes, if you are in a place where you can observe people going by all day, that at the end of the day, only a few faces come before your eyes. In your mental eye you will see or remember the faces which you liked, people whom you know, or people whom you hated. These types will be remembered. Love and hate both are involvements. Love brings a pleasant sensation; hate brings an uncomfortable sensation. It is the uncomfortable that we want to avoid. But here the idea is that impressions in the mind are associated with things or faces with which I am involved, who have created a special impression in me because of some type of involvement, some type of relationship. As an onlooker, the other thousand faces did not make an impression on me.

When you go to a theater, you see many people acting. You have gone there voluntarily. Sometimes you are elated, and sometimes you weep along with the actors and actresses, according to their roles. But in your heart of hearts you know that it is acting, so it becomes an enjoyment. Even when somebody is getting killed in the drama, or somebody is wailing and weeping, you may also shed a few tears, but still, because you are the spectator, and you know it is make believe, it is not the actual situation, your suffering is not acute. The suffering experience probably gives a little catharsis. It is an enjoyment if you can look

upon yourself as the spectator. Otherwise, millions of
people would not spend so much money to go to the
theater.

So this is the advantage of being an onlooker in certain
situations. But as I warned earlier, if you avoid the pain,
you avoid the pleasure also. That is the yogic position. If
you want serenity and calmness, then you can't say, "I will
take the pleasant aspect and avoid the unpleasant aspect,"
which a normal man does. And that's why he prays to the
Lord, "Oh Lord, give me the pleasant and let me avoid
the unpleasant." If God intervenes, well and good. But if
God does not intervene-if you are left to yourself, what is
the way out? The yogis say that if you want to avoid the
pain, to a certain extent you will have to avoid the pleasure
also-the excitement in pleasure. When the mind goes up,
it will surely come down. That is in the nature of things.
You can't all the time remain up, and never come down,
because you are experiencing an emotion. Any emotion will
have its ups and downs. So the yogic idea is to keep the
mind in poise and balance. That will give you enjoyment
in a quieter sense, not in the exhilarating sense.

Another reason why the yogis practice this serenity
and calmness is that when the mind is calm and serene,
then only will spiritual truths flash in the mind. Spiritual
experiences, spiritual truths will flash in the mind when the
mind is calm. The early yogis had an idea-it is a Vedantic
idea, of course-that the truth is there all the time. The spirit
of the Atman is there always, always shining, *but,* we don't
realize it all the time. Why? Because the mind is always in

a turmoil, or always having waves. So the yogic method is to make the mind calm, serene. When the mind is serene, you see the light, as it were. It is like seeing the reflection of the sun or the moon in a pond. If the water is wavy, you don't see it. When the water is calm, you can see it, or see your own reflection. So the raja yogic method is to make the mind calm.

When the mind is calm, the truth of the ultimate reality of one's nature will automatically come. And that is one reason, when you enjoy meditation, when meditation is deep enough, once in a while you feel *a* welling up of joy. Why? You cannot always explain why it happens. You can say that the nerves have been soothed, the body has been soothed, and so forth. These may be contributory causes. But the Vedantins say it is because the obstacles to the manifestation of the nature of the Atman have been removed. The real nature, the basic nature of one's spiritual self, essential self, is *ananda,* bliss. Ananda is one's real nature. Swami Vivekananda argues in one place that it is your real nature so you will have to assert it. Our real nature is being disturbed because of other experiences. According to raja yoga, if you stop the mental waves, the blissful nature of the Atman will automatically come out. And that is why you feel a type of joy, a sense of well-being, when the mind is a little calm.

Another idea is that when the mind is being tossed between contradictory desires or ideas, you are in a state of restlessness. So if you can make a decision, restfulness comes, even if it is the wrong decision. Often you have observed that it is terribly uncomfortable when you are being tossed between two ideas-which course to follow? But the moment you have made a decision, you are better off. In behavioral psychology it has been pointed out that if a man is showing you his fist, threatening to hit you, your whole body becomes tense, all the muscles are tense. But the moment the blow has fallen, you will be bruised, but still, all the muscles again relax. The problem is over. Similarly, suspense makes us much more uncomfortable than having made a decision. From a yogic standpoint, this goal of serenity and calmness is posited, and this itself is one type of enjoyment-a serene enjoyment, not an exuberant type of enjoyment.

Now if a person says, "But I *want* an exuberant type of enjoyment," an exhilarating type, exciting type, go ahead and have that, knowing that later the depression will come. If you are prepared for it, you will not blame yourself so much, or blame all the forces of the world. You will have gone into it knowingly, aware that it has this effect. If you want very much to eat a good dish, go ahead and eat, but know that later your stomach may be upset. Be prepared for it, that is the idea. Once you know that this is the result that may follow, when it happens, you will not be so upset. And that is how the average man adjusts in life. He constructs his own philosophy in some way, based on his experience.

So the emotions are there, but a man of poise, a man of understanding, a man of knowledge is not disturbed, because he knows his real self is untouched, uninvolved.

There is a story about Socrates. Even great souls have adversaries. Socrates was surrounded by his students, Plato and others, when a man came in and went on scolding Socrates, and calling him bad names. "You are a thief, you are a debauchee," and so forth. His disciples became angry and wanted to give the man a thrashing. But Socrates stopped them and said, "Wait. Whatever things he is telling, all are true." "How could it be true?" they asked. "You are the greatest sage of Greece, and to call you a thief or a debauchee is a lie." Socrates replied, "No, it is true, but there is a difference. All these thoughts once in a while come to my mind, because of the impact of the world. They pass through my mind. But the difference between me and other people is that I don't react to them." And he gave this example. Say you have a mound of sand on the seashore, and also a rock. When the waves come in and dash against the mound of sand, the mound breaks down. But when the waves dash against the rock, it is unmoved. That is the difference. Thoughts would arise in his mind, but he did not react. So this is the idea-for a spectator, varieties of things may pass before his eyes, his mind's eye, like a drama. But he doesn't identify himself with them. Or, a man gives up what is called in other language a sense of possession; the things he sees are not for himself, he enjoys them as a visitor, as an onlooker. The moment you want to possess a thing, you are in trouble. That is the position.

This idea of spectatorship, onlookership, can be practiced. A man really can disassociate himself even from the demands of the body and the mind. There is a

story about Swami Vivekananda. I heard this story from
the Professor of Music of Madras University, who heard
it from a person who actually witnessed it. Swamiji was
speaking about this type of complete control, yogic control
over the mind, complete disidentification with the body.
And he cited, as an example to show that it is practicable,
Krishna's driving of the chariot of Arjuna. He had to control
several horses. Swamiji said, "I shall show you how it could
be done." And then, the story goes, Swami Vivekananda
removed his shirt, and with bare body he stood and was
enacting the scene, as if he himself were controlling half a
dozen horses. So much of strength was necessary to control
them! All the muscles of his body bulged out, yet from the
neck upwards, his face was completely calm and serene.
And so, see, it can be done. The idea is that the entire body
could be in great convulsion because of the great activity
going on, but the mind could be kept completely calm.
The face of course, is sometimes the indicator of the mind.
So disidentification is possible. Lessening the sense of
possession is possible.

Now, if an average man tries to live without the sense of
possession he will not have any urge to work. He needs it.
This is accepted. But if the sense of possession is too strong
in him, it brings pain. So, the idea is to try to lessen the
impact. In the devotees' case, the method is to surrender
to the Lord. The Lord is like our father, like our mother,
He knows what is really good for us. We want certain
things very badly. We make all efforts to get them because
God has given us the capability to do so. But if, in spite of
all our efforts, we do not get them, the devotee takes it as

God's will. The Lord knows what is best. Religious people throughout the world say that what God does, does for the best. We also say that, although we often don't believe it. But if we can believe that the Lord knows what is best for us, then at least the pain of suffering is less. For example, if a child becomes sick and is put on a special diet, he may complain that good things to eat are being prepared in the house, but for him there is only the dull diet. But mommy knows better. So this is the same idea - the Lord knows better. I know that I want certain things very badly; I have made all efforts to get them. Still if I don't get them, for some reason or another, I shall have to adjust myself. So the devotional way of facing this idea is just to depend on the Lord.

Also, of course, in the devotional path, the idea of non-possession is often stressed upon. Through centuries of preaching, some ideas can be inculcated in common people's minds. Once it happened in India. I was there at the time-that the Zamindari system in Bengal was being abolished by law. In the Zamindari system some people had a large area of land, and there were tenants who would cultivate the land. The Zamindars were the middlemen for the government, so they would collect all the taxes and give them to the government. That was the arrangement introduced first by Moghul kings and the perfected by the British. So that system was being abolished. That meant that a few hundred thousand people were being affected; their livelihood, the way of life, the style of life would change. And in the assembly discussions were going on, and a bill was to be passed. At that time, in the 1950s,

Marshall Tito of Yugoslavia was visiting India. And he was going around Calcutta. He said, "All these changes are going on, but I don't see any rioting in the streets of Calcutta." The chief minister was there. He explained that it was because of centuries of schooling, people know that too much wealth is not good. Theoretically they know that accumulation of wealth in one place means deprivation somewhere else. So because of these centuries of schooling, the Zamindars felt that they were exploiting others but were trying to get *some* compensation, so that the property was not taken away without any compensation depriving them of their livelihood, as the communists would have done. Tito was very much impressed. That means that if day after day you hear a thing, it soaks into your mind to a certain extent. That's why it is said that the nature of the Atman has to be heard repeatedly. Day after day after day, Atman has to be heard about, repeatedly, reflected about, or meditated upon. Then only it soaks in the mind and becomes a part of one's own nature. The idea is that by repeated practice, gradually we get established in it.

So this is the major point-that in most of the non-dualistic Vedantic literature, there is a discrimination made between our real self, and everything else which is objectified. *Tat* and *twam*. The seer and the seen. *Drikdrishya* it is called. I am different from the things which I objectify. Anything that happens to the things objectified is not happening to me. Disidentification is the method of knowing one's real nature. I must find out my real nature, to see what is essential in me and what is nonessential in me. The outside world, property, land-we know that all these things are nonessential. In times of great crisis, everybody knows that these are nonessential. But to know that even the body and the mind are nonessential, that the body and the mind are not a primary part of my existence, is not easy. It takes time. We have to be theoretically convinced of this position as far as possible, and then we must practice lessening the identification and keeping up this attitude. These will be the major practices in this particular discipline: First, theoretically to get this idea clearer and clearer, as much as possible soaked into the mind, that I am the spirit, I am the undying, uninvolved Atman, which is persistent. The second practice is based on this idea. Whatever is non-Atman I shall try to disidentify with-at least some part of it. And we are to keep up sort of an attitude that whenever identification comes, we *try to* disidentify. It is not that overnight we will be successful. Whenever a painful experience comes about which you cannot do anything, either take the devotee's method-weep to the Lord a little and finish it, or the yogi's method-forget about it, or the jnani's method-disidentify. The devotee's method is surrendering to the Lord, feeling that the Lord does what is best for us. The yogi's method is to take the mind off of the pain, to develop the capacity to master the mind so that at will we can withdraw the mind to something else. In day to day life we do it. Whenever something doesn't seem pleasant, we try to bury ourselves in work, in gardening, in reading, in seeing television, in visiting friends. We try to forget the pain that is coming to the mind. The yogic idea is to develop so much strength of mind that at will you can take the mind off from a thing-especially a painful thing. This is one method. But that is not the jnani's method. The jnani's method is to change the attitude itself. Change the idea about the pain itself. Understand one's real nature, and based on that understanding, disidentify or disown any suffering that comes. This, then, is the idea of the "Witness Self".

PART III
Chapter 11

PEACE AND UNITY THROUGH RELIGION

The mind is everything. If the mind loses its liberty, you lose yours. If the mind is free, you too are free. The mind may get dyed in any color, like a white cloth fresh from the washing house. Study English, and you must mix English words in your talk in spite of yourself. The Pundit who studies Sanskrit must quote verses. If the mind is kept in bad company, the evil influence of it will color one's thoughts and conversations. Placed in the midst of devotees, the mind is sure to meditate on God and God alone. It changes its nature according to the things amongst which it lives and acts.

Sri Ramakrishna

In today's chaotic world, there is a clamor for peace-peace within oneself, peace in the family, peace in the place of work, in the community, in the nation, and in the world at large. We yearn to be free from war and violence. We yearn for a sense of unity that can bring us all together, a sense of oneness that can override our differences.

How can we attain peace and unity in a world that is so fractious and volatile? Various groups in different areas of life are attempting to promote peace and unity, and these efforts help to create the climate necessary for these ideals to bloom. But unless and until religion plays a prominent role in this quest, peace and unity will continue to be an elusive dream. Vivekananda emphasized the importance of religion in society when he said,

Great indeed are the manifestations of muscular power, and marvelous the manifestations of intellect expressing themselves through machines by the appliances of science; yet none of these is more potent than the influence which spirit exerts upon the world.[1]

What are the special contributions of religion to world peace? Religious ideals inspire higher motives and endeavors in man. Religion instills the qualities necessary for peace and unity by inspiring people to be virtuous, loving, sympathetic, altruistic, and non-violent. Religion is the only direct agency to teach people these higher virtues. This is the unique contribution of religion in the social, national, and international arenas.

In spite of his admiration for science, Vivekananda warned us about the dangers of the technological society. For several centuries now, and particularly now, there has been an increased secularization of life. Greed and selfishness run rampant. As the communist countries have demonstrated, love of power and desire for the comforts of life cannot be easily eradicated. They can only be lessened. Nevertheless, an attempt should be made to inculcate a higher ideal, for selfishness lies at the root of all our modern problems.

To quote Rabindranath Tagore:

When we become merely man, but not man-in-the-universe, we create bewildering problems, and having shut off the source of their solution, we try all kinds of artificial methods each of which brings its own crop of interminable difficulties...But this cannot go on forever. Man must realize the wholeness of his existence, his place in the infinite.[2]

Swamiji predicted the fall of secularized society unless it shifted its basis to spirituality. In a society immersed in materialism, bringing back full religious faith may be difficult. But if we do not succeed, we shall lose the major inspiring instrument of our higher life in society. Enlightened self-interest and humanism can help a good deal, but they are not enough. For the vast majority of people, the inspiration of religion is essential in providing the motive power for peace and unity.

The primary social value of religious ideals is that they reduce the self-serving tendencies of secularism. Of course, people have always been self-serving; but they have also been cooperative and self-sacrificing. Three ideas have ruled the world through the centuries: competition in the age of the hunters, cooperation in the age of the agriculturists, and in every age, self-sacrifice, whether biologically engineered or inspired by higher instincts.

In our world today, selflessness, which every religion promotes through the idea of charity, is of paramount importance. Vivekananda said, *"All human action and all human thought, hang upon this one idea of unselfishness. The whole idea of human life can be put into that one word, unselfishness".*[3]

In Karma Yoga, Swamiji further clarified the need

for unselfishness: Every act of charity, every thought of sympathy, every action of help, every good deed, is taking so much of self importance away from our little selves and making us think of ourselves as the lowest and the least, and therefore it is all good...Here are two Sanskrit words. The one is Pravritti, which means revolving towards, and the other is Nivritti, which means revolving away. The "revolving towards" is what we call the world, the "I and mine"; it includes all those things which are always enriching that "me" by wealth and money and power, and name and fame, and which are of a grasping nature, always tending to accumulate everything in one center, that center being "myself". That is the Pravritti, the natural tendency of every human being; taking everything from everywhere and heaping it around one center, that center being man's own sweet self.

When this tendency begins to break, when it is Nivritti or "going away from" then begin morality and religion. Both Pravritti and Nivritti are of the nature of work: the former is evil work, and the latter is good work. *This Nivritti is the fundamental basis of all morality and all religion, and the very perfection of it is entire self-abnegation, readiness to sacrifice mind and body and everything for another being.*[4]

Arnold Toynbee, the well-known historian, said that with the dawn of higher religions, the world has never been the same. Religion has inspired people to great spiritual heights, but it has also been the source of much strife in the world. "Men never do evil so completely and cheerfully", said Blaise Pascal, the French mathematician and philosopher, "as when they do it from religious conviction".[5]

Politically, religion has been used for negative purposes. In democratic countries, religious emotions are stirred up for getting elected, and in totalitarian countries, such emotions are employed to control the people. The emotions aroused, however, are not of the higher quality, but are based on the lower nature of man. Hatred for the "other" is the easier method; loving the "other" is more difficult. So the easier path is taken by both democratic and socialistic countries.

We often find that higher emotions are normally aroused before the independence of a country, but once it is independent, gradually greed and hunger for material goods take hold of the society, and ethical and social values are ignored. Swami Vivekananda foresaw this tendency and warned, *"One may gain political and social independence, but if one is a slave to his passions and desires, one cannot feel the pure joy of real freedom".[6]*

Fundamentalism in religion is a serious problem at present and is the cause of the major conflicts in the world today. This is nothing new: most of the wars that have taken place over the centuries were inspired by religious or ethnic divisions. The proselytizing religions in particular, have been responsible for much of the strife.

It is interesting to note, however, that major conflicts have also erupted without the influence of religion. Vietnam and East Pakistan come to mind. Political ideology was the driving force in Vietnam. And the sheer love of power fractured the relationship in Cambodia and also between East and West Pakistan, causing a terrible holocaust. Other cases in point, where religion was not involved, include Russia and China at odds over communism, and the Muslim countries fighting among themselves.

But Religion has been, and still is, exploited in India, Ireland, Yugoslavia and other areas. *We have just enough religion to make us hate, but not enough to make us love one another*, declared the English satirist, Jonathan Swift. *Unfortunately, religious sentiment can be easily whipped up if mixed with the irreligious sentiment of hate. It is up to society to call on politicians to leave religion out of their rhetoric and to proclaim that "hatred is not religion"*.

In the last century, people believed that the age of reason had come. But in this century, nationalism has become the preponderant consideration, and with it, fundamentalism and parochialism. Vivekananda adamantly denounced the exclusive type of nationalism: *Ours is the Gospel of oneness of all beings, and all national feelings are but wicked superstitions.*[8]

In our world today, nationalism is often mistaken for patriotism. Love for one's country is good, but that love should also extend to the world. As the Mahabharata says, "For the interest of the world, the interest of one's country should be sacrificed".

Because of the development of fundamentalism in religion, people often think that religion should be separated from state as in the democratic countries, or that it should be banished as in communist countries. But religion has a way of creeping in through all barriers set up against it. In Russia, atheism was, in essence, the religion. And yet even Stalin, who destroyed a hundred churches in Moscow itself, had to open churches when thousands of Russians were dying in the Second World War. So many deaths caused untold grief, and there was no consolation other than God and religion.

After seventy years, the Soviet Block collapsed, and there is now a tremendous urge for religious life. But unfortunately, the old struggles between religious and ethnic groups are coming back. It has been established that man cannot live without religion. Yet religion in turn brings about conflict. What is the way out?

There are two remedies. One is the idea of non-violence as preached by Buddha, and Mahatma Gandhi, especially in the national and international fields. "Non-violence is the greatest religion", said Buddha, and Mahatma Gandhi worked out its ramifications, and applied it in national life.

The other remedy is the harmony of religions as preached by Emperor Ashoka and Sri Ramakrishna. "All religions should be equally respected", proclaimed the Ashokan Edicts. And Sri Ramakrishna said, "All these views are but so many paths to reach the same goal".[9] He explained with a telling analogy:

Truth is one; only It can be called by different names. All people are seeking the same Truth; the variance is due to climate, temperament, and name. A lake has many *ghats*. From one ghat the Hindus take water in jars and call it 'jal'. From another ghat the Mussalmans take water in leather bags and call it 'pani'. From a third the Christians take the same thing and call it 'water'. Suppose someone says that the thing is not 'jal' but 'pani', or that it is not 'pani' but 'water', or that it is not 'water' but 'jal'. It would indeed be ridiculous. But this very thing is at the root of friction among sects, their misunderstandings and quarrels. This is why people injure and kill one another, and shed blood in the name of religion. But this is not good. Everyone is going toward God.[10]

Vinoba Bhave, of the Bhudan movement fame, believed that the days of religion were gone and the days of spirituality had come. Spirituality, which engenders virtues, is the essential part of religion. By emphasizing spirituality instead of dogma, the world's religions can inspire rather than incite.

Peace begins with the individual and spreads out from there. "Nothing can bring you peace", said Emerson, "but yourself".[11] Without individual peace, social peace is difficult to achieve, not to speak of world peace. To quote Vivekananda, *The basis of all systems, social or political, rests upon the goodness of men. No nation is great or good because Parliament enacts this or that, but because its men are great and good.*[12]

Individual peace brings national peace, which in turn brings international peace. We are all parts of the whole, and each part contributes to the well-being of the whole. As Vivekananda said,

There is a common platform, a common ground of understanding, a common humanity, which must be the basis of our work. We ought to find out that complete and perfect human nature which is working only in parts, here and there. It has not been given to one man to have everything in perfection. You have a part to play; I, in my humble way, another; here is one who plays a little part; there, another. The perfection is the combination of all these parts. Just as with individuals, so with races. Each race has one side of human nature to develop. And we have to take all these together; and, possibly in the distant future, some race will arise in which all these marvelous individual race perfections, attained by the different races, will come together and form a new race, the like of which the world has not yet dreamed.[13]

On the individual level, peace requires the inculcation of certain personal virtues. Likewise, peace in the world requires certain social virtues. Let us explore some of the virtues necessary for peace.

International peace requires avoidance of war. National peace requires curbing of fissiparous tendencies. And social peace requires a lessening of tensions. Wars, divisions, tensions-all are caused by selfishness. In order to achieve peace, there must be sacrifice on the part of all-the powerful and the weak, the big nation and the small, the rich and the poor.

Some amount of conflict or dichotomy in motivation cannot be avoided. But the protection of society and the world is a desideratum. Modern man is facing a crisis: the possibility of annihilation by nuclear weapons. The nuclear threat has eased somewhat now that the Soviet republic has disintegrated and the two major powers are no longer rivals with distrust as the common bond. But localized conflicts for jurisdiction and self-rule, even by small units, are the cause of much anxiety and, in some cases, much bloodshed. In this area also, the urge for peace and unity must be imbibed by the people. Political, militaristic, economic, and other methods will have to be tried, but they are not enough.

Social, national and international peace requires nonviolence as the basic guiding principle. Nonviolence is not passive tolerance; it is real acceptance based on love and understanding. Vivekananda defined nonviolence or Ahimsa as "never producing pain by thought, word, and deed, in any living being".[14] Only when this lofty principle is firmly adhered to, can there be calm deliberation and mutual understanding, the precursors of peace and unity.

It is no use being a pessimist even if the situation sometimes seems hopeless. The people of the world must keep up hope and try to uphold the higher values in society. In resolving conflicts, the democratic ideas of discussion and persuasion are preferable to brute force.

Various methods of force will not bring peace. Peace will come only when the materialistic and selfish tendency is curbed. To quote Vivekananda, *No amount of force, or government or legislative cruelty will change the condition of a race, but it is spiritual culture and ethical culture alone that can change wrong racial tendencies for the better.*[15]

In our quest for world peace and unity, moral guidance for the political leaders of the world is essential. In today's world, power is concentrated in the political and social systems and is wielded by government, and also by industry, business, and the military. President Eisenhower gave a note of warning that the industrial-military complex has too much hold over government, pushing the latter in its direction. If that is true of a democratic country like America, what to speak of the totalitarian countries of the world? So political and social leaders will have to be influenced with higher ideals and their powers curbed before there can be peace in the world.

It is up to religious leaders, even though they do not have the power to enforce discipline, to inspire the power holders. And it is a noble mission. "Blessed are the peacemakers, for they shall be called the children of God".[16]

Religion has a tremendous hold on the human mind and heart. Widely popular and highly respected religious leaders can influence political and social leaders, many of whom are receptive because of their own religious beliefs and sense of conscience. Furthermore, political leaders, as we have seen throughout history, cannot ignore the will of the people for too long. If the people themselves desire peace and unity, over and above self-centered concerns, their leaders will have to listen, and act.

Churches in the West often try to influence the social leaders when political decisions affect the people by creating religious disharmony or social inequality. If it is not negative and not too political in nature, it may be all right for religion to poke its nose in social affairs. In the recently held Parliament of Religions in Chicago in 1993, the idea of global ethic was very much stressed to bring about global peace and unity.

There is a dream of creating a world body following the previous experiments of the League of Nations and the present United Nations. Without a world body, war, violence, injustice and inequality cannot be removed. An Atmosphere of peace and a desire for unity, beginning with togetherness and open communication, is essential. Complete uniformity and agreement are, of course, impossible. That is why the democratic method, although it tends to encourage division and independence, is better equipped to handle the situation.

The one-world idea of an American politician, Wendell Willkie, had great appeal in the 40s. But the world was not yet ready for it, and instead the United Nations was formed. Evidently, that also is not enough to ease the many conflicts in the world. We must tend towards a one-world government or remain in a halfway-house world with a mixture of enjoyment and suffering.

Unity in the individual and social context is essential
for bringing peace. The message of the Rig Veda, the
oldest available book of the world, was this unity. It said
thousands of years ago:

Be united;
Speak in harmony;
Let your minds apprehend alike;
Common be your prayer;
Common be the end of your assembly;
Common be your resolution;
Common be your deliberations;
Alike be your feelings;
Unified be your hearts;
Common be your intentions;
Perfect be your unity.[17]

Swami Vivekananda believed that some great souls
have been born with the grand idea of unifying the world.
The unification was usually attempted through political
and militaristic conquest. Swamiji considered Alexander,
Chengis Khan, and Napoleon to be such great souls who
were no mere power mongers, but who dreamt of unifying
the whole world.

Governmental unification may be a fantasy, but some
type of unification is necessary for world peace. It was, I
think, Paul Carus who suggested the division of the world
into six large units, each with enough resources to be self-

sufficient. Evidently it is not possible. From the examples of Yugoslavia and the republic of Russia, we find that some amount of pressure, in the form of military force, is necessary to keep the various units together. Religion, democracy, and persuasion, however can lubricate the machine and prepare the minds of the people to accept the ideals of peace and unity.

While peace begins with the individual, unity involves more than one person. Inter-personal relationships in the family, the work areas, and society as a whole, require face-to-face discussion and persuasion without creating tension or violence.

Before any group can live together without the kinds of tensions that lead to bloodshed, there must be an atmosphere of tolerance, trust, understanding and sacrifice. Above all, the concept of world unity needs to be addressed in the light of Monistic Vedanta, or the oneness of all existence. To quote Swami Vivekananda:

'In every nation the truth has been preached from the most ancient times-love your fellow-beings as yourselves-I mean, love human beings as yourselves....But no reason was forthcoming, no one really knew why it would be good to love other beings as ourselves. And the reason why, is there in the idea of the Impersonal God; you understand it when you learn that the whole world is one- the oneness of the universe- the solidarity of all life- that in hurting any one I am hurting myself, in loving any one I am loving myself. Hence we understand why it is that we ought not to hurt others'.[18]

World peace begins with each one of us. If we live a life dedicated to nonviolence, tolerance, and selfless service to God manifest in humanity, our lives will inspire those around us. The ideals around which we center our own lives will gradually expand our family, our community, our nation, and finally, our world.

(1) C.W. 3:137.
(2) Sadhana, p.10.
(3) C.W. 1:182.
(4) C.W. 1:84-86.
(5) Blaise Pascal, *Pensees*, Sect, XIV, No. 894.
(6) C.W. 5:419.
(7) Johnathan Swift, Thoughts on Various Subjects.
(8) C.W. 8:375.
(9) M. The Gospel of Sri Ramakrishna, trans. Swami Nikhilananda p. 748.
(10) M. The Gospel. p. 423.
(11) Ralph Waldo Emerson, Essays: First Series. Self-Reliance.
(12) C.W. 5:192.
(13) C.W. 8:56-57.
(14) C.W. 1:189.
(15) C.W. 3:182.
(16) The Holy Bible, Matthew 5:9.
(17) The Rig Veda, Mandala X, 191, 2-4. *Vedic Prayers*, trans. Swami Sambuddhananda, Second ed. (Bombay: Sri Ramakrishna Ashrama, 1945) p. 34.
(18) C.W. 3:129-130.

PART III

Chapter 12

SELF EXERTION IN SPIRITUAL LIFE

Achievement of a goal requires effort whatever that goal may be. The progress that has been made in the fields of science and technology, communication and commerce, or even arts and letters is the result of tremendous effort by humanity for many centuries. In the field of religious life also effort is necessary. What exactly is the place of self-effort in spiritual progress? It is often believed that the theories of karma and grace are opposed to the idea of self-effort. The theory that circumstances are predetermined also seems to conflict with the idea of self-effort. And free will, which is essential for self-effort, is recognized as having limitations. Therefore, the ideas regarding these principles must be clarified first in order to appreciate the role of self-exertion in spiritual life.

The doctrine of divine grace, which is held supreme by the followers of the devotional path, says that self-surrender to God is the only thing necessary for spiritual realization. It paves the way for the incoming of divine mercy. Furthermore, as even the smallest detail of the functioning of the world takes place through God's will, how can there be provision for any endeavor on our part? Divine grace is an important principle in religious literature. But it is also pointed out that certain qualities of character are necessary before a person is ready to receive divine grace. The devotee's whole-souled surrender itself purifies his character and develops these qualities. Even when one is only a novice in spiritual life and one tries to direct one's whole mind to God, what is the eventual result? One forgets even one's body. One's whole center of life shifts from oneself to God. Selfishness, egotism, greed and other impediments are cast off unknowingly, and higher qualities take possession of one. These pure (*sattvic*) qualities are mentioned in the *Bhagavad Gita*:

Fearlessness, purity of heart, steadfastness in knowledge and yoga, alms giving, control of the senses, performing sacrifices, reading scriptures, austerity, uprightness;

Non-injury, truth, absence of anger, renunciation, tranquility, absence of calumny, compassion to beings, lack of covetousness, gentleness, modesty, steadiness;

Boldness, forgiveness, fortitude, purity, absence of hatred, absence of pride; these belong to one born to achieve a divine state, O descendant of Bharata (Gita, XVI, 1-3)

Sri Ramakrishna has described beautifully how these virtues are automatically conferred on a devotee simply through the devotee's intense love of the divine:

'What are the indications of God's advent into the human heart? As the glow of dawn heralds the rising sun, so unselfishness, purity, and righteousness announce the advent of the Lord. Before visiting a servant's house to receive his hospitality, a king sends the necessary articles, like seats, ornaments, and food from his own stores so that the servant may be enabled to receive the master properly and show him due honor. In the same manner the Lord sends love, reverence, and faith into the yearning hearts of the devotees before He makes His advent'. (*Sayings of Sri Ramakrishna*, 937-938).

These qualities of character are the same ones developed consciously and directly through spiritual disciplines and austerities by other aspirants following other paths. So we see that though there may not be conscious self-effort on the part of the devotee, except for the whole-souled love for God, actually he undergoes the same purification of character as is enjoined on any spiritual aspirant. Yet he does not consider the effort involved in such disciplines to be his own; instead he is impelled to do it by a higher force.

The Law of Karma

The law of karma is sometimes regarded as conflicting with the ideal of self-effort. The law of karma is no doubt operative. But what exactly does it mean? As we sow so we reap; every cause must produce a proportionate effect. So the results of all our actions must be experienced by us in this life or in a later one. Every action leaves an impression in our mind (*samskara*), which creates a tendency for the action to be repeated in the future. Viewed thus, the doctrine of karma provides a great incentive for self-effort, for every new action creates a new tendency. Religious actions will produce religious tendencies, this making the mind more and more fit for realization. Furthermore, though a particular *samskara* may be a compelling influence for some time, the experience of pain or pleasure may weaken its influence, and by the exercise of one's will, better *samskaras* can be made predominant.

Sometimes we may feel helpless in the face of our bad *samskaras*. But the great teachers have encouraged us, saying that by thinking of the divine, our bonds are loosened and the mind slowly becomes stronger and better able to make further efforts towards God. The greatest merit of the theory of karma is that no one can be regarded as beyond hope. Everyone will reach the highest goal, even if it requires a succession of lives. And no effort goes in vain. Even a little effort becomes the starting point for great good. Hence we see that the theory of karma can be a great incentive for self-effort. Moreover, God, the giver of the fruits of karma according to the devotional schools, is not only a great judge, but also, as the devotional schools maintain, the repository of mercy.

"If an aspirant goes one step toward the Divine Mother", says Sri Ramakrishna, "She comes a hundred steps toward him". The evil effects of karma can be minimized or even canceled. Again, from the *advaitic* (non-dual) standpoint, a person of realization, even if his karma is not mitigated, does not actually suffer the fruit of his karma because he does not identify himself with his body and mind. This is what Sri Shankacharya's line of argument in discussing *prarabdha karma*, karma which has already become operative and must be experienced even by a realized soul. The inoperative karmas of a realized soul have all been burnt by the wisdom and need not be experienced.

Consecrated Action

Self-effort implies work. Does work not bind an individual? As it is said in the *Gita*, it is a person's nature to work. Yet since every action leads to a new action, it seems there can be no end to the chain of work and its effects and hence to the cycle of birth and death. On the other hand, it has been pointed out in the *Gita* that consecrated action does not bind a person; in fact, it releases one from the thralldom of karma.

The world is bound by actions, other than those performed for the sake of yajna (sacrifice); *do thou, therefore, O son of Kunti, perform actions for yajna alone, devoid of attachment.* (*Gita*: III: 9)

A person who is unattached feels that the work is being done by the senses, by the *gunas* (thought modifications), or by *prakriti* (matter). To cease identifying oneself as the agent of action and separating the real "I' from the acting "I" is the suppression of the ego. If we do not think of ourselves as doers nor anticipate the results of our actions, the main causes of our bondage are removed:

Do thou perform obligatory action, for action is superior to inaction, and even the bare maintenance of thy body is not possible if thou art inactive (III: 8)

Therefore, always perform actions which are obligatory without attachment; by performing action without attachment, one attains to the highest (III: 19)

Renouncing all actions to Me, with mind centered on the Self, free from hope and selfishness, fight free from mental fever. (III: 30)

The theory of predetermination is akin to the devotional attitude that everything is done through God's will. It is also similar to the idea of *karma-phala*, that every action leaves an impression which will bear a fruit in the future. However the theory of karma posits that one's karma can be changed by one's present actions, whereas the theory of predetermination does not allow that possibility. Whether one accepts the theory that everything is done through God's will or that everything is predetermined by some other force, scope for self-effort is still left. As we cannot know what is ordained for the future, we can only endeavor to lead our lives in accordance with the teachings of the scriptures and the dictates of our conscience. And this effort in its turn guides us towards the goal.

Free Will

There is a great deal of discussion in religious literature about free will, particularly posing the question: "If everything is preordained, where is the scope for free will?" In any given circumstance there are alternatives between which a person is free to choose, but there is no free will in the ultimate sense. Sri Ramakrishna has beautifully pointed out both the range and the limitations of free will with the analogy of a cow that is tied to a post with a long rope; it can either remain near the post or roam as far as the rope allows. Similarly, a person is free to act, but only within the radius determined by his physical and mental circumstances. Therefore free will does have a place in our spiritual efforts, giving us the possibility of choosing at any given moment the alternative that leads us Godward. Advanced spiritual aspirants, who have practice in attuning their will to God's will, find that it is really God's will that operates through them as they act. For others, divine inspiration often comes through their own purified minds. As Sri Ramakrishna says, the mind eventually becomes the guru.

Although, as we see, self-effort has an essential role in spiritual life, the importance of God's grace must always be recognized. God is the self-willed sovereign. He is not bound by any conditions. But self-effort paves the way for the grace of God to be operative. Of course, by stressing self-effort we should not become more egotistic, for God has given us the body, mind, and senses with which we serve Him; how can we feel self-important? The task of a spiritual aspirant is to forget his ego by identifying with the higher Being or by surrendering to Him. Egotism is identification of ourselves with the body and mind, forgetting that we are really the Self. This is not conducive to spiritual progress. On the other hand, as Sri Ramakrishna said, there is no harm in thinking of oneself as the child or servant of God.

'If you find that you cannot drive off this feeling of "I", then let it remain as the servant "I". There is not much to fear from the ego which is centered in the thought, "I am the servant of God; I am his devotee". Sweets cause dyspepsia, but not sugar candy which is an exception. The "servant I", the "I" of a devotee, the "I" of a child- each of these is like a line drawn with a stick on the surface of water, this "I" does not last long'. (*Sayings of Sri Ramakrishna*, 121).

In his teachings Sri Ramakrishna fully recognizes the power of divine grace and yet strongly encourages self-exertion. He says:

'Adopt adequate means for the end you seek to attain. You cannot get butter by crying yourself hoarse, saying, "There is butter in the milk". If you wish to get butter, turn the milk into curd and churn it well, and then you will have butter. Therefore, if you long to see God, take to spiritual practices. What is the good of crying, "O God!'?

(*Sayings* 582)

Shankara speaks of three prime necessities for spiritual realization: human life, intense desire for liberation, and guidance from a great teacher. The first condition is already fulfilled. The second is also in our hands, although to a great extent it requires self-effort. If that is satisfied, the third also is automatically fulfilled. That has been found to be the spiritual law.

Buddha stressed self-effort, saying:

Exertion is my beast of burden; carrying me to nirvana *he goes without turning back to the place where having gone one does not grieve.* (Kasi-bharadvaja-sutta)

Christ also spoke of self-effort when he said:

And I say unto you, ask, and it shall be given to you, seek, and ye shall find, knock, and it shall be opened unto you. For everyone that asketh receiveth; and he that seeketh findeth; and to him that knocketh it shall be opened. (Luke 11:9, 10)

The spiritual disciplines enjoined by all religions, the practices of austerity, self-control, *japa*, and meditation, are all forms of self-effort used for spiritual development. Hence we see that self-effort is consistent with the theories of free will and karma and even grace, for as long as we do not feel the effects of grace, we must exert effort to achieve the highest goal.

PART III
Chapter 13

The Clarion Call

Oh India! Forget not that thou art born as a sacrifice to the Mother's altar; say, the ignorant Indian, the poor and destitute Indian, the Brahmin Indian, the Pariah Indian is my brother. O Thou. Mother of Strength, take away my weakness, take away unmanliness, and Make me a Man.

I have seen castes in almost every country in the world, but nowhere is their plan and purpose so glorious as here. If caste is thus unavoidable, I would rather have a caste of purity and culture and self-sacrifice than a caste of dollars. Feel, therefore, my would-be reformers, my would-be patriots! Do you feel? Our ideal is the Brahmin of spiritual culture and renunciation.

Shall India die? Then from the world all spirituality will be extinct; all moral perfection will be extinct.

India will be raised, not with the power of flesh, but with the power of spirit; not with the flag of destruction but with the flag of peace and love, the garb of a Sannyasin. Call up on the divinity within you, which will enable you to bear hunger and thirst, heat and cold. Mother has awakened once more, sitting on her throne rejuvenated, more glorious than ever. Proclaim her to all the world with the voice of peace and benediction.

Vivekananda (culled)

Swami Vivekananda was an energizer. He himself was energy personified and action was his message to humanity. He has been hailed as an awakener of souls, and his words form a clarion call. Romain Rolland and others have spoken about the inspiring quality of his words. With a great zeal he wrote: "Up, up, the long night is passing, the day is approaching, the wave has risen, nothing will be able to resist its tidal fury. ... Believe, believe, the decree has gone forth, the fiat of the Lord has gone forth. ... Arise, awake, and stop not till the goal is reached."[1]

A man who understands and believes in the Impersonal gets his inspiration from that. John Stuart Mill, for example, may say a personal God is impossible and cannot be proved. Swamiji admits with him that "a personal God cannot be demonstrated. But He is the highest reading of the Impersonal that can be reached by the human intellect, and what else is the universe but various readings of the Absolute? It is like a book before us, and each one has brought his intellect to read it, and each one has to read it for himself."[2]

One of the major things in life is to build up character. The best character is based on the ultimate reality of man's real nature. Man is not merely physical; that is a temporary aspect. He is not merely mental; again it is a temporary aspect. Man's ultimate nature is the Spirit, the deathless Atman which is within everybody. Vivekananda advocates that we must attune ourselves to that idea; and from that attunement all strength and power will come.

The duty of religion is to produce good people. When good men are produced, society will automatically look after itself. Mahatma Gandhi said when India had just become independent, "I would feel that if we succeed in building the character of the individual, society will take care of itself. I would be quite willing to trust the organization of society to individuals so developed." Because intellectual and bright people are always available with money, but not good people. And later history has proved it.

Vivekananda advised people to serve the poor, the illiterate, the ignorant, the afflicted. Let these be your God, said he, service to these alone is the highest religion.[3]

He was a prophet of strength. "Strength, strength is what the Upanishads speak to me from every page. This is the one great thing to remember, it has been the one great lesson I have been taught in my life; strength, it says, strength, O man be not weak."[4] Strength is what is essential.

"Weakness is the one cause of suffering. We become miserable because we are weak. We lie, steal, kill and commit other crimes, because we are weak."[5]

"What I want is muscles of iron and nerves of steel, inside which dwells a mind of the same material as that of which the thunderbolt is made. Strength, manhood, kshatra-virya + Brahma-teja."[6]

"We are the children of the Almighty, we are sparks of

the infinite, divine fire. How can we be nothings? We are everything, ready to do everything, we can do everything, and man must do everything. ... Therefore, my brethren, teach this life-saving, ennobling, grand doctrine to your children even from their very birth.'[7]

As a result, Vivekananda considered self-confidence to be paramount. "He is an atheist who does not believe in himself."[8]

In his famous oft-quoted message he reminded India not to forget the ancient ideal and asked them to "Repeat and pray day and night, 'O Thou Lord of Gauri, O Thou Mother of the Universe, vouchsafe manliness unto me! O Thou Mother of Strength, take away my weakness, take away my unmanliness, and make me a Man!'"[9]

His call to the youth to love India is reverberating still. He has been hailed as a great patriot. He had patriotism because unless India becomes independent the spiritual message of India, which is the real message of eternal India, will not be accepted by the rulers. So India must become free first. In India he spoke about freedom and strength. In foreign countries, America and other places, he spoke about the universal ideas and the glory of the soul.

He was a great believer in service. "Doing good to others out of compassion is good, but the seva (service) of all beings in the spirit of the Lord is better."[10] "Even the least work done for others awakens the power within;

even thinking of the least good of others gradually instills into the heart the strength of a lion. I love you all ever so much, but I wish you all to die working for others — I should rather be glad to see you do that!"[11]

Sacrifice is the law of life. "Great things can be done by great sacrifices only;" "The essential thing is renunciation."[12]

Morality, sacrificing one's self-interest, is essential for the functioning of society. "And where is that eternal sanction to be found except in the only Infinite Reality that exists in you and in me and in all, in the Self, in the Soul? The infinite oneness of the Soul is the eternal sanction of all morality, that you and I are not only brothers ... but that you and I are really one."[13]

"Unselfishness is more paying, only people have not the patience to practice it."[14]

The worthwhileness of life is in doing something tangible for the society. Swamiji said, "Fight on bravely! Life is short! Give it up to a great cause."[15]

How to get strength? To this Swamiji replies, "Think all of you that you are the infinitely powerful Atman, and see what strength comes out."[16]

Romain Rolland mentions about the thrilling quality of his words. The Editor of the Tribune newspaper, Nagendra Gupta, a contemporary, said "What struck me most was the intensity of Vivekananda's feelings and his passionate devotion to the cause of his country."[17]

Swamiji said, "Until India becomes politically free there is not the slightest chance that our religion will be appreciated by the English people. Not the slightest chance."[18] Swami Satprakashananda, the founder of our Saint Louis Center, said when they first came and went to Washington DC, it was a town of clerical people; the city was not developed at that time. He said they did not have much prestige there, because India was a slave nation, but the moment India became independent, others began to listen. In the early days when they would travel by bus, nobody would give them a seat. But after India became independent — and probably because millions of American boys and girls went to different parts of the world, especially to India, and found that Indians are an educated, highly civilized people — they began to be recognized and respected. So now whenever they would board the bus, the young people would give them seats. A sense of prestige came, and young people became more liberal also. They began to appreciate the greatness in other places. So political freedom is connected with recognition of religion and other ideas.

Even in the early days Swamiji was recognized and honored. That was because of his personal demeanor and lectures. Reporters spoke about his majestic personality as "The calm, self-controlled, large and majestic figure of Swamiji, clad in ocher robe and turban, began to radiate a rare radiance on all sides."

How interesting is his approach towards games which engender courage and boldness. One day a question was raised about which game is the best. Swamiji answered, football (or soccer in America). Why? Because in that game there is a counter kick against a kick. So if a ruler gives you a kick, you must give a kick in reply. Interestingly 26 billion people watched the last World Cup football game.

Bipin Chandra Pal, who was a great orator himself and one of the leaders of the nationalist movement, wrote, "He is indeed the greatest preacher and prophet of Indian nationalism." He elevated patriotism to the practice of religion, as Mahatma Gandhi did, who said he entered into politics because of religion. Swamiji felt that service of the people is itself the expression of religion.

Aurobindo said that the going forth of Vivekananda was the first visible sign to the world that India was awake, not only to survive but to conquer—of course through spiritual ideals. Why was India so important to Swamiji? Because, "If India lives, who dies? If India dies, who lives?"[19]

Vivekananda had a two-fold mission, as his Irish disciple Sister Nivedita realized: nation-making and man-making. He advocated having men without frontiers. India was certainly the "queen of his adoration", but as Nivedita saw, yet his vision was always universal. In one place he says, "Whose India? Who cares? Everything is His."[20]

Vivekananda further said, "If I am grateful to my white skinned Aryan ancestor, I am far more so to my yellow skinned Mongolian ancestor and, most so of all, to the black skinned Negritoid!"[21] "Everything must be sacrificed, if necessary, for that one sentiment, universality."[22] "There is but one basis of well-being, social, political or spiritual, — to know that I and my brother are one."[23] "Doubtless I do love India. But everyday my sight grows clearer. What is India, or England, or America to us? We are the servants of that God who by the ignorant is called MAN. He who pours water at the root, does he not water the whole tree?"[24]

Vivekananda envisions globalization. "The problem of life is becoming deeper and broader every day as the world moves on. The watchword and the essence have been preached in the days of yore when the Vedantic truth was first discovered, the solidarity of all life. One atom in this universe cannot move without dragging the whole world along with it. There cannot be any progress without the whole world following in the wake, and it is becoming every day clearer that the solution of any problem can never be attained on racial, or national, or narrow grounds. Every idea has to become broad till it covers the whole of this world, every aspiration must go on increasing till it has engulfed the whole of humanity, nay, the whole of life, within its scope."[25]

The total civilization must embrace the totality of ideas. It must not be one-sided. "It is not that we ought to learn everything from the West, or that they have to learn everything from us [the East], but each will have to supply and hand down to future generations what it has for the future accomplishment of that dream of ages — the harmony of nations, an ideal world."[26]

Even in politics and sociology, problems that were only national twenty years ago can no more be solved on national grounds alone. They are assuming huge proportions, gigantic shapes. They can only be solved, looked at in the broader light of an international perspective, through international organizations, international combinations, international laws. They are the cry of the day. They show the solidarity. The proof of this is that within a few years of the First World War came the idea of the League of Nations trying to harmonize, bring people together. Then again, after the Second World War, came the idea of the United Nations. The world is struggling after every bad experience, discovering that unification and common understanding is more important, though nationalism still rules the world. Nationalistic supremacy is the goal of most of the politicians still, but gradually they are learning that one world will be the ideal. At one time after the Second World War, the one-world idea developed so much, that an American aspirant for Presidency, Wendell Willkie (1892–1944), stood on that platform; however, he was defeated. The present effort to unify the European countries is a positive step in that direction.

We must have the broad idea of the one world. America and Russia had that idea of one world, but with their supremacy. But that will have to go, the world will not agree to anybody becoming too strong. America thought that they were very strong, but they are burning their fingers. Nobody can be so supreme that the rest of the world will accept them. The only idea is understanding. Swamiji said it more than a hundred years ago, that this idea became more and more apparent, more clear that globalization is necessary. Later, it was even supported by other scholars. Teilhard de Chardin said, "The Age of Nations is now over. The time has come for men to shake off their ancient prejudices and turn as one Man to building the earth."

Religion brings quarrels. So Vinoba Bhave said that the day of religions has gone, the days of spirituality have come. Vedanta claims that it represents the essence and core of religion. A famous thinker of Japan said that nations today should sign a treaty not of independence but of interdependence.

The Hindu can worship any sage and any saint from any country whatsoever. Why not? Because ours is a universal religion. Some of you are aware that when a Pope came to India, two hundred thousand people were there to receive him. He never expected that, as a foreign religious leader, so many people would have thronged to see him. That made him a little more liberal. The theologians cannot be too liberal. But there was a social consideration. So now the Catholics recognize four religions as valid. The Pope wanted all religions to join together to fight against irreligion and communism.

There was a conference of comparative religions in Los

Angeles. The Pope came, and I was invited to be one of
the representatives of Hinduism. India showed the way
that you can be religious and at the same time liberal.
The counter-argument is that devotion may not develop
much unless there is concentration — as a woman may like
many people, but will have to have only one husband. All
sectarian religions have this idea. They are not as bad as
the fundamentalists, who cannot tolerate anybody else.

But Vivekananda said, "Our watchword, then, will
be acceptance, and not exclusion. Not only toleration ...
I accept all religions that were in the past, and worship
with them all; I worship God with every one of them,
in whatever form they worship Him."[27] "We not only
tolerate, but we Hindus accept every religion,"[28] knowing
that "all the religions, from the lowest fetishism to the
highest absolutism, mean so many attempts of the human
soul to grasp and realise the Infinite, each determined by
the conditions of its birth and association, and each of
these marks a stage of progress."[29]

These many quotations have actually summarized what
Swami Vivekananda's inspiration is. The point is, in the
life of a person, spirituality means life's transformation.
It is not merely accepting a theory. That is the beginning
of expanding spiritual life. Appreciate your own religion,
but then expand it to embrace all religions, anchored on
the core of religions.

Many people nowadays are born without any religion.
Many people come and say, "We have no religion

because our parents did not go to a church." Such people, especially very intellectual ones, require a very logical religion. To them Vedanta appeals, but once they become Vedantists, they begin to appreciate other religions. Our Swami Atulananda, who was a Dutch American, wrote in his early days that he saw Swami Vivekananda in the beginning of the 20th century. Later he said, "I did not believe in Christianity, but I accepted Vedanta and through Vedanta, I began to accept Christianity and Christ also."

Vedanta explains very scientifically that different teachers can manifest the truth in different ways. So through that I am appreciating other teachers also. That is the difference between Christianity or any other sectarian religion. Vedanta is the core of Hinduism. In Hinduism also, there are sectarian ideas among the orthodox type. But the liberal people try to accept others also without converting them. Conversion is more political and social in nature. We must recognize that religion is meant for producing good people, not Talibans and other violent ones. Every religion has a record of producing good people; that is the purpose of religion.

The core of every religion must be good. The extraneous things will have to be eliminated to make a person more universal. That does not mean that all rites and rituals will have to be given up, because Swamiji defends them: through many of the rituals and other things, great people have been produced. So they have a demand on human nature. The majority of people cannot live on pure philosophy; they like to do something. They ask,

"I understand that religion is true, but what am I to do now?" That is the question.

Swamiji said that shows human nature demands some type of expression. I love you, but how to prove that I love you? You must do something to prove it. If the mother says "I love you, I love you," but doesn't feed the child, that will not do—she will have to feed the child. Doing something is the social expectation from the ideal that you are striving for. Vivekananda is trying to go to the root of the thing. He advocated social service, but social service with the idea of God in man. But even normal social service is based on the idea of renunciation. The national ideals not only of India but of the world are renunciation and service.

Life is based on renunciation. How? Even the idea of the institution of marriage was introduced for the upkeep of society, for regularizing society, and that is based upon renunciation. A person who is free to choose from any number of women is told, "You may have only one wife." That is tremendous renunciation and austerity, and that means socialization. And secondly, the idea of giving freedom to other people is called equality, democratic socialization.

If a child in his own home is hungry; he can jump on the food. But by the time he grows up, the mother says, "No, you can jump on the food in your own house, but in another house you must ask the mother of the house, 'Can I take it? May I have it?'" This is called socialization, which again is based on giving up one's self-consideration. The society says that you are not absolutely free. Wherever your freedom restricts the freedom of somebody else, you will have to restrain yourself. Socialization is being one with the society, adjusting with the society.

Absolute freedom is not possible in manifestation. Will Durant, in his *Story of Philosophy*, says Voltaire advocated absolute freedom. He ought to be made the superintendent of a prison of 26 prisoners. He then would see that full freedom is possible for people who are morally elevated, who have the understanding of other people's needs.

Mahatma Gandhi was in favor of non-violence, and it began to go into every area of his life, interpreted not merely as physical violence, not hurting anybody, but not even to exploit anybody. But money-earning is based upon exploitation. One may be more liberal and his exploitation may be less, but still it is based upon exploitation. He gave up milk because it exploited the calf. But then when he became sick the doctors persuaded him to take goat's milk. That is of course observing the vow in the literal sense.

When the Round Table Conference took place in London, Mahatma Gandhi got down from his ship with his goat! Every newspaper published it. Now his major supporters of course were rich people. Some owners of factories contributed to the national cause. Jamnalal Bajaj and others came to him. "Can we earn more money?" they asked. Even in the Bhagavata there is a sloka, *"Whatever you acquire beyond your need is stealing"*[30]; that type of extreme saying is there even in earlier religious books. So they practised the spiritual ideal. But when that idea was put to Mahatma Gandhi, he said that yes, you can earn more money, but you must think you are the trustees of the excess money and reserve it for the poor. Such compromises were necessary for the upkeep of society.

Swamiji brought that idea of love for all people and gave two lectures on Vedanta and privilege. He said that there should be no privilege of money, social privilege, or religious profession. Why? The Gita says we should love everybody because the same Self inhabits all.[31] There is a famous word called *ātmarāma*. It means bliss in the Self. So you go within. That is the normal position taken by commentators. Swami Tyagishananda, following Swamiji, wrote that *if you see Atman everywhere then worship and service is the only way to appreciate other beings*. The presence of Atman is everywhere, not merely within. That means serving other people, remembering that they are Atman, they are God or God's manifestation. And that was Vivekananda's special message. This idea is applicable to philanthropic and moral activities.

Psychology and other studies consider man as a creature. Whenever you stray away from animality, you are going away from nature. That is why you have got all mental and social troubles. That being the basic idea, selfishness is natural. Darwin and other people have asserted that man is also an animal. As a result you will have to have self-interest and the idea of compensation. Nowadays they talk about the selfish gene; but in the society it is there. If all the people in a society are selfish, that society will not survive.

The social necessity of religion is there to make a person to some extent unselfish, which in modern language is often put as "enlightened self-interest. And what is it? If my neighbor's house is unclean, children may fall sick, then my children will also fall sick, so I go to clean his house. It is not direct self-interest, but enlightened self-interest. If some part of the world is poor, communism may develop, so America goes with its money, lessening its selfishness. Of course if there is a conflict between enlightened self-interest and one's own interest, we follow the self-interest.

The important idea Swamiji asserted is that renunciation is the basis of life. Wherever there is accumulation of money, you are cajoled to give up the money. If you don't give up, you will be forced to give up. That is called taxation. What is taxation? Money is getting accumulated in a certain group; the government knows that if we accumulate too much money, and other parts of the world are deprived, there will be trouble later. So you must squeeze people to give money. Nobody gives money willingly. So in the taxing system, you will have to give certain percentage of your earnings. You are all aware that if you give money to a church, or museum, you get a tax exemption. That is a great incentive for people to part with money. Because you may be losing $100 in taxes, but if you make a charitable contribution, you may lose $125. So really you lose more money, but you feel great pride in yourself. There is a satisfaction also.

Anyhow, Swamiji stressed the ideas of renunciation and service. But his major contribution is creating enthusiasm and inspiration. As a result, that energy can manifest in different directions. All need not do it in an especially spiritual way.

I had an experience of a well-known writer who began to study Vivekananda. One day early in the morning he came to see me. That was not the time for meeting people, but he came with so much zeal that I had to meet him. He said, "Swami, I could not contain myself. I had a great experience last night." What happened? "I was reading Vivekananda till 12 o' clock last night. Suddenly I felt an upsurge of enthusiasm. Now at midnight what could I do? So I sat and wrote three short stories." It was wonderful, because for more than two years, he could not write anything. He felt dry, because he was engaged in building a house. Those of you who have supervised building your house know that it is a whole time job. Anyhow, he was very impressed.

So your going within, or getting inspired, will manifest itself but will depend upon your mental composition. If there is a particular direction you are especially interested in, you will develop in that direction. In the *Ramayana*, Kumbhakarna was tamasic, which means he was of a lazy type and an expert in sleeping. He could sleep for six months at a stretch and eat for six months at a stretch. He did it because he also made tapasya. These are of course exaggerations. But these are the main occupations of life, are they not? All of you spend eighty percent of your life for getting good food, and security of food, and a good house with protection. The other twenty percent is spent on a little idealism, social service, and a little name, fame, and enjoyment. But the main two are sleeping and eating. So Kumbhakarna was the ideal! But of course we don't like to go too far, like him. So the thrust of the story is that your natural tendency will manifest if you meditate or have inner thinking. This is called intensification of emotions. So Raja Yoga says that it is a secret and the Gita says it should not be taught to unregenerate people. It is because austerity and knowledge gives special power.

If unscrupulous people become educated they can do more harm to society than the unlettered, simple people. That is why the majority of the soldiers in every country are young. Often they have not finished school or are from the agricultural community. Officers are educated people, but all the general soldiers are all less educated with simple faith. Young people have more zeal and enthusiasm. Often they love their country and are inspired by patriotism; and they don't think too much about their future. Elders are not often so.

I remember an interesting observation made by Swami Premeshananda. He was of a very inspiring type, so many people came to see him. A teacher used to bring his young students to see the swami. One day the teacher told about a boy, that he was very intelligent but very timid. Vivekananda liked bold young people. So the teacher thought timidity was a bad quality. But Premeshanandaji saw it in a different light. He said, no, he is not timid, he is intelligent. How? The other boy is a stronger one, he can visualize what will happen to him after two minutes. So because of his farsightedness he does not enter into a fight. Have you heard the definition of a hero? It is the one who remains in the battlefield for five minutes more! Is it not? If you recede five minutes earlier you become a coward though you save yourself.

For Rajputs, at one time, skin beauty was no beauty; courage, prowess, freedom, that was beauty. Every society has its own idea of valuation, what you praise in people.

When India fought for independence, austere life was praised. Khaddar, a rough type of cloth, was a must. Very rich politicians used silken clothes in their homes and rough khaddar in public meetings. Austerity was recognized as patriotism, so it was prestigious.

Renunciation and service ideas will be accepted more and more if society gives prestige. If the society does not lionize them, who will go and sacrifice? So they say, "My dear young man, come and risk your life for the country. If you die, we will put up monuments for you; if you are wounded, we will look after you your whole life, or your family." These are all compensations.

Swamiji gave specific instructions about things but his major contribution was creating zeal. And once zeal comes the energy will be manifested in different directions. That is how a person and his society get benefited. In spirituality also he gains for his unselfishness or his dedication to God

Let us read Swamiji's books and get energized. At one time the books *Letters of Vivekananda* and *Lectures from*

Colombo to Almora were very popular. They gave strength, courage, and enthusiasm, which make life worth living and valuable. This message of Swamiji is the source of all higher qualities.

1. The Complete Works of Swami Vivekananda, 5.35
2. 2.337
3. cf. 6.288
4. 3.237
5. 2.198
6. 5.117
7. 3.376
8. 2.301
9. 4.480
10. 5.325
11. 5.382
12. 5. 34; 5. 382
13. 3.189
14. 1.32
15. 5.37
16. 6.276
17. Nagendranath Gupta, Seven Noble Lives (Hind Kitabs, 1950), 177
18. See Marie Louis Burke, Swami Vivekananda in America: New Discoveries, 6.403
19. Attributed to both Mahatma Gandhi and Jawaharlal Nehru.
20. 9.35
21. 9.420
22. 6.285

23. 8.350
24. 8.349
25. 3.269
26. 3.171
27. 2.374
28. 1.331
29. 1.17
30. Srimad Bhagvata,14.8
31. Gita, 6.32

Biography and Books

Swami Swahananda, a senior monk of the Ramakrishna Order of India, is the minister and spiritual leader of the Vedanta Society of Southern California. He joined the Ramakrishna Order in 1947 and received sannyasa, final vows, in 1956.

After joining the Order, he served in the Belur College and then in the Madras Math and as editor of the Order's scholarly publication, the *Vedanta Kesari*. Then he was Head of the Delhi center, the premier center of the Ramakrishna Order in the capital of India. He came to the United States in 1968 as the Assistant Minister of the San Francisco Vedanta Society and was later appointed head of the Vedanta Society of Berkeley, California.

In December of 1976 he was transferred to Hollywood, the headquarters of the Vedanta Society of Southern California, which has branches in Santa Barbara, Trabuco, Pasadena and San Diego.

With his encouragement several centers have been started in Greater Washington D.C., Ridgely, San Diego, San Jose, Phoenix, Dallas, Raleigh and Pittsburgh.

He spoke in conferences and lectured on spiritual life and Vedanta in Russia, Western Europe and Asia.

By The Same Author

Translated from Sanskrit with commentary

* Chandogya Upanishad
* Panchadasi of Sri Vidyaranya Swami

Translated from Bengali

* Go Forward: Letters of Swami Premeshananda
* Swami Premananda
* Swami Akhandananda

* Hindu Symbology and Other Essays
* Meditation and Other Spiritual Disciplines
* Service and Spirituality
* Mother Worship
* Monasteries in South India
* Vedanta and Ramakrishna
* Devotional Lyrics in Indian Literature (edited)